A Cross-Cultural Look
at Death, Dying, and Religion

The Nelson-Hall Series in Social Work
Consulting Editor: Charles Zastrow
University of Wisconsin—Whitewater

A Cross-Cultural Look at Death, Dying, and Religion

Edited by

Joan K. Parry

San Jose State University

and

Angela Shen Ryan

Hunter College School of Social Work

Nelson-Hall Publishers / Chicago

Project Editor: Dorothy Anderson
Typesetter: Fine Print, Ltd.
Printer: Capital City Press
Cover Painting: *Spirit of the Mountain,* Tom Brand

Library of Congress Cataloging-in-Publication Data

A cross-cultural look at death, dying, and religion / edited by Joan
   K. Parry and Angela Shen Ryan.
      p.   cm.—(The Nelson-Hall series in social work)
   Includes bibliographical references and index.
   ISBN 0–8304–1333–2
   1. Death — Religious aspects — Comparative studies. 2. Death — Cross
-cultural studies.   I. Parry, Joan K.   II. Ryan, Angela Shen.
III. Series
BL504.C76   1995
291.2'3—dc20   94-42941
                                              CIP

Manufactured in the United States of America.

10 9 8 7 6 5 4 3

CONTENTS

v

Contents

PREFACE

The United States continues to change rapidly, and as the term "minority groups" enlarges, many groups need to be accounted for when examining death, dying, grieving, and religion. These groups include men and women, those who practice different religions, those whose sexual preference varies from the norm, and those of varying ethnic backgrounds. Psychiatrists, psychologists, social workers, medical physicians, nurses, and other health professionals need to know how terminal illness, death, grief, and religious belief affect the various minority individuals or families with whom they work.

The chapters in this book represent five different religious belief systems: Roman Catholic, Jewish, Protestant Christian Fundamentalist, Islamic, and Buddhist. There is a chapter on gays and one on lesbians. There is a chapter on women and another on Mexican-American women in particular. There are several different ethnic groups represented: Chinese, African American, Korean, Filipino, and Dominican.

The chapters are written by psychiatrists, psychologists, and social workers. Some writers are from academia, and some are in practice.

This text is a guide for practitioners, educators, and students who are concerned about helping persons who are dying and families who are grieving, and about understanding why minority groups react as they do to such events. Readers will learn how each minority group copes, what rituals are important, and the roles ascribed to various family members. Death, dying, and religion are experiences of major importance to every group.

INTRODUCTION

This is a book about death, dying, and religion and how these subjects are integrated into the belief systems of various cultures. The minority groups that are written about in this book are African Americans, Buddhists, Roman Catholics and other Christians, Chinese, Dominicans, Filipinos, Christian Fundamentalists, gays, Muslims, Jews, Koreans, lesbians, Mexican Americans, and women. Although some groups, such as gays and lesbians, are not "ethnic" groups, they are oppressed minorities. In today's world of AIDS, the concern each group has about death, dying, and religion can certainly be understood within the cross-cultural mix that makes up the American multi-varied scene. While women are not an ethnic group, the particular roles women play when a family member is dying makes the gender issue of crucial importance.

This book provides information that will be very helpful to students in many fields, to professional counselors, to clergypersons, and to all types of health personnel who deal directly with patients and their families. When we as mainstream helpers encounter ethnicities, religious beliefs, and/or life-styles outside of our own experience, we must be careful not to act on expectations that could very easily be completely off track. For example, if we examine the state of widowhood in a traditional Hindu family, we find that when a husband dies, his widow is expected to observe traditional customs of seclusion. These include no encounters with men except her father-in-law and brothers-in-law. She is not permitted to remarry. If Hindu men are widowed, they are encouraged to remarry. This denigration of women contrasts sharply with beliefs of many other cultures, including the American culture (Tseng and Hsu, 1991). Thus, when working with a young

Hindu widow, a helper can anticipate severe depression due not so much to the loss of her husband but to the loss of her own future. This is but one of many special reactions created by the culture that sets down rules of conduct for all family members when dealing with death practices.

Perceptions of Death

The meaning of death is similar among varied cultures, although it is also quite diverse. Dying, or life-threatening illness, is a similar biological experience but is responded to in multifaceted ways; in fact, what people experience, believe, or feel while loved ones are dying and after their death varies enormously from culture to culture (Rosenblatt, 1993). It is important to note that there are variations within ethnic groups, as well as among them; for example, Grollman (1993) states that there are unifying concepts in the way "many Jews approach death and dying; there are also significant variations even within Orthodox, Conservative, Reform, and Reconstructionist Judaism" (p. 29).

There has been much written in the area of death and dying during the last twenty-five years, but it is only recently that the literature has begun to look at the cultural differences and how such differences affect behavior, affect, and cognition. The United States preferred to view itself as a "melting pot" until more recently, when one's "roots" became a more urgent concern. There has been much intermarriage of some of the original European ethnics who first migrated to this continent. There was also forced mixing of women slaves with white slave masters, which created many differences in skin color and other characteristics among African Americans.

African Americans, Caucasians, and other groups have all intermarried. Asian Caucasians and Asian-African Americans have become more common as well. Mixed racial marriages are accepted on both the east and west coasts more readily than in the center of the country. However, there has never been a thorough melding of cultural and racial differences in this country. The United States, like many other countries, is still multiethnic and not yet multicultural. "Some minority cultural groups have survived for centuries within multiethnic societies in spite of dominant pressures upon them to assimilate. Others were exterminated, yet others managed to survive but have been socially marginalized" (Irish, 1993, p. 2).

Belief Systems

The Catholic belief system is church and priest centered and suggests the concept of salvation. In a broader context of physical anthropology, archeology, and history, Platt and Persico (1992) quote from a volume by Humphreys and King (1981) that demonstrates the extreme cultural diversity of beliefs and behaviors related to the general phenomenon of death. However, the findings provided evidence of a number of shared cultural similarities among various Western and non-Western societies. The most common conceptual linkage among the seventeen societies surveyed in the volume was "that death confronts human beings with an awareness of their own transience, to which they react with attempts to salvage out of this disturbing experience some residue to which permanence can be attributed" (p. 5).

As one examines this idea, it can be noted that this is probably the reason that drives many of the rituals of death with which we are all familiar. It can be simply put as the fear of death. The fear of death drives many people to look for support in rituals and religion.

A Jewish dying person may seek out his or her Rabbi, and the Catholic dying person may wish to see his or her priest for last rites. The Hindu dying person will seek out union with *Brahmin,* described as a state of ecstasy (Parry, 1990, p. 4). The African-American experience with death is a constant, from the hulls of slave ships to the tainted needle that brings oblivion and AIDS, and he or she will seek out the church and extended family. The Mexican-American dying person may also seek out family, the healer, and the priest. In some cultures, such as Samoan, older persons who are dying adhere to traditional practice by going to their own healers, and younger Samoans tend to use Western medicine (Parry, 1990).

We can observe that the fear of death is attenuated by religious rituals, customs, native healers, and strong family support. Kapp (1993) comments that there are all sorts of personal and social policy conundrums that confront Americans today from a variety of religious backgrounds, and it is a struggle to reach a working accommodation among competing ethical and legal forces representing the tug of modern secular views against that of traditional teachings.

Professional Helpers

As the trend of cultural diversity in the 1990s increases and grows exponentially into the next century, professionals who previously have had little opportunity to know or serve the dying and bereaved will, in the future, need to serve this expanded client base. However, existing curricula in disciplines that serve the dying and bereaved are still giving scant attention to cultural differences (Irish, Lundquist, and Nelsen, 1993, p. 181). They further suggest changing public policy surrounding cultural diversity so that it will make certain that services related to death, dying, and grief "become both more sensitive and more accountable to a client base that is becoming ever more culturally diverse" (p. 182).

There has been some understanding of the importance of ethnic and racial information for physicians when making diagnostic assessments. Some of the following statements were made in a report (Leary, 1990):

> Race and ethnicity can and should be factors in evaluating symptoms while reaching a diagnosis and in determining treatment and how the patients fare. . . .
>
> . . . It has become almost impossible to properly deliver medical care without considering the ethnic background of the patient, including the effect of both genetic and socioeconomic factors [Dr. Robert Murray, Jr., Professor of Medicine, Howard University].
>
> Failure to acknowledge the racial or ethnic background of a patient is in itself a kind of discrimination [Dr. Richard William, Adjunct Professor, U.C.L.A. Medical School].

Nurses have been speaking up about the fact that they are the professionals who are often the ones who spend the most time with dying patients and their family members. They have been writing about their concerns for many years (New, 1965; Peoples and Francis, 1968; Richard and Shepard, 1981; Vachon, 1987). Nurses have been expressing their dissatisfaction with the way care for the dying has been provided for a long time.

> They have been advocating that optimal care of the dying and of their families calls for a new kind of egalitarian, holistic, and supportive collaboration among nurses, physicians, and other professionals and non-professionals in which the "humanly authentic" needs and defenses of the caretakers, as well as of their patients and clients, are more fully recognized and more responsively handled. (Fox, 1981, p. 48)

However, learning the cultural patterns of various groups can become a stressor for nurses in a variety of settings, in that they often are not sure of what should or should not be accepted within the culture of their hospital. For example, "Staff in a pediatric hospital were horrified when an Italian family started dressing in black when told their son had leukemia" (Vachon, 1987, p. 110).

Then there are the clergy. In some particular cultures residing within the United States, there is usually a clergy person who is fully aware of the needs of the particular ethnic groups. For example, in Samoan deaths, the clergy person knows that the deceased must wait several days to be buried to accommodate cultural services lasting those several days; a Cambodian monk is present during the dying and during the funeral, which can take from three to seven days (Party, 1990).

When we work with clergy who are involved with more acculturated groups, such as Roman Catholics, Protestants, and Jews, Doka and Jendreski (1986-87) comment that many clergy are unfamiliar with the nature and symptomatology of grief. Clergy were much more likely to accept affective symptoms than behavioral, physical, or cognitive symptoms. Not many clergy recognize emotions such as relief as normal or physical symptoms such as shortness of breath as normal, and very few consider hallucinatory experiences to be normal (pp. 156-57).

This failure to recognize symptomatology of grief can cause survivors to feel increased pain. Clergy may increase pain when they are insensitive to the duration or nature of grief; pain can also be increased when clergy are unaware of the social context of a death. Some of these are nontraditional relationships (Doka and Jendreski, 1986-87). Cullinan (1993) asks, "Should persons with pain arising out of grief seek solace only from clergy or the church, especially when they may not be the best source of support?" (p. 195). Clergy often have trouble listening to persons who question "God" because of grief and find it hard to accept these human reactions when they are unaware of the dimensions of the grief process. There is a need for clergy of all denominations to have access to, and participate in, death education courses.

> A great need exists today for both clergy and secular clinicians to become more sensitive to the spiritual (as well as the psychological) needs of the bereaved, to become aware of their own death attitudes, and to obtain adequate training to do effective grief counseling. (Cullinan, 1993, p. 204)

AIDS

Any book written today on death, dying, and grief cannot be complete without a discussion of AIDS. What are some of the issues clinicians and clergy need to be aware of when working with PWAs (Persons with AIDS), their lovers, family members, friends, and the larger community? AIDS is a disease from which people die while in the prime of life. Such early deaths leave grief-stricken children, siblings, parents, spouses, lovers, other relatives, and friends. Stigma, fear, and anger are part of the emotions of discrimination against PWAs. "AIDS-related discrimination in issues associated with dying often extends beyond the end of life" (Huber, 1993, p. 230). Many funeral homes refuse to take the remains of individuals who have died of AIDS. When a funeral home accepts the remains of an individual who has died of an AIDS-related death, it often discriminates in the services it provides. Some of these are refusing to perform embalming, conducting funerals with empty caskets, and assessing extra charges (Huber, 1993).

Unfortunately, people of color have become sick with AIDS in greater proportion than their numbers in the population. It is pointed out that Puerto Ricans in New York City represent the group most severely affected by AIDS, with cumulative age-adjusted mortality among males significantly higher than among African Americans, Caucasians, or other Latino males (De La Cancela and McDowell, 1992, p. 109).

One of the larger problems for health-care workers who are involved with PWAs is the perception of people of color that they are victims and powerless. These attitudes tend to limit an individual's ability to change behavior or assume responsibility for actions taken. For many people of color, AIDS-prevention campaigns and HIV tests and treatments are not trusted, since AIDS is perceived as government neglect aimed at genocide (De La Cancela and McDowell, 1992). There are several chapters that address the issues related to AIDS. Clearly, if human service professionals are to provide ethnic-sensitive help, then they need to receive multicultural education for themselves and their clients.

Grief

There have been extensive writings in this area, but they tend to be exclusively about Caucasian, middle-class people. The question becomes: How much of this information has any relevance in the cross-cultural context? There is one formulation that presents a grief chart and includes the following: disbelief, shock, sobbing, crying, physical symptoms, denial, repetition, reality of death, confusion, idealization, identification, anxiety/panic, bargaining, relief, depression, expectations, lowered self-esteem, preoccupation, guilt, anger, loneliness, despair, sadness, helplessness, envy, frustration, hatred, bitterness, resentments, limbo, hope emerges, missing, struggle with new life patterns, and life is worth living (Schoeneck, 1991). In another formulation, grief is categorized in four stages: (a) shock and numbness; (b) yearning and pining; (c) depression and intense grief; and (d) reintegration (Parry, 1989, p. 86).

But do such formulations apply to other cultures? There are many cultures that strongly believe in life after death. If such beliefs of the hereafter are part of a culture, then survivors' reactions to the death of a loved one may be very different. Still, the mourning process does seem to be a remarkably stable phenomenon throughout different cultures (Cooklin, 1989). "It is known that people who are able to show and share sadness and distress and secondarily to receive support in showing and sharing this distress . . . will have fewer symptoms than those who do not" (p. 90). Different cultures in the context of the above mean different European cultures. In all cultures, Western and Eastern, the rituals of funerals, burials, and post-burial rites are very important in attenuating the severity of grief reactions. Societies that perform final ceremonies some time after a person's death do not experience severe grief, and societies that lack final post-burial ceremonies have more prolonged grief (Tseng and Hsu, 1991).

A discussion of Eastern religion in relation to death, dying, and grief will make the above observations more clear.

Religion, Death, and Dying

The importance of religion to Asian society is indicated by the high density of temples and shrines in all parts of Asia; for example, in Southern China, in Kwangtung province, there is Nanching village which, in 1950, had eight temples for its 240 families, or one temple for each thirty families (Yang, 1973). Traditional religion in Asia has been represented by Hinduism, Buddhism, Confucianism, and Taoism. There are also other cultural/religious beliefs found in all major Asian groups (Yang, 1973). Ancestor worship is an example: belief in the souls of departed ancestors is part of the concept of family perpetuation; its mortuary and sacrificial rites form an important part of the family rituals.

Hinduism

The spiritual source of Hinduism lies in the *Vedas,* a collection of ancient scriptures written by anonymous sages. There are four *Vedas.* Each consists of several parts that were composed at different periods, probably between 1500 and 500 B.C. The oldest parts are sacred hymns and prayers. Subsequent parts deal with sacrificial rituals connected with the Vedic hymns, the last called the *Upanishads,* which have elaborate philosophical and practical content. These scriptures teach the belief in *karma*—that every act of a human being, even an internal act such as a desire, has an effect on what that person becomes. Also, there are endless series of creations, dissolutions, and re-creations. Besides this fundamental belief in *karma* and rebirth, the *Upanishads* also teach that beyond these transient worlds and creations, beyond the cycles of life, there exists a Supreme Being. An important relationship exists between the Supreme Being and the individual self with its consciousness. This Supreme Being exists in the universe in individual souls and is the ultimate end of all things.

One consequence of these basic Hindu beliefs is that fear of death is considered to be based on a false identification of the true soul with the temporary self of this life. Another belief is that moral effort will not only affect one's state after death but also one's ability to obtain release from the cycle of birth and death. One should accept one's present situation as just retribution for past *karma* and respond to the moral challenges of the present in the hope of making spiritual progress (Ryan, 1993).

Buddhism

According to Buddhist tradition, Siddhartha Gautama, the Buddha, lived in India in the middle of the sixth century B.C. Buddhists believe that it was the sight of a dead man, in part, that led Buddha on his six-year search for truth. The truth he discovered and passed on in the celebrated form of the Four Noble Truths is that life is filled with the pain of grief because humans constantly desire that life not change, that death not occur. This is a fundamental ignorance of reality. Thus, the First Noble Truth states that the outstanding characteristics of the human situation, *dukha,* which is suffering or frustration, comes from difficulty in facing the basic facts of life, that everything is transitory. In the *Dhammapoda,* a Buddhist scripture, the Buddha said, "All things arise and pass away." The notion that flow and change are basic features of nature lies at the roots of Buddhism. Suffering arises from resisting the flow of life and trying to cling to "fixed" forms that are actually impermanent (Capra, 1984).

The Second Noble Truth deals with the cause of all suffering, *trishna,* which is clinging or grasping. Buddha described the origin of life's pain as "craving," or more commonly, "desire." Trying to cling to things that we see as firm and persistent but that in fact are transient and ever changing, we are trapped in a vicious cycle where every action generates further action, and the answer to each question poses new questions. This vicious cycle is known as *samsara,* the round of birth and death, and it is driven by *karma,* the never-ending chain of cause and effect. What lies at the root of all sorrow is the notion of ego and a concomitant dualism of self and other. These, in turn, lead to craving for things to satisfy the demands of the ego and clinging to those things as though they were substantial and enduring instead of in a state of continued change and decay. Because impermanence is the law of life, sooner or later we must part from what we try to hold, and this parting is painful (Kaplcau, 1989).

The Third Noble Truth says that suffering and frustration can be ended. It is possible to transcend the vicious cycle of *samsara,* to free oneself from the bondage of *karma,* and to reach a state of total liberation called *nirvana.* In *nirvana,* the notions of a separate self disappear, and the oneness of all life becomes a constant sensation. To reach *nirvana* is to attain awakening, or Buddhahood. The cessation of suffering is the complete cessation of desire. If we can forget personal wrongs and desires and shift our focus to the greater expanse of life outside ourself, our pains and frustrations will subside.

The Fourth Noble Truth is Buddha's prescription to end all suffering. The Eightfold Path of self-development is simply right view, right thought, right speech, right action, right livelihood, right effort, right mindfulness, and right concentration (Bowker, 1970).

During his lifetime, the Buddha instructed his followers to contemplate death as a means of understanding impermanence. In some Buddhist countries, monks are instructed to meditate on decaying corpses as a way to understand impermanence and free themselves from sensual attachment.

The state of the mind of the dying person at the moment of death is thought to influence the rebirth process. The better the state of mind, the better the chances of a good rebirth. Chanted aloud, the teachings of Buddha are thought to have a calming effect on the minds of the dying. They also serve to protect the listener, driving away evil influences and directing the mind to the teachings (Truitner and Truitner, 1991).

The elaborate preparation for the dying also serves as an initiation of the dead or dying person to the transition from death to rebirth. There are instructions to be read to the dying person and later to the corpse to help guide it through the transitional state between life forms. The goal is to initiate the consciousness of the dying one to the great opportunity of enlightenment that lies ahead.

Most Buddhists think that it is difficult to attain *nirvana.* Some Buddhists, particularly the Mahayana Buddhists, believe that saviors offer to help suffering humanity when death is near. This form of Buddhism is known as Pure Land Buddhism. Pure Land Buddhism is also called the Western Paradise, founded by Amida Buddha, who attained *nirvana* but was overcome with compassion for his fellow humans who were unable to attain it. Amida Buddha created a Pure Land as refuge for all who have faith in him. Pure Land Buddhists believe that if they call to the Buddha, who was a human who achieved *nirvana,* he will bring them to his Pure Land when they die, where they can obtain *nirvana* more easily than on earth (Ryan, 1993). The dying person, therefore, should focus his or her mind on the Pure Land and on Amitabha Buddha. This form of Buddhism is found in China, Korea, and Japan.

Confucianism

During the sixth century B.C., two distinct philosophical schools of Confucianism and Taoism developed in China. Confucianism was the philosophy of social organization, of common sense and practical knowledge. It provided Chinese society with a system of education and with distinct conventions of social etiquette. Confucius's teachings proposed to form an ethical basis for the traditional Chinese family system, with its complex structure and its rituals of ancestor worship. Taoism, on the other hand, was concerned primarily with the observation of nature and the discovery of its way, or *Tao.* It emphasized that human happiness is achieved when one follows the natural order, acting spontaneously and trusting one's intuitive knowledge (Capra, 1984).

Confucius was interested in improving social relationships and believed in hierarchical structure and right ways of interacting. Social rituals were ways of expressing respect for parents and the ruling members of society. He emphasized that they should be the right ways of relating to others.

> Death does not sever the relationship of the departed with the living; but merely changes it to a different level. Far from being

characterized by fear, the attitude of the living toward the departed members of the family or clan is one of continuous remembrance and affection. (Chan, 1963)

Confucius emphasized the value of rituals. One should attend to the rituals that relate the living with the dead. One keeps alive the memory of one's parents and ancestors through regular rituals of remembrance. While performing the rituals, one expresses emotions of grief and affection; one provides specific ways of expressing grief — ways that follow the middle way, avoiding extremes. "Ritual reveals the ultimate dignity of human relationships, the moral perfection implicit in achieving one's ends by freely choosing to deal with others as having equal dignity" (Ryan, 1993).

In expressing memories of one's parents and ancestors, one receives the gift of life that is passed on from the dead to the living.

Taoism

Lao Tzu, the father of Taoism, began his book with: "Existence is beyond the power of words to define; terms may be used but none of them absolute" (Bynner, 1944). Lao Tzu was concerned with the origin and meaning of life and determined that no man's explanation of it is absolute. Taoism focuses on nature — not on man, as Confucianism does. Instead of emphasizing the value of social conventions and rituals, Taoism offers a way of transcending the limits of one's world. Taoists concentrate their attention on the observation of nature in order to discern the "characteristic of the *Tao*," the way of life. They believe that transformation and change are essential features of nature. Death is part of this natural change. Chuang Tzu, a Taoist, wrote,

> Life is the companion of death, death is the beginning of life. Who understands their workings? Man's life is a coming together of breath. If it comes together, there is life; if it scatters, there is death. And if life and death are companions to each other, then what is there for us to be anxious about? (Watson, 1968)

Lao Tzu himself wrote,

> Death is not a threat to people who are not afraid to die; but even if these offenders feel death all day, who shall be rash enough to act as executioner? Nature is executioner. When man usurps the place, a carpenter's apprentice takes the place of the master,

xix

and an apprentice hacking with the master's axe may slice his own hand. (Bynner, 1944)

The Taoists saw all changes in nature as manifestations of the dynamic interplay between the polar opposites, yin and yang. They believed that any pair of opposites constitutes a polar relationship wherein each of the two poles is dynamically linked to the other. This notion that the movements of the Tao are a continuous interplay between opposites suggests that whenever you want to achieve anything, you should start with its opposite. The opposites include the concepts of good and bad, which are interrelated in the same way as yin and yang.

Recognizing the relativity of good and bad, Taoists do not strive for the good; rather, they try to maintain a dynamic balance between good and bad, between yin and yang. Each force constantly transforms into its opposite. There is no evil without good, no life without death. To rebel against death and not to recognize that it is inevitable is to lack a fundamental understanding of life.

Although Buddhism, Taoism, and other religions are separate faiths in practice, they intermingle freely in the religious lives of the people of Asia. China, for instance, is a land of eclecticism and polytheism, and often the focus of religious interests is practical function, not necessarily of theological identification. A man might pray one day to the Buddhist gods for the begetting of a son and another day to the Taoist medicine god for the return of health.

Ancestor Worship

Religion in its diffused form serves as an integrative force, particularly for Chinese and Korean social institutions. This can be seen in ancestor worship in relation to the family system, which has been a structural core in traditional Chinese and Korean society. Failure to practice ancestor worship would invoke moral condemnation.

The basic function of ancestor worship was to maintain the continuity and cohesion of the family organization by using the memory image of deceased kinship members as an integral symbol of perpetual memory. The process began with mortuary rites at the death of an adult family member. The first act was to report the death to the Earth God and the God of Five Roads, who, as guards, would facilitate the admission of the soul of the dead to the world of spirits. The rites continued for as many as forty-nine days, depending upon the family's wealth. Other rites included dressing the corpse in the best garments available, and burning paper money, clothing, house, and furniture for the purpose of serving the needs of the soul in the other world.

There were other rituals, such as the eldest son, the chief mourner, crossing the paper Bridge of Sigho from which the deceased could take a long look at the world of the living before passing into the world of the dead. Buddhists and Taoists would perform chanting sessions so that the soul would enter the paradise of happy land. Mortuary rites provided the psychological process and the emotional effect of affirming the belief in the continued existence of the soul of the deceased and providing a lasting symbol for long-term integration of the family group (Yang, 1973).

Organization of the Book

The authors who contributed to this book were asked to examine seven issues. The issues were to be used as a guide only.

1. How death is viewed within an ethnic group, and how it interfaces with American mainstream values that stress youth.
2. Does the ethnic group encourage open discussion, or is there a conspiracy of silence?
3. How do families deal with a dying member and death? What is the role acculturation plays in where people die?
4. Funeral practices.
5. What are the group's responses to mainstream medical care and to pain? What about traditional healers? Use of rituals?
6. How is grief expressed? How is it dealt with?
7. How are an ethnic or religious group's death practices similar or different from mainstream America's death practices?

Some authors adhered to the issues guide, and some did not. However, all chapters provide interesting and perhaps new information and ideas on how culture affects death practices. This book has sixteen different authors; some address the same groups but from a different perspective. The authors are psychiatrists, psychologists, social workers, practitioners, and academics.

In chapter 1, a very important point is made about how most discussions on death and dying overlook gender. Merdinger notes that research (Stillion, 1985) suggests that gender plays a significant role in all aspects of death, grief reactions, and outcomes. The various roles gender plays in nurturance, care-taking, and responsibility are discussed in detail. Women perform more care-taking if a child is sick or dying; daughters are more likely than sons to help ailing or dying parents; and the principal caregivers of terminally ill cancer patients are women. There is a good discussion about the differences between widows and widowers. Gender is also described in a multicultural perspective to show that many cultures depend on women to be the caretakers of the ill, to be supportive, and to be the wailers (the persons who express grief openly). In general, this chapter presents issues that should be part of the concern of the following chapters.

In chapter 2, Gerty discusses a response from the National Conference of Catholic Bishops to the many faces of AIDS and the need for compassion and responsibility. The Bishops' documents issued five calls — to compassion, to integrity, to responsibility, to social justice, and to prayer and conversion. The author discusses each of these calls. Services to persons with HIV/AIDS are discussed. Fear, depression, guilt, and a sense of stigma are talked about in terms of how to provide services. Several church programs are described, and the chapter highlights several different programs, including one in Uganda. The chapter also covers education, prevention, and confidentiality.

Chapter 3 fully describes the Jewish experience with death and dying. Getzel states that the Hebrew Bible describes death as a natural part of life that all human beings should expect. Death is a finite end to a part of God's ongoing creation. It includes an extensive discussion of rituals and how they are used to help patients and family members. Judaism encourages repentance, confession, and getting one's affairs in order. This enables terminally ill Jews to die with dignity and meaning (Parry, 1990, p. 13). Getzel points out that Jews place a high value on physicians and efficacy of medicine. A dying Jew is not to die alone; it is the obligation of the community to attend to the dying. The treatment of the body, the funeral, the burial, and the mourning period are all detailed clearly in the chapter. There is a brief piece related to modernity and its effect on contemporary Jews. The chapter concludes with several case examples, including that of AIDS. The chapter gives the reader a broad sense of Judaism and its relation to dying, death, and religion.

Chapter 4 provides an excellent discussion of the stark contrasts in the Protestant Fundamentalist approach to death and dying. The most important premise is the belief that the Bible is the authoritative, literal word of God. One is either assured of eternal life with God or doomed to hell. Death is often seen as a product of sin. AIDS would be seen as a product of sin. Death is subject to God's rule; death has been conquered by Jesus Christ; the person who dies will be judged and rewarded for his or her faithfulness while alive on earth.

The primary event after death is the funeral service, which resembles a church service with music, readings from the Bible, and a sermon. Grief is complex; if one expresses any negative feelings such as guilt, doubt, anger, fear, or sadness, one might be judged as less solid in one's faith. On the positive side, strong religious faith may make the death easier to bear.

The author, Gary Anderson, gives guidelines for therapists working with Protestant Fundamentalists. It is a chapter that has much that is challenging and new.

Chapter 5 gives the Islamic approach to death and dying. Sakr first gives the reader background information. The human life cycle is detailed in eight stages: life in the womb; life on this planet; life in the grave; rebirth; Assembly Day; Judgement Day; life in hell; and life in paradise. While one is on earth, one has to have good intentions. One should be sincere, honest, and try to please God. One has to accept death as one accepts daily sleep. We are travelers who are passing through this life before reaching our other life.

It is recommended that sick women go to women doctors and sick men go to men doctors. Sickness has specific prescriptions. There are fifteen recommendations provided when a person is in a state of dying. After death, the body is washed and wrapped. Special prayers are said; the funeral, burial, and after-burial rituals are performed. The widow's waiting period is noted. This is followed by sections on life in the grave and rebirth. This chapter is very different from the previous chapters and gives the reader a thoroughgoing sense of another culture.

In chapter 6, Yeung, a psychiatrist who is also a Buddhist monk, presents the Buddhist perspective on death and dying and an introduction to the Buddha and his teachings. Buddhists look at death as part of life's process. Yeung emphasizes the compassion and wisdom of Buddha, and Buddha's teaching of enlightenment as it related to death and dying. The chapter also discusses the concept of *karma* and its relation to fear of death, medical care, funeral rites, and bereavement.

In chapter 7, Paulino provides insights into the Dominicans living in the United States. The demographics of the group are presented along with a general discussion of Latino culture. The resources used by Dominicans, bereavement, and the use of community, such as church, family, and friends, are included. The use of case material helps to flesh out the information on this ethnic group's dying and mourning practices. There is a good discussion of spiritualism, which is a large part of the religion of this group.

In chapter 8, Mexican-American people are considered by Silva from an historical perspective that examines the time of the Spanish conquest and the influence of the Indian cultures such as the Mayans. Particular emphasis is placed on Mexican-American women, and their varying roles — from the traditional role to the acculturated role — in the United States. Mexican-American women are further described as caretakers of families, of crises, and of the terminally ill.

Religion is a combination of Catholicism and folk medicine. Folk medicine is called the system of *curanderismo*. The author details the change in the *curanderismo* system from high to low utilization by Mexican Americans in the United States. There is extensive discussion on "role" and a chart included on role adaptation. There is also a chart on Mexican-American women's role variables related to dying and death. Traditional dying and death rituals are presented, as well as the "Day of the Dead." The wake and the funeral are also described.

In chapter 9, Housel sets about establishing two important principles: "spiritual" does not mean identification with a particular organized religious belief system or dogma; and "gayness" transcends one's sexual life — it is a personal identification that influences one's perception of, and interface with, the world. The author presents an overview of homophobia from historical, legal, and social perspectives. He points out that sex-phobia pervades this country and has been institutionalized in the Judeo-Christian religious dogma and the medical model. He states that when a gay person "comes out" to his family, he risks rejection and ostracism from the very system that is supposed to support him.

When the author discusses illness and medical care, he stresses how difficult it is for gay men because of societal notions about rugged individualism and the Protestant work ethic. Gay men view dying and death much the same way as mainstream America does — as something to be avoided. The funeral plans presented are those that most gay men formulate, although many plans are complicated by family nonacceptance of the lover of the deceased.

In discussing grief, the author points out that gay men experienced loss before AIDS, when they went through the process of "coming out." Specific bereavement groups are detailed, and the concept of survivor guilt is part of the grief discussion. There are some excellent case examples.

Chapter 10 helps the reader begin to understand lesbian women as the invisible minority. It is noted in this chapter, as well as the chapter on gay men, that lesbianism is an all-encompassing life-style, not just a sexual preference. Prior to 1962, homosexual behavior was a criminal act in all fifty states. Today, the legal status of lesbians in this country is determined on a state-by-state basis. The criminalization of homosexual behavior not only affects those who are apprehended but also legitimizes discrimination by other parts of society. A subculture has developed in which lesbians, unhappy with the bar scene, set up lesbian rights organizations. The Gay Rights organization did not become "Lesbian and Gay" until the 1980s.

The authors, Evans and Carter, discuss levels of visibility in terms of the coming-out process, which is composed of five developmental stages. The concept of loss related to the coming-out process is discussed as well. Lesbian family issues may be seen as single-parent families, as adoptive or foster parents, and as unmarried couples with or without children. Lesbians, like gays, have, for the most part, rejected organized religion. There are a handful of national organizations that serve a multi-faith community. In 1990, Reform and Reconstructionist Judaism approved admitting homosexuals as rabbis. The Reconstructionists, in opposition to all other branches of Judaism, have come out in favor of sanctioning same-sex unions. In terms of medical care, a lesbian was stigmatized as having a mental illness and referred to a psychiatrist. Concerns for terminally ill lesbians include whether "exposure" will negatively affect the quality of care, whether the patient's definition of family will be respected, and whether or not there will be social and/or psychological support for her.

Chapter 11 on death and dying in the African-American community by Bolling suggests that all African Americans have dual-belief systems. One is influenced by the Western European world view. The other is the Africentric world view, which he calls the soul-centered world view and which has been overshadowed by the Eurocentric aspects of African-American character and development. The soul culture consists of organized systems of symbols and images, known as soul forces, *orishas, obosum,* and so on. In Africentric belief, these organized systems of invisible forces govern and regulate the everyday interactions and relationships between the material world and the spiritual world, between the living and the dead. Death is a rite of passage wherein the soul passes into another phase of existence. Bolling describes how this conceptual framework is played out in the way African Americans approach death and dying and in grief and bereavement.

Another view of the African-American experience of death and dying is described in chapter 12 by Sullivan. Several principles of African philosophy and culture help us understand how African Americans experience death and dying. The core concept is that of dual unity, wherein opposites — death and life — are viewed as reciprocal and unifying rather than dichotomous. Another concept is that spirit and matter cannot be separated. Group orientation, including family centeredness, is key to understanding African-American culture. The concept of time, as influenced by fatalism, influences the dying patient's acceptance of death. Sullivan presents several clinical practices in which these principles can be traced, both in working with dying persons and with their families.

Two chapters, 13 and 14, focus on Chinese-American culture. Lee reviews major religious beliefs among Chinese and the influence of Confucianism, Taoism, Buddhism, and ancestor worship on Chinese civilization. He describes death and dying from a Chinese religious and cultural perspective, and the ritualistic nature of death and dying, expression of grief, and the significance of death for the living.

Tanner not only describes mortuary practices of the Chinese but also compares them to mainstream American groups' rituals, particularly those of the Irish American. She discusses their similarities and differences, gives clinical examples, and delineates the role of the health professions in working with terminally ill Chinese.

Chapter 15 is organized around traditional Korean practices and Korean Americans' adaptive modes in dealing with loss and grief. Traditional funeral rituals, as well as contemporary practices of burial and ancestral worship, are described. A study of eighty-one Korean Americans' attitudes on death and dying is presented. The majority of Korean immigrants hold on to their religious beliefs while adapting to their adopted sociocultural environment. Clinical implications of the findings concerning bereavement, loss, and grief processes are examined from several approaches — cognitive, cultural, existential, and spiritual.

In chapter 16, Weber comments that death in Filipino culture provides an opportunity to examine one's life, whether it is good and productive or whether it is full of shortcomings. Death is seen not only as one of the normal stages of life development but also as a transition from life in the present to eternal life in the spiritual world. Grieving is influenced by the family as well as the community. Funeral practices relating to wakes and burial rites are viewed in relation to Catholicism. Weber remarks that the degree of acculturation plays an important role in determining how traditional values and practices are expressed.

CHAPTER ONE

Women, Death, and Dying

Joan M. Merdinger

When consideration is given to the topics of death, dying, and how people are affected by or deal with these issues, the discussion often overlooks gender. Earlier writings on the stages of grief proposed by Kübler-Ross (1969) and Weisman (1972) suggest a universality of reactions, both by the person who is dying and by the survivors, regardless of sex.

Just as Broverman, Vogel, Broverman, Clarkson, and Rosencrantz (1972) discovered that definitions of mental health meant *male* mental health, universal discussions often refer to men. It is critical to analyze the effects of death and dying on women in order to understand their unique experiences, special roles, and difficulties, as well as the gains and positives from having faced death and dying personally or through intimate connections. New research and recent literature (Stillion, 1985) suggest that gender plays a significant role in all aspects of death, grief reactions, and outcomes.

In order to understand issues particularly relevant to women, it is important to consider the significant roles that they assume, while looking at the special stresses they experience. Belle's (1982) important article on the stress of caring outlined a "support gap" experienced by women who provide social support to others, at some personal cost, and find themselves not reciprocally nurtured. Because death and dying call for interpersonal support, the issues of caring and caretaking are particularly important to examine.

Other issues to consider include the effects of death and dying on women if the person who is dying is a family member, partner, spouse, or friend, and how gender might play a part in roles and reactions. It

1

is also important to look at differences between widows and widowers to determine the longer-term effects of death of a spouse.

Culture needs to be considered as well, in order to understand the similarities and differences of women of dominant and non-dominant cultures as they face issues of death and dying. Finally, having defined some of the problems women face, a consideration of the implications for policies and programs can point to direct ways in which women can be assisted with the work of death and dying.

Caring and Caretaking

In an era of "time poverty," according to Schor (1991), men and women in the United States are working an extra month yearly, in comparison to twenty years ago. The number of workplace hours has risen more dramatically for women than men during this same period. Thus, the time gap for women is increasingly a problem from the perspective of work alone.

Recently, Hoschild (1989) reported on the "second shift," the additional month each year that mothers with paid employment labor in the home to meet the needs of their families. Schor (1991) and Hoschild report independently that women's labor has increased more than that of men and that time, for women, has critically diminished in recent years.

In addition to the dramatic decrease in time for women with children employed outside the home, Schor (1991) found that fathers are also working longer hours in the labor force. Although fathers perform slightly more work at home than in the past, their home work does not balance out that of the overworked mother (Hoschild, 1989).

Finally, there is the issue of the "sandwich generation," the "adult children of the aging—that segment of the population between roughly forty-five and sixty years of age" (Miller, 1981, p. 419) who are simultaneously responsible for growing children and aging parents. Those women, "sandwiched" by having children at increasingly later ages, may be facing the combination of even younger and more dependent children on the one hand, and aging parents on the other.

With the increase in time at work, the continuing responsibilities of the home, and the increase in the aging population, who takes on the role of caring? Who provides the nurturance, support, and the time to be with the person who is dying? It is most frequently women: mothers, wives, daughters, daughters-in-law.

2

Although extensive literature exists about death, dying, and children (Kalish, 1985; Aiken, 1985; Kastenbaum and Kastenbaum, 1989), there are only a few references that offer glimpses into the effect of a child's death on the parents, by gender. Rando (1984, 1985) proposes that fathers and mothers may grieve differently due to their sex-role socialization and the sex of the deceased child. It is most likely, however that the mother was the parent who spent more time with the dying child and performed more of the caretaking than did the father.

In a study reported by Cartwright, Hockey, and Anderson (1973), wives were found to provide nearly two times as much support to husbands as husbands did to wives. Lopata (1987) states, "It is usually the wife who cares for the husband since he tends to be older in age and since women tend to outlive men" (p. 393). Cartwright, Hockey and Anderson also found that more daughters provided help than sons, and if children lived outside of the home, daughters were more likely to help than sons: "Daughters were not only more likely than sons to have helped at all, but when they did so they also helped with more things" (p. 149). Lopata also found that daughters supported parents and widowed mothers more than sons, who were most likely to provide "household repairs or advice in business matters" (p. 387).

In the National Hospice Study reported by Mor, Greer, and Kastenbaum (1988), the researchers found that 72 percent of the principal care-givers of the terminally ill cancer patients were women. Other researchers (Cartwright et al., 1973) have found that wives were more likely to give up work altogether to deal with the terminal illness of a spouse, while husbands reported taking time off work, in contrast. Finally, Lopata (1987) points out that "in our society, the daughter-in-law is the primary care-giver in the household where a son has assumed responsibility for the ill or very old parent" (p. 388). Thus, even if a son makes a commitment to care for his aging and ill parents, it is his wife who actually does most of the caretaking.

An interesting new trend, documented in a study conducted by the Commonwealth Fund (Teltsch, 1992), indicates that although women provide the most caretaking, men's roles are increasing. The number of caretaking men is expected to grow "because women as care-givers are reaching the saturation point and the need for care-giving continues to increase" (p. C1).

In light of the "time gap" for women documented by Schor (1991) and Hoschild (1989), the increased need for male caretakers seems inevitable. It is interesting to note that men's reactions to care-giving seem to differ from those of women. Hooyman and Ryan (1987) report,

3

"Even when women and men share tasks equally, women are more likely to experience care-giving. . . . Men are better able to distance themselves physically and emotionally, focusing primarily on their economic responsibilities" (p. 157). These differences indicate the special burden that women carry, perceiving a heavier load than a male counterpart doing the same amount of care-giving.

Another issue to consider is the "contagion of stress." If women are the most likely caretakers for children, husbands, parents, and parents-in-law, they also seem to take on stress from other sources as well. Wethington, McLeod, and Kessler (1987) found that

> women seem to cast a wider net of concern and so are affected emotionally not only by the well-being of their immediate family but also by lives of those to whom they may be less intimately related. Men, by comparison, are less affected emotionally by events occurring to people outside their immediate family. (P. 150)

Kessler and McLeod (1984), finding that some women are more affected by network events than men, concluded that "men know more people than women do, yet women are aware of more of the crises that occur to the people around them" (p. 625).

Widows and Widowers

An important fact of life for married women is that they are more likely to live alone after the death of a spouse than are their husbands: "One-third of women in the United States are widowed by the time they reach age sixty-five. At age seventy-five, well over half are widowed, and by eighty-five, over 80 percent are" (Holden, 1989, p. 143). The death of a husband puts older women at risk for moving into poverty (Holden, 1989), an important stressor that coincides with mourning and grief.

In addition, there are important differences in the way that widows and widowers deal with the affective aspects of death. Stroebe and Stroebe (1987) note:

> It is much less acceptable in our culture for men than women to express personal feelings or verbalize intimate thoughts with regard to feelings of loneliness or a need for companionship. Due to these constraints, men are more likely to rely exclusively on their wives as confidants, while women frequently have confidants

4

outside their households. As a consequence, widowers are less likely than widows to have somebody to whom they can talk freely about their anguish and pain and who, by merely listening, helps them to work through their grief. . . . While stressful life experiences motivate women to actively search for emotional support, men seem to react by trying to distance themselves through their work. (P. 179)

These findings mirror the work of Veroff, Douvan, and Kulka (1981), who report that wives have friends for support; husbands rely almost exclusively on their wives.

Stroebe and Stroebe (1983) have also reported that being widowed is associated with higher death rates for both men and women, but that "bereavement has more dire effects on widowers than widows" (p. 291). It appears that widowers are more likely to have difficulty adjusting to a spouse's death in the immediate aftermath, while widows experience problems later. These findings seem best interpreted in the light of "interpersonal protection theory," as explained by Stroebe and Stroebe (1983):

If one assumes that same-sex friends are more important to a person in overcoming the initial period of bereavement, whereas relations with the opposite sex help one to adapt to the widowed role, then the greater number of widows as compared to widowers may contribute to the finding that widowers have their greatest problems in the first six months of bereavement, whereas widows seem to suffer most during the second year. (P. 298)

A Multicultural Perspective

In addition to looking at studies that capture the experiences of the dominant culture and how death and dying are viewed by the majority of Americans, it is important to look at nondominant cultures in the United States and how culture attaches a new lens to the same phenomenon (Parry, 1990). Additionally, how do women of nondominant cultures, or cultures new to the United States, relate to death and dying?

Salcido (1990) reports that Mexican-American women are more likely to rely on relatives than the Mexican-American men when they are grieving. Women are also more likely to be emotional, calling upon medical care for assistance. Finally, women are most likely to make funeral arrangements and plan other supports at the time of death.

Campos (1990), in discussing the Puerto Rican family, uses several case examples demonstrating the expectation that the woman is the caretaker and the one who shows the most open grief reactions. Campos also cites the fact that women, children, and the elderly can openly cry or discuss their pain; that is not true for Puerto Rican men. Finally, Campos reports that "as might be expected, there is a significant difference between the sexes, with the Puerto Rican woman more likely to turn to relatives for practical assistance in times of grief and males more likely to depend on no one" (p. 139).

Brown (1990) and Devore (1990) discuss the effects of death and dying on the African-American community, noting the engagement of extended family when care is needed for a person with terminal illness. Brown states, "The care and concern for the terminally ill person is always a family affair, encompassing the active involvement of the extended family, friends, and neighbors. Family members are willing to go to extremes to insure that the terminally ill person receives adequate and personal care" (p. 73). When death has occurred, Devore notes, during funerals "the wailing is most often done by the women. . . . The grief of the men is evident in their silence and tears with bowed heads" (p. 59).

Hirayama (1990) notes that in Japanese culture, it is usually the female family members who provide for the ill person: "The female caretakers care for the ill family member without much help from their spouses or mothers-in-law. When a wife becomes terminally ill, her daughter-in-law or her own daughter is expected to take care of her physical needs as well as her emotional needs" (p. 167). So clearly defined is the woman's role as caretaker in Japanese culture that if a man is forced into the caretaker role, role conflict is the result. Hirayama reports on a recent occurrence of husbands killing their ill wives — a result of cultural attitudes about death, intense role conflict, and lack of other supports.

In Cambodian (Lang, 1990), Samoan (King, 1990), and Vietnamese (Ta and Chung, 1990) cultures, women are expected to be primary caretakers of ill family members. Women are also able to express their emotions more openly than is permitted for men of these same cultures.

Some interesting differences emerge in the Chinese-American families described by Wilson and Ryan (1990). They found that language ability and gender together help to determine which family member is responsible for an elderly relative. Often it is the oldest son who is listed as next of kin and who deals with agencies on behalf of the aging mother or father. Wilson and Ryan report that "the female patients do not express their feelings readily or make decisions even about their own care. . . . They do not resist family or staff decisions, as they are fearful of alienating them" (p. 154).

It appears that culture *and* gender are two very important areas of concern when looking at issues of death and dying. Most authors (Salcido, 1990; Campos, 1990; Brown, 1990; Devore, 1990; Hirayama, 1990; Lang, 1990; King, 1990; and Ta and Chung, 1990) note that women are most likely to provide nurturance, support, and emotional release when confronting death and loss.

Conclusions

It appears that women, as mothers, spouses, daughters, daughters-in-law, friends, and companions, deal with death and dying in a way that is different from that of men of both dominant and nondominant cultures. Women experience a "support gap," "time poverty," the "sandwich phenomenon," "the second shift," and "stress contagion"—all issues related to caring for and caretaking. The literature that reports on this burden of caring cites little that offers much in the way of support, other than that men will start to do more only because women cannot do more.

If we take seriously the concept that for women, personal is political, we may need to look at the caring that women do in the areas of death and dying and find new mechanisms to promote more personal ways of dealing with death, dying, and loss. This means that being emotional, being connected, is important and special. A close friend and colleague faced with cancer recently told me that what she has learned most from the women's movement is that "personal is important, that nurturing and being nurtured are valuable and need valuing."

We need to continue documenting the ways in which more nurturing can be given and gotten. Gottlieb (1980) suggests programs that work with the strengths that women have in order to build on existing skills and help in the development of new abilities. Her case examples of the Widowed Information and Consultation Service and Women in Midstream provide an in-depth look at programs that meet the special needs of women at different stages in the life cycle. These programs indicate that women can improve their lives by using their abilities positively.

We cannot overlook the problems of caretaking only by reframing the concept and look at the positive aspects. We need to create new programs that provide help to helpers, to sustain the nurturing that is needed by everyone, regardless of sex. We need to help men to be more comfortable nurturing, to share the load of the most important work in life: living and dying.

CHAPTER TWO

The Roman Catholic/Christian Church and AIDS

Ursula M. Gerty

The urgency of the pandemic of HIV/AIDS, with its life-threatening effects among literally millions of people on all continents, calls for a response from the Christian churches.[1] The need on a purely human level is so great that help in all forms — medical, psychological, and social — is needed in all parts of the world. The slow acknowledgment of the existence and the virulence of the disease has aroused some considerable delay in responding to the disease quickly and adequately.

Throughout history, Christian churches have represented a compassionate arm of humanity wherever known crises arose. The plagues of the middle ages, the needs of the people in times of war and devastation, have elicited the help of religious organizations and groups. The history of the world shows that Christian churches have always provided services to care for human needs. In our own time, there is a greater imperative to assist the victims of HIV/AIDS, especially since persons of religious faith clearly recognize that services to others is essential to their faith beliefs.

The efforts of Christian churches have now become known through publications of numerous books, pamphlets, and articles. The need to inform, to counsel, and to proclaim the principles of justice for the sick is being met through the dissemination of a considerable amount of written material.

Impediments to Services
to HIV/AIDS Victims

Characteristic of this particular epidemic is the lack of resources for care and the lack of knowledge surrounding the extent of the problem in the United States. Diagnosed cases in the United States in 1989 were more than 100,000. In 1993:

> More than 30,000 AIDS cases were reported in the first quarter of 1993, an increase of 204 percent over the number reported for the same period in 1992, the Centers for Disease Control and Prevention said in a report. (*New York Times,* April 30, 1993)

Undiagnosed cases may be equal in number to the known number. The nature of HIV infection may be unknown to many individuals for several years, and therefore the threat of infection to other persons will continue over a period of time.

In addition to the lack of knowledge of HIV infection and how the disease is transmitted, there appears to be a phenomenon of discrimination toward persons with HIV/AIDS because of moralistic attitudes toward drug users and homosexuals, who constitute many of the victims. This type of discrimination prevents many people from becoming involved in supporting services and also causes disinterest in a serious public health problem that would normally become the concern of all people.

The victim's response to discrimination includes the anxiety of being rejected by family and friends, further withdrawal and isolation, and fear of becoming known to medical facilities. The latter results in extreme stress about the progress of the disease when serious symptoms develop.

Churches have already demonstrated a firm conviction of the human dignity of each person and a nonjudgmental attitude toward any behavior that might be associated with the incidence of the disease. However, the churches' position needs to be publicized as well as demonstrated in action.

Church Policy
toward HIV/AIDS Victims

In 1987, the United States Catholic Conference, and in 1989, the National Conference of Catholic Bishops, each published a policy statement. The publications are entitled "The Many Faces of AIDS, A Gospel Response" and "Called to Compassion and Responsibility, a Response to the HIV/AIDS Crisis," respectively. Both documents attest to the dignity of the human person and to the need for compassion on the part of every person for our affected brothers and sisters. The key concept of compassion serves as the focus of the proposed policies recommended for the Catholic church and its members.

"Called to Compassion" demands that *everyone* become aware of the facts concerning HIV/AIDS and become involved on a national, local, and/or community level in supporting services to the victims. Treatment of the problem demands governmental effort in medical research, as well as financial support for patients in need. For the churches and the members, a compassionate response can be made on a diocesan level, or on a parish or community level.

The Bishops' documents issued five calls "to compassion, to integrity, to responsibility, to social justice, and to prayer and conversion" ("Called to Compassion," 1989, p. 9). The call to compassion envisions more than action; rather, it encourages an attitude of wanting to alleviate suffering, with the model of the Good Samaritan (Luke 10:30-37) as a type of person who carries universal appeal. The call to integrity ("Called to Compassion," p. 11) specifies the need for self-respect and respect for others. The Bishops recommend the practice of chastity as exemplifying integrity and avoidance of exploitation of human persons. The ideal of chastity in and out of marriage is presented not as a principle of AIDS prevention, but as a principle of living and of relationships between men and women. Chastity is defined as "an expression of moral goodness in the sexual sphere" and is depicted as "an authentic appreciation for human dignity" (p. 13).

The call to responsibility refers to behavioral changes that may be needed but are based on objective ethical principles. These behaviors include drug addiction and sexual behavior between homosexuals and between heterosexuals outside of marriage. The call to responsibility at the same time recognizes addiction as an illness for which there is treatment and hope and urges a compassionate response in all communities to assist those who suffer from addiction.

Without being judgmental, the Bishops' statement reiterates the teaching of the Church on homosexuality. The doctrine recognizes that some adults have a homosexual orientation, but it requires that such persons remain celibate. Homosexual activity is seen as "immoral behavior," and the Church teaches that heterosexuality is normative.

11

The call to social justice (p. 20) is a call to the United States government for continued research and to a system of medical care for HIV/AIDS patients, which includes the integration of all needed services: hospital care, home care, and auxiliary care services. To insure that discrimination is eliminated, all persons with HIV/AIDS, including immigrants, the disabled, and their families, are to be served if justice is to be honored. The human rights of every individual are recognized as part of the program, and guidelines are prepared for maintaining confidentiality.

Finally, the call to prayer and conversion (p. 24) is urged upon all. The Catholic church teaches as doctrine that God is a loving and saving God who receives us as the biblical father received his prodigal son (Luke 15:11-32). The portrayal of the father who looked for his son every day and who welcomed him upon his return, unconditionally, with joyful love, is like God our Father who always waits for us and welcomes us with open arms.

Services to Persons with HIV/AIDS

If we fully accept the principle that we have a responsibility to assist the victims of AIDS and their families, we are then confronted with the practicality of the need for offering specific services to the AIDS population. Services to patients at any stage in the disease may be offered by a religious minister, by a social worker or other therapist, or by trained volunteers.

The emotional state of a person facing a period of severe illness and ultimately death will surely benefit from pastoral care and/or the help of a therapist who understands the patient's total needs. In some instances, a team of therapists and pastor can offer spiritual help and emotional support, thus fulfilling the needs of the total person. Pastors and social workers, with their complementary skills while exercising their special roles and functions, can assist the ill person with their many feelings about spirituality and their emotional reactions. Patients experience many interacting psychosocial and spiritual reactions that can create stress, and these stresses can be incessant.

The emotional stresses of AIDS patients are discussed and their interconnectedness graphically depicted by Perelli (1991).

Fear exists among all persons afflicted with AIDS. Not only is there the fear of death and the fear of loss, but fear exists along each

12

step of the progress of the illness. The victims' caretakers experience fear also as they observe the debilitating effects of AIDS as symptoms advance. Patients are abandoned by their families; fear is increased by the sense of rejection that ensues. In some centers, mother substitutes, who are volunteers, supply emotional support to alleviate this phenomenon. The churches need to be aware that such abandonment may be perceived by the patient as a rejection by God; the patient needs realistic reassurance of God's love at the crucial time of this illness.

Fear and depression are intermingled, and therapists, whether pastors or social workers or others, play an important role by responding to this type of reaction. A depression affects the patient's general well-being and surely inhibits recovery efforts and the general mental health status of the patient.

Guilt is a severe emotional reaction experienced by AIDS patients and by those related to them. The feeling of guilt appears to be associated with the community's attitude toward behavior that might have led to the AIDS infection. Sexual behavior, especially homosexual behavior, and drug use are considered "bad" behaviors by some persons in society and lead to negative criticism and rejection of AIDS victims.

Guilt exists among those who may feel that they transmitted the illness or who feel responsible for failing to prevent the infection by lack of assistance in the patient's earlier life. The pastoral counselor or therapist who can relieve destructive guilt can help the patient to deal with other rational issues. Guilt feelings of parents and others who believe that they have "failed" their child or friend are also destructive, and it is important for the helping person to provide a more appropriate response to the patient and his or her situation.

A sense of *stigma* is often felt by families of AIDS victims, and this can lead to secrecy and to alienation from the afflicted person. The incidence of stigma leads only to a temporary and false solution to the reality of the threat of loss and grief and is an unhealthy attempt to deal with inner feelings. Again, the counselor can help through demonstrating his or her own full acceptance of the patient and through reassurance offered to families.

Exemplars of Church-Sponsored Programs to Assist HIV/AIDS Victims

Numerous publications describe various programs that serve as models for church-related services to AIDS-infected persons and their families.

The Salvation Army provides shelter services throughout the United States in large cities. The Anglican church conducts an annual national conference to exchange information about its services to those in need. Other examples of AIDS programs include the following:

Model One

The Church of St. Francis on West 31st Street, New York City, offers a variety of services to the poor of New York. The Franciscan Friars have provided a "bread line" for over fifty years that is well known to New Yorkers. More recently, three residences for the homeless, many of whom are mentally ill, have been established and have been acclaimed as models for other social service agencies. In 1987, a support program was provided for a number of persons with AIDS who needed basic services. In 1992, St. Francis House on West 26th Street, New York City, was opened as a "drop-in" center. Staff include a full-time social worker, a religious sister, peer-group counselors, and volunteers. "Spiritual, material, and emotional needs are met by caring and trained personnel" (Bulletin of the Church and Friary of Saint Francis of Assissi, 1993).

A unique feature of the program at St. Francis House is a creative writing group where clients are encouraged to participate in a workshop and to express feelings in writing. The program for the clients is summarized in the words: "Above all, what we offer at St. Francis House is compassion, presence, and hospitality."

Model Two

A Trinity Mission Brother (Trinity Missions, 1993), Howard Piller, in New Orleans, Louisiana, is a family nurse practitioner in the HIV Outpatient Program of the Medical Center of Louisiana. Brother Piller works with outpatients but continues to see patients in or out of the hospital. Brother Piller writes with great feeling as he describes a sense of loss when one of his patients expires. Brother Piller believes that he has made a difference in the lives of the persons he serves. The example of this religious brother offers a model of possibilities for health care personnel to work in a nonsectarian setting, thus providing the presence of the church for the AIDS patients.

Model Three

In the *Maryknoll Mission Journal* for April 1993, the article "How Uganda Battles AIDS" is presented. The National Ministry of Health for Uganda has developed a policy of openness about the causes of AIDS and a program to halt the spread of the disease. The national government is assisted by a number of auxiliary groups. UNICEF and the United States government have both provided financial and other assistance for the anti-AIDS program in Uganda. The article further states that "Catholic hospitals, diocesan departments of social services, religious organizations and individual parishes conduct programs that complement government and NGO [non-governmental organizations] efforts."

An AIDS support organization (TASI) offers psychological as well as medical and material support to AIDS families. Kitoyu Catholic Hospital offers counseling and education for AIDS families. At another hospital, a missionary established a program for AIDS' widows and an Orphan Family Support. Yet another group offers a special program to assist orphans. The magnitude of the problem in Uganda is so great that many young children who are deprived of two parents need permanent homes with grandparents or with foster parents.

Education about AIDS

It seems to be a simple truism to state that everyone needs to know about AIDS. Until a cure and a method of prevention that carries certainty can be developed, a plan for education, especially for the at-risk group, is urgent.

As we develop services, there is a need for education for counselors, pastors, and others who will become counselors. Finally, there is a need for *all* members of the Christian churches and for the general population to be knowledgeable about AIDS.

The high-risk group is most vulnerable and most in need of knowledge of the means of transmission and of prevention. While these factors are thought to be commonly understood, the continued high rate of the number of persons newly infected suggests that the high-risk group is not fully informed or is unmotivated to avoid infection. For drug users, the lack of care in the use of needles or in the sharing of needles may be symptomatic of ignorance or an attitude of invulnerability, or a reflection of emotional need that abandons caution.

Of those who seek sexual contact with a partner who may be infected, many may also be ignorant of the possibility of infection or, like the drug user, may disregard caution because of a sexual need.

15

Whenever possible, individual guidance in outreach programs for drug users and active homosexuals is highly desirable. For heterosexuals who are or may be at risk, the only resource for conveying educational information is the public forum and the media. The recent emphasis on "safe sex" may, in fact, reach a large number of people, but this number remains unknown. The need for privacy in sexual matters constitutes a handicap in educational planning for at-risk heterosexuals.

In a general sense, all members of the Christian churches, as members of a compassionate community, need an ongoing educational program, whether on a parish level or other local level, as we all share in the AIDS crisis. Education will help us to share the church community's burden of the afflicted members. As members of a church, we are responsible for the wellness of all, and our spiritual and emotional support is needed by those who are sick.

What is true for members of a church community is true also for members of the general population. With more knowledge and greater understanding, it is hoped that there will be a reduction in prejudice and intolerance, and a recognition of the human dignity of AIDS victims. Opportunities for individuals and families to learn more about the AIDS experience will provide all persons in the general population with the facts of AIDS and hopefully will elicit compassion and help for those who need it. If we believe that all the members of a community are our brothers and sisters, the appropriate response is one of love and assistance.

Prevention

All aspects of prevention are related to education. If we can assume a greater involvement of people and communities in education, we might expect that preventive measures will be used by at-risk persons and others. However, it may be less difficult to change attitudes than to change behavior.

Since we are certain of the means of transmission of the HIV virus, we can indeed make a plea to drug users to use clean needles only and to avoid the sharing of needles or other nonsterile supplies.

The issue of infecting others when one is unsure of the presence of the HIV virus in oneself remains a problem yet to be solved. Questions have been raised about whether or not new laws may be needed for the protection of persons from those already infected. But a second question emerges of whether or not such laws can be enforced or are practical from a legal and financial point of view.

Confidentiality

Ethicists are concerned with the individual's right to privacy and to confidentiality. There may be circumstances in which confidentiality may be suspended. Recognizing the *right* to confidentiality is the first step. This right may be in conflict with the rights of another person, for instance, when there is a need to prevent infection of the other person or the need to provide medical care for the HIV-infected person. In both instances, the disclosure of the situation should consider the right of a person to *know,* and the disclosure should be made to that person only.

Conclusion

Because there are no immediate expectations for a cure for HIV/AIDS, there will be a need for all churches to continue their efforts to serve AIDS patients and their families. It is hoped that all persons of goodwill will continue to meet the challenge of this very serious illness.

Note

1. Christian churches are discussed here as organized services.

Judaism and Death: Practice Implications

George S. Getzel

In Arnold Schoenberg's great opera, *Moses and Aron,* the tension between death and immortality within Judaism dramatically unfolds. In a plodding and inarticulate manner, Moses quests for a personal encounter with the One-ness of God, the Source of Truth; Aron, his priestly brother, argues with him that such a quest is beyond the ordinary people who need and demand rites, rituals, and formulae to assuage their mortal fears, even if the consequences will be mindless observances and the danger of idolatry. For Moses, God's commandments bring people closer to the transcendent and ineffable Presence; no formula of righteous conduct can guarantee goodness and success in and of itself. The direct experience of God subsumes the question of death and immortality.

Modern men and women who, like Schoenberg, are drawn to their ancestral faith, are fascinated by the complex tensions between the Jewish concepts of life, death, and immortality. The struggles over these ideas are addressed over twenty-five hundred years of Jewish biblical commentary and debate.

Objectives

This chapter examines Jewish perspectives on death, with special attention to the ways in which Jews experience the occurrence of illness, dying, and death. This can be seen as a daunting task, if you begin by trying to define: What is Judaism, and who is a Jew? In the past and in the modern period, these questions have been and are currently the subjects of debate, controversy, and schism. In reality, a Jewish perspective on illness, dying, and death is an array of perspectives that have evolved and that reflect common understandings and points of departure that emanate from differing belief systems, cultural traditions, and historical factors that comprise the heterodoxy of the Jewish people within the United State. Jewish identity has always combined the concept of faith, peoplehood, and nationhood. Contemporary Jews may consciously ascribe to all, to one, or to particular combinations of these identifications. For example, a religious and a secular (nonobservant or atheistic) person can be identified as a Jew; to make things more confusing, a deeply religious and an atheistic Jew can be anti-Zionist.

Jews currently can and do express their Jewish identities in these contrasting ways. As the tired joke among Jews goes, "If you have *two* Jews, you have *three* points of view." This discussion and analysis assumes such variation among Jews as a given and does not take a position as to which expressions of Jewishness are preferable. However, some Jews cannot allow for such variation of perspectives under the designation Jew or Judaism; to advocates of that viewpoint, I plead for their indulgence, if that is possible.

One last point: no discussion about Judaism and Jewish identity can bypass the fact of assimilation among American Jews, as evidenced by the high rates of intermarriage between Jews and people of other religious faiths (Herzberg, 1960; Malcolm, 1991). For many Jews, knowledge of Jewish thinking and the practice of traditional customs are very rudimentary or nonexistent; their responses to life-threatening illness, dying, and death are an admixture of Jewish and secular and non-Jewish expressions.

A brief overview of Jewish perspectives toward illness, death, and dying will be presented using traditional sources and Jewish religious customs; their significance will be related to Jewish attitudes and behaviors. Clinical intervention with Jewish people will be described and analyzed through case examples. An understanding of religious and cultural perspectives should help social workers and other practitioners intervene with more understanding when Jewish clients face illness, dying, and death.

Traditional Sources

Hebrew writings of consolation give ample testimony to Judaism's recognition of death as an inextricable aspect of living and human existence. The classical statement of Ecclesiastes is, "A season is set for everything, a time for every experience under heaven: A time for being born and a time for dying" (Ecclesiastes, 3:1-2).

The Psalmist comforts the grieving: "Man, his days are like of grass; he blooms like a flower of the field; a wind passes by and it is no more, its own place no longer knows it" (Psalms, 103:15-16). The God of Israel is eternal; humankind created by God is not!

The Psalmist (Psalms, 90:3-4) notes God's power to determine the length of life:

> You return man to dust;
> You decreed, "Return you mortal!"
> For in Your sight a thousand years
> are like yesterday that has past,
> like a watch of the night.

The Hebrew Bible describes death as a natural part of life that all human beings should expect. Death is a finite end to a part of God's ongoing Creation. Thus, death, while certainly sad and not an occasion for celebration, can be construed as the appointed time of ending a solitary life: God completes the life of a human being. The argument offered, from this perspective, is that the quality of a life can be judged only when it is concluded (Heschel, 1974; Reimer, 1974; Lamm, 1969).

Also implicit here, and quite explicit throughout the Bible, is death's association with human failure or sin (Genesis, 19:18-30). Death is common punishment for serious offenses to God: sometimes death is implemented through ordinances of capital punishment done by believers (Leviticus, 20:9-16). Quite clearly, there exists a conflict in seeing death as a natural occurrence, perhaps a relief from the pain and the struggles of ordinary existence, and death as a punishment for sins.

The death of Moses, the greatest Hebrew prophet, epitomizes the complexity and the subtlety of the Jewish perspective on dying and the completion of the good life (Deuteronomy, 32:48-34:10). In many respects, it serves as a paradigm of Jewish dying; rabbinic commentary on this extract of biblical text has become an interpretative basis for Jewish attitudes, mores, and customs (Plaut, 1981).

The biblical narrative indicates that Moses lived a full life of 120 years; however, he could not visit the Promised Land—an irrevocable impediment to his worldly mission. Moses was allowed to be within sight of his goal but was not allowed to reach it; the goal was to be completed by another. Moses's plight can easily be seen as a metaphor for the good life and how human mortality frustrates us with the unfinished tasks and unfulfilled aspirations (Getzel, 1983). The greatest Hebrew prophet died alone and was buried in an unmarked grave. The glory of heavenly immortality is not mentioned — only that Moses would be forever revered by his followers and their ancestors.

Told by God that he would die and not reach the Promised Land, Moses gave evidence of his frustration as he implored his people to abide by his teachings — but Moses also indicated that he knew that his followers would forget what he had taught them. In effect, there is no guarantee that the revelation, to which he dedicated his life, would be remembered. Moses demonstrated a humbling human understanding of the fragility of all human efforts. Human understanding of the divine is particularly fragile.

Rabbinic commentary indicates that Moses asked his followers to forgive him for making difficult demands on them; they, in turn, sought Moses's forgiveness, because they were not sufficiently mindful of his teachings. The advent of death occasions mutual forgiveness, which makes leave-taking less burdensome and guilt-ridden. A death with outstanding recriminations cannot be a restful departing. Moses is said to have helped prepare his successor, Joshua, which also suggests Moses's acceptance of his own death (Plaut, 1981).

Other rabbinic commentary suggests that Moses entered into a long argument about why he should die and why God should be more forgiving. God was not moved by Moses's arguments, and God told His prophet that he would die for the sins of intemperance when he castigated his people and for the slaying of the Egyptians. The rabbis indicate that death is the punishment for human shortcomings, and it is not for human beings to question God's judgment (Plaut, 1981). In short, fighting the judgment of God's decree is an honored prerogative of the Jew and is seen not as a lack of faith but as an understandable grievance with God. Life is viewed as a valuable gift from God, which should not be disposed of quickly and mindlessly.

One of the most dramatic portrayals of a grievance with God appears in the Book of Job. The reader is told that Job was righteous and without sin; his faith was tested by God. Job lost his children, wealth, and health. Neither rational arguments nor imploring succeeds in changing God's action against Job. Finally, God proclaims that His omnipotence is an argument that precludes human understanding of suffering which, in its wake, can include the righteous (Job, 38: 1-39:30).

Ritual Responses

Judaism, as a religious tradition, focuses on a system of *mitzvot* (deeds that are commanded by God) and prayer, which are expressions of faith in God. Judaism, unlike Christianity, does not use elaborate statements of creed or articles of faith as a central part of its ritual (Baeck, 1948; Selzer, 1980; Trepp, 1962).

Rabbi Abraham Joshua Heschel (1954), Jewish religious philosopher, stated that *mitzvot* bring the Jew together with God. *Mitzvot* cannot be judged by their efficacy or rationality, but by their potential to spiritually transform the moment. Jewish observance of ritual arises from the commandments specified in Jewish law, which have been elaborated and interpreted over the centuries. Traditional Jews closely observe these rituals; Conservative and Reform Jews are more apt to adjust observances to the conditions of modernity and contemporary value considerations.

The *mitzvot* related to serious illness, dying, and death have a coherence and unity that have developed over the centuries. In large measure, they revolve around the Jewish belief that life is a gift — God's Creation — and it must be sanctified through the completion of appropriate *mitzvot* and traditional customs (Liebman, 1946; Heschel, 1974, Solveitchik, 1974; Meier, 1988). *Mitzvot* can be seen as expressions of Jewish virtues that are the building blocks of Jewish personality. To be a good Jew is to observe *mitzvot* freely and even with a sense of joy, because they bring you personally closer to God (Heschel, 1954).

Serious Illness

A period of serious illness represents a personal and spiritual challenge to the traditional Jew. *Pikuach nefesh* (to save an endangered life) and *bikur cholim* (to comfort the ill) are *mitzvot* to be followed, and their enactment puts Jews in frequent and close proximity to the fragility of life. Jewish traditions place a high value on the preservation of life, which becomes the reciprocal task of the sick, to actively try to get well, and of family members and friends, to support them in their recovery (Trepp, 1962; Rosner, 1991). It is not unusual for even the poorest Jewish family to go to great extremes to seek medical attention, and the community is also believed to have a collective responsibility to make certain the poor have proper medical care. The *mitzvot* of communal responsibility is *Kol Yishrael averim zeh bazeh* (each Jew is responsible for every Jew). This was a strong ethos that Eastern European Jews brought with them to the United States and explains the presence of hospitals under Jewish auspices in cities with significant Jewish populations (Zborowski and Herzog, 1952).

From the Jewish perspective, illness is a fearful occurrence because of the high value placed on human life; illness is invested with the inscrutability of God's actions in all human events, which can include retribution for human shortcomings. Dread of disease creates a spiritual and emotional challenge that occasions self-scrutiny and guilt, particularly if some past or current action can be linked to the cause of an illness.

Consequently, Jews place a high value on physicians and the efficacy of medicine. Among extremely pious Jews, rabbis are called on to recommend physicians. The *mitzvot* to save an endangered life can supersede in importance the enactment of other ritual requirements; for example, a Jewish doctor can work on the Sabbath (breaking an important *mitzvot*) if it means that he or she will be saving the life of a critically ill person (Rosner, 1991).

The *mitzvot* of saving an endangered life and comforting the ill present significant ethical dilemmas for Jewish doctors, especially in cases of painful terminal illness, that closely resemble the familiar medical ethical concerns about defining the parameters of dying and death, and deciding when to start palliative care and when to discontinue active treatment in cases of painful terminal illness. Needless to say, such decisions for Jewish families can be fraught with conflict and guilt, which have personal and traditional origins (Silver, 1974; Kaplan, 1974; Rosner, 1991). The field of Jewish medical ethics has grown more complex as it has had to respond to new, sophisticated diagnostic and treatment technologies. Efforts of Jewish medical ethics to reconcile current medical interventions to Jewish Law through rabbinic commentary is also known as *responsa* (Rosner, 1991).

Dying

If death seems to be approaching, an ill person is to be comforted by kin and friends. The visitor benefits from the fulfillment of a *mitzvot* that also eases the isolation and psychic pain of the ailing kin or neighbor. The kin and members of the community pray for the well-being of sick members by intoning special prayers during the synagogue services or by the recitation of psalms.

A dying Jew is not to die alone; it is the obligation of the community to attend to the dying. Consequently, the living know that at the period of their dying, they too will not be alone. In addition to family members present at the time of death, a community group of very pious men and women called the *Chevra Kadisha* (Holy Society) plays a special role. The *Chevra Kadisha* attends to needs of the dead and the mourning family, and membership gives them the highest prestige and respect of the community by their fulfillment of the *mitzvot* of *kevod hamet* (honoring the dead), which includes ritually preparing the body, or *mit,* for burial according to religious principles and traditions; their ministrations are done without compensation and are perceived to be holy in their own right, even if the grief-stricken family fails to thank them (Lamm, 1969; Goodman, 1981).

A very sick person should be judiciously encouraged to arrange his or her affairs without incurring the assumption that he or she is going to die soon. No procedures required after a person dies should be commenced until the death actually occurs. A dying person is to confess his or her sins; if unable to confess verbally, he or she should be encouraged to confess silently. At the point of death, tradition indicates that a Jew should try to recite the *Shema*—the affirmation of the Unity of God, central to the Jewish faith (Milligram, 1977).

The discussion of death in Judaism is fairly open: there are biblical examples of Joseph, Moses, and David who openly discussed the imminence of their deaths with their kin, including children (Meier, 1988). Preparation prior to dying includes the writing of a formal will for the disposing of possessions and wealth and also an "ethical will" that specifies the spiritual legacy to be carried forth by surviving children and grandchildren. The ethical legacy is viewed as more important than the material one among observant Jews (Abrahams, 1926; Reimer and Stampfer, 1983).

Death

After the moment of death occurs, the laws for formal mourning, known as *keriah* and signifying the rending of garments, take over. Traditionally, the mourner, while standing, tears the top part of his or her garment. The members of the *Chevra Kadisha* and others stand vigil with the body until its burial, which is to take place within twenty-four hours, except on the Sabbath and significant Holy Days, when burial takes place after their conclusion, early the next day (Lamm, 1969; Goodman, 1981).

Traditionally, the *Chevra Kadisha* ritual prepares the *mit* for burial by carefully following the rules called *taharah* (purification). The body is placed on a plank and carefully washed with large quantities of water from the head to the lower body, and appropriate prayers are recited. The *mit* is uniformly dressed in special burial clothing, with no distinction due to the status of persons prior to death. Judaism sees death as a democratic leveler, which makes no distinction among people because they are all created in God's image. Burial clothing consists of a simple white linen or cotton shroud — trousers, a long smock, and a skullcap for men or bonnet for women. A man's shoulders are covered with his *tallit* (prayer shawl), which he wore during religious services. The fringes of the *tallit* are cut when it serves as part of the shroud (Lamm, 1969; Goodman, 1981).

In the same democratic spirit, the *mit* is placed in a simple, unlined casket made of wood, with a bag of earth from the Holy Land, following the religious principle that the body should return to the earth from which it came, as mentioned in the story of Creation (Genesis, 2:6-7). The casket is seen as a temporary abode for the body as it gradually becomes part of the earth. (Holes are sometimes drilled into the casket to abet this process.)

The body in the coffin is never to be left alone until burial; traditionally, the community maintains vigil. Jewish tradition does not permit the viewing of the body — it remains in a closed coffin. This is done as a recognition of the finality of death and to protect the dead from idle and irreverent comments from the living.

No cosmetic treatment or embalming of the body is allowed. Traditional Jews do not allow cremation under any circumstances; burial in earth is mandated. Rabbis determine if a death is a volitional suicide, in which case the body is buried near the cemetery gate. A Jew can voluntarily kill him- or herself only to demonstrate fidelity to the belief in God, in the situation of forced conversion or apostasy.

A funeral service generally occurs in a funeral parlor and not in the synagogue. Brief prayers are recited and psalms are read. Typically, eulogies are said that reflect on the virtues of the deceased and that offer comfort to the bereaved. The service includes a memorial prayer, *El Malei Rachimim,* which beseeches God to accept and protect the soul of the dead "under the shelter of Thy wings . . ." — a metaphorical reference to the immortality of the soul, which returns to its Source.

Burial, in its most traditional form, includes kin and friends digging the grave, the manual lowering of the coffin so that it rests gently on the earth, and family mourners and friends participating in the filling of the grave before leaving the cemetery. The irrevocable commitment of the dead to the earth is directly and powerfully experienced by all. The *Kaddish* prayer, which sanctifies God's name and affirms God's omnipotence, is recited by mourners after the filling of the grave. Another version of the *Kaddish* is recited at memorial services throughout the year by the principal mourners (Lamm, 1969).

Rabbi Maurice Lamm (1969, pp. 78-79), in his eloquent book on traditional Jewish death and mourning, identifies five stages of Jewish mourning: (a) prior to burial is a period of intense grief, in which mourners are exempt from the demands of ordinary religious observance; (b) the three days after burial, when mourners can demonstrably lament and weep about their loss — visitors are discouraged during this intense private period; (c) during the last four days of *shiva* (the first week of mourning), mourners can have visitors expressing condolences and accept comfort from the community, although men are unshaven and, with women, wear rent clothing; (d) following *shiva,* mourners observe *sheloshim,* thirty days of diminished expression of mourning and encouraged reentry into the flow of life's routines; (e) for one year after *shiva,* life can become routine in the fullest way, but in the case of the death of a parent, entertainment and amusements are to be avoided. After this period, mourning is to cease except for traditional memorial services held for the dead on Jewish Holy Days.

Observance of these traditions provides a carefully specified process of transition for grief expression (Solveitchik, 1974). Emotional expression is encouraged and condoned early in the mourning process, with specific behavioral requirements that demand progressively greater involvement with others, who are required to provide instrumental assistance and emotional support throughout the period of mourning. Prayer and reflection that offset the strong naturalistic burial ritual are integrated into the Jewish paradigm of mourning, reenforcing a sense of finite human existence. Judaism lacks very specific visualizations and definitions of immortality and resurrection, in contrast to Christianity and Islam.

Inroads of Modernity

In the United States over the last fifty years, adherence to the traditional paradigm of understanding and responding to death has significantly changed. What might be called American or Christian customs have entered the practice of many Jews. For example, the Jewish tradition of having no flowers at memorial services or burial is widely disregarded, and the use of the simple wooden coffin has been displaced by elaborate and ostentatious wooden or metal, lined caskets in which the embalmed body, attired in worldly clothing, is to be viewed by family members and strangers. Ritual prayer and the elaborate mourning customs have been abbreviated or discarded.

Geographical mobility of principal mourners, the priority of commercial activity over religious obligations, the use of professional funeral services, and the diminished observance of Jewish traditions are some explanations offered for these changes. Interestingly, avoidance of flowers and of open caskets have recently been adopted by many non-Jews in an effort to avoid the excesses of the modern funeral, which offend the aesthetic, spiritual, and economic sensibilities of many people. There is even a small movement among Conservative and Reform Jews to revitalize the concepts of visiting the ill and honoring the dead (Goodman, 1981).

Traditional Jews have had to accommodate to governmental requirements for autopsies and have had to grapple with the acceptability of organ transplants — invasive approaches using the organs of the dead (Lamm, 1969; Goodman, 1981; Rosner, 1991).

Discussion

From this synoptic view of Judaism's viewpoints about death and dying, generalizations must be carefully drawn when examining the reactions and behaviors of Jewish people to terminal illness, death, and dying. Of necessity, Jewish responses are conditioned and nuanced by personal, cultural, and religious factors in the following case illustration.

Mrs. Oppenheim, an eighty-four-year-old Jewish woman, became seriously confused and anxious living alone at home; she cried piteously, wanting to see her son and asking her social worker where he went. The fact was that her only son visited her every day, and she seemed to disregard this. A consultant was called in to check Mrs. Oppenheim's mental status. She told him that she felt safe in her apartment, protected from the Nazis, but she was worried because she didn't know if her son was dead or alive. It turned out that the son Mrs. Oppenheim was talking about was a courier who relayed messages to

Resistance fighters during the siege of the Warsaw Ghetto. Her living son told the consultant that her first son probably died in April 1943, when the Ghetto was destroyed. Each year, her surviving son would take Mrs. Oppenheim to *Yizkor* (Memorial Service) held during the Passover service; she would cry as if her son had just died.

The consultant realized that it was approximately the time of year that her son was lost, and Mrs. Oppenheim was reliving the trauma. She was especially agitated now that she was becoming mentally confused and disoriented.

The consultant asked the old woman if it would be acceptable for the social worker to speak with a rabbi. Upon seeing the rabbi, Mrs. Oppenheim began to confess her guilt in letting her son risk his life. Later, her surviving son said *Kaddish* with the rabbi at Mrs. Oppenheim's bedside. She quietly smiled, and tears flowed down her cheeks.

A central task for the Jew in dealing with the finality of the death of a loved one is to find a ritual outlet for pent-up emotions—Jewish ritual allows expression for that emotion. Recognition of bodily dissolution, abetted by Judaism's naturalistic characteristics in confronting death, invites emotional and spiritual reflection. Mrs. Oppenheim was denied seeing her dead son and a fuller sense of the reality of her loss. The Memorial Service provided for remembrance of the martyrs of the Jewish people collectively and individually.

The full life of three score and ten was exceeded by Mrs. Oppenheim, but denied her son. The guilt she felt haunted her life and was aggravated in old age. The deaths of 1.5 million children during the Nazi Holocaust create a special burden of remembrance for the Jewish people, collectively and individually (Rosenbloom, 1988).

The Case of AIDS

In recent times, the AIDS pandemic has emerged as a special challenge to, and opportunity for, Jewish response to the issues of illness, dying, and death (Bogot, 1987; Schlindler, 1989; Rosner, 1991). The following case example points to some of the issues encountered:

Ronald Weiss was a forty-five-year-old Jewish man diagnosed with AIDS; he had become more disabled, with bouts of uncontrollable diarrhea and visible lesions from Kaposi's sarcoma (a skin cancer associated with AIDS) over most of his body. Even with the visibility of lesions, Ronald did not tell his eighty-two-year-old father that he was gay and had AIDS. About six months after his diagnosis, he was able to tell his older brother that he had AIDS. Ronald's brother was married, with grown children, and was a leader in the Jewish community. Ronald felt his gay life-style and illness would only be construed by the Jewish community as a mark against his family. When Ronald revealed his condition at a midday lunch in Manhattan, his brother cried and offered material and emotional support, which Ronald experienced with shocked pleasure.

Ronald told his social worker that he was unable to tell his elderly father, with whom he had frequent contact, about being gay and seriously ill, because he felt that his father, unlike his deceased mother, was always remote and not openly affectionate toward him, even as a child.

Recently, Ronald discussed the possibility of converting to Catholicism because of his affectionate feeling for St. Francis of Assisi: he had studied the lives of saints and was moved by their ability to endure pain and tribulation. Becoming more ill, Ronald had very vivid dreams of dying and entering heaven to be reunited with his mother and his lover, who had committed suicide when he was diagnosed with AIDS. Ronald said that he was strongly ambivalent about conversion, seeing the decision as a repudiation of his family. In addition, Ronald did not feel sanguine about the Catholic church accepting him as a gay man, but he wondered if that would matter now that he was dying of AIDS.

Religion had become for Ronald a metaphorical expression for his sadness and sense of rejection for being gay and having AIDS. The remoteness of his father seemed to be related to his moving away from his Jewish identification. Ronald apparently likened the withdrawal of his father to the removal of God's protection; nothing, he reasoned, could reverse the course of AIDS, which daily brought new indignities. Confusion about his Jewish identity was further evidenced in his wish to be buried in a Jewish cemetery next to his mother.

Ronald discussed with his social worker a plan to leave a substantial amount of money to his godchild, a child of friends; the money would be given to her when she became eighteen years old. Ronald said with resignation, "At least one person will remember me." At the time, he felt his immortality was very uncertain.

Ronald's quest to be remembered after his death was usually associated with repeated perturbations over his father's inability to remember the suicide death of his lover. His father had met his lover on several occasions, introduced always by Ronald as a close friend.

When Ronald became too weak to leave his apartment, he needed constant medical attention and household assistance. His family and

29

friends organized a group to always be near him so that he would never be alone — a secular *Chevra Kadisha.*

With the help of the social worker, friends asked Ronald's father if he ever wondered why Ronald never got married. His father said in a matter-of-fact way that that could not happen because Ronald was gay. The old man then recounted, by name, all of Ronald's lovers over the last twenty years and said that he never discussed Ronald's homosexuality because Ronald never seemed comfortable telling him that he was gay. His father said that he loved both of his sons equally and always tried to be evenhanded in the treatment of his children.

Ronald's friends and the social worker told the old man that Ronald was not sure about his father's reactions to him as a gay man. His father, without ceremony or hesitation, went into Ronald's bedroom. He told him that he had long known that his son was gay and loved him very much. His father then kissed Ronald on the forehead. Ronald smiled as tears filled his eyes. Unable to speak, Ronald said all he had to with his eyes. A week later, Ronald was buried next to his mother.

This case reveals how the internalization of Jewish values and sentiments can become symbolically significant in understanding the complexity of human emotion arising in the family context. AIDS, with its inevitable association with homosexuality, reenforces historical and cultural issues for the family and the community. Judaism's antagonism to homosexuality becomes hypothetically at odds with the *mitzvot* of *bikur cholim* (comforting the sick) and of *shituf betsa'ar* (empathy to human pain and suffering).

In Ronald's situation, the reconciliation of father and son was through the ritual called the *Vidui* (deathbed confession). Their reciprocal confession at the approach of death provided greater certainty of their emotional tie and that Ronald would be remembered in the context of the love of two parents.

Conclusion

Judaism, a system of beliefs, values, and behaviors internalized by adherents, assumes a great deal of importance throughout the life cycle, including dying and event of death. Complicated emotional reactions are related to Jews' understandings of God's actions in the world and of human responsibility. Ritual and expressions of faith comprise the Jewish responses to death, which permit emotional expression and self-examination in contemplating the vagaries of immortality. The naturalistic elements of Jewish funeral rites give a stark depiction of bodily dissolution and the irrevocability of human life. Liturgy provides naturalistic motifs and declarations of the soul's spiritual return to God.

Walking Through the Valley of the Shadow of Death: Grief and Fundamentalism

Gary R. Anderson

Culture is defined and shaped by religious beliefs and expressions. The stronger the belief system—due to its pervasive quality and time and energy commitment—the greater the contribution to the cultural context and individual fiber of the believer. Understanding a family's religious background and perspective on life is crucial for any person working in the area of loss, grief, and death (Rando, 1984).

One of the strongest religious systems in the United States is Fundamentalist Protestant Christianity. Fundamentalism is sometimes portrayed as an eccentric fringe aspect of American society and the religious landscape; however, to trivialize its impact in the United States or to underestimate its importance in believers' lives would be a serious oversight. With as many as 50 million Americans describing themselves as Born-Again Christians, understanding this religious orientation is important for persons seeking to assist and comfort people who are grieving (Lifton and Stozier, 1990).

This chapter will address the grieving process and Fundamentalist Christian expressions. After defining Christian Fundamentalism, the meaning of death and loss will be described. Practices with regard to grieving, rituals, and funerals will also be discussed. The implications for counselors are significant, as persons with Fundamentalist beliefs and others who do not identify themselves as Fundamentalists but share common areas of belief and concern face an often complicated grief process.

Fundamentalism Defined

Historically, Fundamentalism was a movement against the theological modernization or liberalism of Protestant denominations. This modernization questioned or overturned the fundamentals of the faith. These fundamentals include: (a) the inspiration, authority, and inerrancy of the Bible; (b) the virgin birth of Jesus; (c) the deity of Jesus; (d) Jesus's physical resurrection from the dead; (e) His substitutionary atonement for sin; and (f) the literal second coming of Jesus Christ (Marty, 1981; Lightner, 1986). Fundamentalists defended these beliefs and separated themselves from others who diluted or rejected them. In addition to adherence to "fundamental" beliefs and separation from modernists, Fundamentalist religious groups have often created strong prohibitions governing certain behaviors (the use of alcohol, for example) and life-styles.

Fundamentalism has been used to designate a class of Christian groups sometimes called conservative or the Christian Right. A variety of other descriptive terms are used: Fundamentalists, Charismatics, Evangelicals, and Pentecostals (Denton, 1990; Lowenberg, 1988). These terms encompass a wide spectrum of beliefs and practices, many of which conflict with one another. So Fundamentalism can be defined broadly, encompassing many conservative Protestant viewpoints ("born-again"), or more precisely, differentiating between groups such as Fundamentalists and Evangelicals (Dobson, 1986; Lightner, 1986). The most important premise for this discussion is the belief that the Bible is the authoritative, *literal* Word of God.

The Fundamentalist Christian church culture is sometimes described as isolated, insulated, and maintaining a "we-versus-them mentality." This separation from others, with various strong prohibitions, often leads to a negative perspective on Fundamentalism. This description overlooks the strengths of the Fundamentalist church— opportunities for socialization, feelings of belongingness, increased status and role opportunities, forgiveness, ability to relinquish responsibility for one's actions and problems, and spiritual guidance in the form of rules, values, and rituals (Denton, 1990; Ness and Wintrob, 1980). Responding to death and loss may be a strong point for Fundamentalism, as death has meaning, and with meaning comes assurance and hope for believers. It is possible to offer consolation and comfort grounded in a Fundamentalist interpretation of the Bible. However, with a literal belief in the Bible, there is the danger of eternal damnation in hell as well as the possibility of eternity in heaven.

The Meaning of Death

In the Fundamentalist view of life, there are answers to life's questions and guidance for living. Ernest Becker (1975) noted the role of religion in explaining death:

> Religion solves the problem of death. . . . Religion, then, gives the possibility of heroic victory in freedom. . . . Religion alone gives hope, because it holds open the dimension of the unknown and unknowable, the fantastic mystery of creation that the human mind cannot ever begin to approach, the possibility of a multidimensionality of spheres of existence, of heavens. . . . (Pp. 203, 204)

For the person with a Fundamentalist faith, the solution is clear, the mystery is less mysterious, and "heavens" is singular. Death has a variety of interlocking meanings: (a) death is a product of sin; (b) death is subject to God's rule, but His ways are sometimes difficult for mortals to comprehend; (c) death has been conquered by Jesus Christ; (d) upon death, the believer is assured of eternal life with God; (e) the person who dies will be judged and rewarded for his or her faithfulness while alive on earth; and (f) the person who does not believe in Jesus is doomed to hell.

Death Is a Product of Sin

Why is there death, and why do people have to die? A Fundamentalist might answer that death entered Creation at the time of Adam and Eve's disobedience to God in the Garden of Eden, as described in the biblical book of Genesis. A conservative theologian, Henry Thiessen (1969), explained:

> When God said that for disobedience man would "surely die," He meant also as to the body. Immediately after the trespass God said to Adam, "Dust thou art, and unto dust shalt thou return" (Genesis 3:19) . . . the constant teaching of Scripture that physical death is a result of Adam's sin; and since the Scriptures are final authority in all matters, it is necessary to regard physical death as the penalty of sin. (P. 257)

Death has entered into the world due to man's sinfulness, and at times, death is a specific outcome or punishment for disobedience to God:

34

> Does God pervert justice? Does the Almighty pervert what is
> right? When your children sinned against Him, He gave them
> over to the penalty of their sin. (Job 8:3,4)

If pain, suffering, and death are deserved punishment for evil actions,
then the sufferer must repent and live rightly:

> If you will look to the Almighty, if you are pure and upright,
> even now He will rouse Himself on your behalf and restore you
> to your rightful place. (Job 8:5,6)

Is all suffering and death to be interpreted as sent from God to pun-
ish a sinful person? While acknowledging that all people are sinners,
there is still a sense that some people suffer unfairly—that the righteous suffer. So how is the suffering of the young, innocent, or pious
explained?

Death Is Subject to God's Rule

The God of Fundamentalism is not a distant observer of human history and experience. He has a purpose and plan for people's lives:
"Death is not an accident; it is an appointment" (Wiersbe and Wiersbe,
1986, p. 42). His actions, however, are not always comprehensible to
humans, so some deaths may not be readily understood:

> My thoughts are not your thoughts, neither are your ways my
> ways, declares the Lord. As the heavens are higher than the earth,
> so are my ways higher than your ways and my thoughts than your
> thoughts. (Isaiah 55:8,9)
> Because He is so much greater than we are, we can trust
> Him though we do not understand everything which happens.
> (NIV Notes, p. 883)

For the Fundamentalist Christian, nothing happens by accident:
God either causes or allows things to happen. As some of these events
are hard to understand, the believer must have faith in and trust this
personal, planful, superior God, so that when a believer dies it is possible to proclaim and be comforted by the statement, "The Savior took
her home" (Rice, 1971, p. 21). A child interviewed by Robert Coles
(1990) noted, "I might just be hoping I'd die. I'd not pray to God that
I die, no . . . because He's the one who decides; it's not up to you"
(p. 137).

Death Has Been Defeated by Jesus's
Literal Resurrection

The Christian is victorious, as death has been conquered by Jesus, because He died for humanity's sins and returned to life after being dead. Consequently, for the Fundamentalist, there is hope, and death is not the end of life and is not to be feared:

> For the trumpet will sound, the dead will be raised imperishable . . . the perishable has been clothed with the imperishable, and the mortal with immortality. . . . Death has been swallowed up in victory. "Where, O death, is your victory? Where, O death, is your sting?" But thanks be to God! He gives us the victory through our Lord Jesus Christ. (I Corinthians 15:52-57)

> For the Christian, however, death is no longer a penalty, since Christ has endured death as the penalty of sin. To him it becomes a sleep as to the body and a gateway as to the soul through which he enters into full communion with his Lord. (Thiessen, 1969, p. 271)

> Christ Himself has experienced the worst that life has to offer, all that death holds, and now stands victorious on the other side of both in eternal glory. So for the Christian the providence of God is a vital reality. The Savior has blazed a trail before him. (Adams, 1971, p. 76)

For the Fundamentalist Christian, the ultimate victory is the second coming to earth of Jesus Christ and the end of death:

> They will be His people, and God Himself will be with them and be their God. He will wipe away every tear from their eyes. There will be no more death or mourning or crying or pain, for the old order of things has passed away. (Revelation 21:3b,4)

A number of studies have been conducted to explore the relationship between death anxiety and religious belief. A survey of high school students found less death anxiety for Christians than non-Christians but could not distinguish between born-again Christians and those students who identified themselves as Christian but not born again (Young and Daniels, 1980). Another study noted that "fear of death decreased with increasing depth of religious experience, with strength of belief in life after death, and with religious ritual" (Leming,

1980, p. 347). It concluded that religion arouses death anxiety and then alleviates this anxiety!

The Christian Will Go to Be with God upon Death

Death is the gateway to eternal life. Adams (1971), a Christian counselor, proclaimed, "The Christian's hope brings him the assurance that because Christ died for his sins he shall have eternal life, and that at death his spirit shall be made perfect" (p. 138). Giving advice on how to explain death to a child, the *Fundamentalist Journal* ("Family Living," 1986) recommended: "Our bodies are like seeds. We plant the body in the ground in the cemetery ('God's acre'), and one day it will be raised in glory and beauty, a new body fitted for eternity" (p. 54).

The faithful believer is assured of eternal life in heaven with Jesus:

> Do not let your hearts be troubled. Trust in God, trust also in me. In my Father's house are many rooms. . . . I am going there to prepare a place for you. . . . I will come back and take you to be with me that you also may be where I am. (John 14:1-3)

There is also the assurance of a reunion with loved ones who were Christians and have already died. This expectation of being reunited can inspire anticipation and powerful sentimentality: "Tell mother I'll be there, Heaven's joys with her to share, yes tell my darling mother I'll be there!" (Rice, 1971, p. 21). Going to heaven is going home for the believer.

Death Moves One to a New World and Life That Is Influenced by One's Actions Prior to Death

The Fundamentalist believes that the Bible teaches that, upon one's death, there is a day of judgment on which the person's life and decisions are reviewed by God: "No life is a success unless it has been used as a preparation for the next life. Regardless of the accomplishments a person makes his life is a failure unless he is prepared for dying" (Hyles, 1974, p. 36). This time of review and judgment may result in praise and rewards for faithful believers:

> I have fought the good fight, I have finished the race, I have kept the faith. Now there is in store for me the crown of righteousness, which the Lord, the righteous Judge, will award to me on that day—and not only to me. (II Timothy 4:7,8)

37

Blessed are you when people insult you, persecute you and
falsely say all kinds of evil against you because of me. Rejoice
and be glad, because great is your reward in heaven. (Matthew
5:11,12a)

How the believer lives his or her life while alive on earth has eternal
consequences, potentially determining the quality of one's heavenly
status and, even more basically, whether or not the person will spend
eternity in heaven or hell.

Hell Is Certain for Those Who Do Not Believe in Jesus

In addition to teaching that the believer will have an eternal life in
heaven, the Fundamentalist Christian believes that the Bible teaches
that the person who does not accept Jesus as his or her Savior (i.e.,
is not born again) will spend eternity in hell. This belief in a literal
hell, as well as a real Satan, distinguishes Fundamentalism from other
religious viewpoints. Religious liberalism erased references to hell and
damnation, but Fundamentalists insist that these consequences of
unbelief are biblically based and valid (Farrell, 1982).

There are a number of images used in the Bible for heaven and
hell sufficient to communicate the desirability of one and the pain-
fulness of the other. In part because the consequences of not being
a believer are so severe, the Fundamentalist Christian is expected to
warn others and try to convert them, a process called evangelism (Falwell, 1986). George Gallup defined an "evangelical" as a born-again
person who believes that every part of the Bible is the actual Word
of God, and this person has encouraged someone else to accept Jesus
as their Savior (Galanter, Larson, and Rubenstone, 1991).

With regard to young children who die, as they have not reached
an "age of understanding" in which they can be held accountable for
accepting or rejecting Jesus, it is generally believed that young children go to heaven.

Rituals and Funerals

There are few formal rituals or events associated with death apart from
a funeral service. Although there may be a viewing of the body and
meeting the family at a funeral home, there is no formal "wake" as

in the Roman Catholic tradition. Although generally not expressly forbidden, cremations are not common.

The primary event is the funeral service itself. This service is often conducted at the church and resembles a church service, with music, reading from the Bible, and a sermon. It is the sermon that may most distinguish a Fundamentalist person's funeral from other funerals, for the time of a person's death is an opportunity for the minister to remind surviving believers to be faithful:

> Grief offers an important opportunity for a pastor to reorient lives according to biblical patterns. Death demands changes; why shouldn't those changes be in the direction of greater devotion to Christ? When one's life is disintegrated it can be altered much more readily, much more rapidly, along biblical lines than at any other time. (Adams, 1971, p. 171)

It is also a time to present an evangelistic message to persuade people at the funeral who are not Christians to become Christians.

In addition to the sermon, the content of the funeral service typically includes reading biblical passages that address death and eternal life (for example, Romans 8; I Corinthians 15; II Corinthians 5; Revelation 21), or favorite family passages (for example, Psalm 23). A variety of reassuring hymns that affirm God's faithfulness and love are often sung by the congregation or guest musicians. There are also ministerial prayers, often thanking God for the deceased person and seeking comfort for mourning survivors. There are no prayers for the dead, as these are considered meaningless and ineffectual. There is no purgatory or status between heaven or hell.

While affirming that no one can know another's inner thoughts and that people can turn to Jesus upon their deathbeds, a Fundamentalist minister would find it difficult to extend assurances with regard to a person who died and was, to the best of the minister's knowledge, not a believer. To believers, there is considerable hope and assurance given as to the meaning of death and the security of eternal life in heaven. In addition, the context of a funeral is a time for the church to become very cohesive and to support and encourage the family through concrete assistance (such as providing food), prayers and words of comfort, and attendance at the funeral. There are no formal commemorations or remembrances of the deceased, nor is there a formal period of mourning. There may be opportunities to make donations, such as floral arrangements, in memory of the deceased at later points in time.

A Complicated Grief Process

Comforting a mourning Fundamentalist family requires a culturally sensitive response. This includes understanding the meaning attributed to death and dying and the potentially troubling messages that may subtly or overtly be intertwined with the meaning of death:

1. If death is a result of Adam and Eve's disobedience of God, is all suffering and death attributable to disobedience and human failure? It might be quite natural for a Fundamentalist person to wonder if a loss is a form of punishment for his or her transgressions. This attitude might be evidenced with an illness such as AIDS leading to the assertion that an illness and death are punishment from God or in some way deserved due to one's sinful life-style or behaviors. This linking of death and sin may result in guilt and shame.

2. If God is in control of His creation, experiencing a loss might lead to questioning God's behavior: Why did He allow suffering and death? Such questions might be prominent when the sufferer is young or has lived a sacrificial and caring life. For the Fundamentalist Christian, doubting God and questioning His actions, or even His existence, might be equated with losing his or her faith and rejecting God—how can one be a believer and also have doubt? A research study noted, "Doubts of any kind leave them confused about their own faith and susceptible to powerful anxieties concerning death and extinction" (Lifton and Stozier, 1990, p. 24). It may be even more troubling if the person is angry with God. Such anger may be viewed as unacceptable by the person or as un-Christian by other believers in the community.

3. If death has been defeated by Jesus's resurrection, what if the grieving believer feels fear rather than triumph and assurance? A fear of death or the desire to live a long life and avoid death might be interpreted as a weakness in faith and failure to truly believe that death has lost its fearful hold upon the committed Christian.

4. If the believer will go to heaven upon his or her death, some members of a Fundamentalist community might find it difficult to accept great sadness and sorrow by people experiencing a loss. There may also be self-doubt and confusion—if the person I love is in heaven, why do I feel so sad? Such sadness might be even

harder to accept when it persists beyond a short period of time. It may lead to questioning the sincerity or depth of one's religion: "The literature addresses the danger that the death of friends or loved ones will bring about a grief that leads to loss of faith" (Lifton and Stozier, 1990, p. 25).

5. If there is a judgment day, at which time one's actions and choices are reviewed and judged, the believer must live his or her life in careful obedience to God. If present actions have eternal consequences, any behavior short of perfection might be particularly troubling.

6. If there is an eternal hell, how does a person reconcile this belief with his or her everyday life? To doubt its existence is to question the foundation of one's faith based on a literal interpretation of the Bible. To accept its accuracy compels one to fervent evangelism or coping with the uncomfortableness of believing that some friends, family members, and associates are eternally damned.

In summary, the Christian Fundamentalist belief system about death may pose a number of complications to the grieving process. Foremost may be the difficulty in recognizing, acknowledging, or expressing a range of emotions that are categorized as negative and viewed as incompatible with true faith, such as guilt, doubt, anger, fear, sadness, and confusion: "If I am angry at God, doubting, fearful, sad, confused, or guilty, I have lost or am losing my faith. If I lose my faith in God, I have nothing. I am lost and alone and without hope."

Reflecting on the role of religion in grieving, Therese Rando (1988) observed:

> It is quite common to be angry at God, to lose faith in your religion or philosophy of life after the death of someone you love. . . . This distress over the failure of your value system, religion, or belief in God to sustain you in your grief can become a major stumbling block in your grief process, leaving you to cope with intense anger and a profound sense of betrayal. (Pp. 31, 32)

In situations where the believer can acknowledge and accept such emotions, he or she might be misunderstood by others in the community, who may judge them to be less solid in their faith. There may also be losses that are not accepted or understood by one's religious community, such as an AIDS-related death of a homosexual child or a divorce, or an action such as abortion, suicide, or sexual abuse. When the relationship, loss, or griever is not recognized, the resulting secrecy, isolation, and exclusion can be called "disenfranchised grief." Disenfrancished grief complicates mourning by intensifying anger, guilt, and powerlessness while also removing or minimizing sources of support (Doka, 1989).

So some Fundamentalist persons may face a grief process characterized by suppression that doesn't allow, or quickly brings a halt to, troubling emotions provoked by a loss. A stoic response to loss may be appropriate, but there also seems to be an expectation that the grieving person is confident, comforted, and peaceful because of his or her faith.

A Facilitated Grief Process

Some aspects of Fundamentalist beliefs and practice may complicate mourning; other features may assist a person and family. Strong religious faith may make traumatic events easier to bear through the establishment of a relationship with a divine being — God — and the provision of a system of meaning and existential coherence (Ellison, 1991). Religious beliefs encapsulate an illness or loss by controlling the meaning of the experience. Coping strategies include maintaining an optimistic viewpoint, endowing the illness or loss with meaning, affirming life, and a philosophy of life that allows family members to continue living after a death (Birenbaum, 1990). The believer may also be able to redefine potentially negative life events as opportunities for spiritual growth or define losses and trauma as part of a broader divine plan.

For the Christian Fundamentalist family, the meaning of death is relatively clear and hopeful. The believer can trust a powerful and loving God, can appeal to a divine person who has experienced grief ("Jesus wept") and death, can hope for a better eternal life and reunion with those who have died, and the survivor has a sense of purpose in this present life.

Strong religious faith offers a powerful framework for interpreting one's daily experiences as well as major life events and traumas. It provides a tool for constructing meaning and coherence. One author noted that this might "compensate for the lack of more sophisticated cognitive resources," suggesting that the "effects of divine relations and existential certainty on well-being may be strongest among persons with lower levels of formal education" (Ellison, 1991). To portray Fundamentalist people as uneducated is a negative stereotype; however, they may have lower levels of formal education compared to members of other Protestant affiliations.

As noted earlier, there may be a correlation between death anxiety and religious practices and beliefs. Although studies sometimes report no significant lessening of anxiety, others have noted more effective coping by persons who use religious beliefs and prayer during stressful situations. A study of seven hundred senior citizens concluded: "Elderly individuals who employ intrapsychic or cognitive religious behaviors to deal with stressful or difficult life situations appear to more effectively cope with anxiety and fears surrounding death" (Koenig, 1988).

The Fundamentalist Christian also often has the experience of being part of a supportive community that provides concrete assistance (food, money, and so on), friendship, and encouragement when coping with loss. This combination of social support, a divine relationship, and existential meaning has potentially helpful features for Fundamentalist families. This may contrast with Rando's (1984) observation that for those lacking strong, positive family ties and other supportive group interactions and experiencing a waning of faith, "death no longer signals atonement and redemption as much as man's loneliness and a threat to his pursuit of happiness" (p. 7).

Implications for Mental Health Professionals

A Fundamentalist Christian may be hesitant to seek out a therapist or counselor due to a mistrust of secular psychology and psychotherapy. There may be the perception, and for some, the experience, of having their belief system either misunderstood or ridiculed and attacked. A person might be more likely to seek out his or her minister, a church leader, or a person identified as a Christian counselor. Although it is not necessary that a helping person have a similar background, a cultural sensitivity and "religious affinity" would provide the attitude necessary to decrease the Fundamentalist person's initial resistance and distrust (*AIDSline,* 1982).

There are several points to highlight in a therapeutic response to the Fundamentalist griever:

1. Explore and recognize the strengths of the person's belief system and the potential assurance and comfort it might provide (Millison and Dudley, 1990).

43

2. Be aware of the role of the church community in the person's life and the social network, status, and support that these fellow believers might provide.

3. Listen for the complicating messages and accompanying defenses (such as repression, denial, and reaction formation) that make it difficult for the person to grieve and mourn a loss because such feelings are equated with losing one's faith.

4. Explore the events accompanying the loss, as the formal structure of the church service/funeral may not provide sufficient ritual for grieving, or the time frame for expressing grief may be too short and limiting.

5. Seek out the advice and cooperation of the family's respected religious advisors. Many Fundamentalist leaders and writers are aware of possible harmful responses to people in grief. One minister advises:

> Be swift to hear, slow to speak, and slow to react to words and feelings that may appear "un-Christian." Do not try to explain everything. . . . Remember that grieving is a difficult process that takes time. Be patient with those who mourn and don't ask, "Aren't you over it yet?" (Wiersbe and Wiersbe, 1986, p. 42)

A study of pastoral counseling activities of the clergy pointed out the lack of communication and networking between conservative clergy and mental health professionals. Evangelical ministers were the least likely to refer counselees to mental health professionals. On the other hand, community mental health and psychiatric professionals rarely, if ever, referred clients to clergy of any theological orientation (Mollica, Streets, Boscarino, and Redlich, 1986).

6. Respect the family's religious behaviors that have significance for them, such as praying, reading the Bible, or attending church services (Wilson-Ford, 1992). A survey of Christian psychiatrists found that Bible reading and prayer were judged to be the most effective intervention modality in treating grief reactions (Galanter et al., 1991). Do not be surprised if families with a critically ill member expect, or pray for, a miraculous recovery or express confidence in faith healing.

The helping person might want to be aware of specific Bible verses or stories that could be briefly shared with a family. For example, there are many examples of expressing sadness, confusion, and anger with God in the book of Psalms (see chapters 13, 28, 39, or 43), or the example of Jesus when learning of the death of his friend Lazarus (John 11). Some knowledge of metaphors and acknowledgment of a relationship between family members and God may be helpful (Denton, 1990; Griffith, 1986).

The helping person must also be aware of his or her own reactions and responses to people with strong religious convictions (Bergin, 1991). For some therapists, it may be difficult to understand the importance of these beliefs, as well as their content. Some may have to recognize and control stereotypes or negative reactions to Fundamentalism. Some have rejected their own more conservative upbringings; for example, the founder of Fundamentalists Anonymous characterized Fundamentalism as having simple thought processes, closed-mindedness, and a compulsion to impose their beliefs on others (Hunsberger, 1991). The religious counselor may face other challenges with regard to boundaries, posing expectations for the family, or unknowingly complicating the process for the family that may not want to expose its doubts to another believer.

Finally, as with all cultures, it is important to individualize the person and the family. Although certain generalizations may guide the thinking of the helping person, it is important to assess the family to learn each family member's own experience, meanings, and behaviors related to death and loss. There may be varying degrees of adherence to beliefs and religious practices. The grief process is further shaped by a range of key variables, including gender, race, ethnicity, and socioeconomic status.

Conclusion

A strongly held belief system that shapes thoughts and behaviors and orders the social world and relationships should not be ignored when working with families:

> From the cradle to the grave, many American families are intimately involved in religion. Failing to note this, some of our family theories and therapeutic interventions have limited relevance and impact on those whose family paradigm is constructed with religious beliefs and values. (Abbott, Berry, and Meredith, 1990, p. 447)

An attitude of openness and respect is essential if one is to gain trust and provide a setting in which healing can be facilitated. Understanding and responding to the Fundamentalist Christian family poses a challenge for helping professionals, as the family's beliefs may introduce both complications and contributions to the grieving process.

CHAPTER FIVE

Death and Dying: An Islamic Perspective

Ahmad H. Sakr

Islam is the religion of God (Allah[1]) revealed to prophet Muhammad[2] when he was forty years of age, and for a period of twenty-three years (610–632 c.e.). Muslims are those people who follow and abide by the teachings of Islam. The sources of Islamic teachings are the *Qur'an*,[3] the sayings (*Hadith*[4]) of the Prophet, and the life history (*Sirah*[5]) of the Prophet (570–632 c.e.). The main beliefs of Islam are: one God (Allah), Day of Judgment, angels, prophets and messengers that came before Muhammad, books of revelations, and destiny. However, there are five main pillars (practices) in Islam. These are: pledge of allegiance (belief in Allah and in Muhammad as His final prophet and messenger), daily prayers of five times (*salat*[6]), fasting (*sawm*[7]) the month of *Ramadan*, praying the religious charity (*zakat*[8]), and performing pilgrimage (*haji*[9]) to the city of Makkah in Saudi Arabia.

Islam is a total and complete way of life; it is a system and a code of rules and regulations. It deals with every aspect of life, including religion and state. Hence, the concept of life, death, and the hereafter are among the main issues with which Islam deals, giving information and solutions.

What is life? What is death? What is life after death going to be? These are perplexing questions that have been raised by so many people since the creation of mankind.

Life can be explained by religious people, philosophers, scholars, educators, or by scientists, including biologists, anthropologists, or other professional groups of people. Each group may look at life, death, and the life after from their own corners and specialties.

47

According to Islam, life is the combination of soul and flesh. The characteristics of life are exemplified by movement, respiration, sensation, hearing, speaking, thinking, seeing, eating, drinking, urination, defecation, perspiration, reproduction, and so on. Someone may lose one or more of these essentials of life and still may function as a living creature. The most important characteristic of life for a human being is his intellect, his brain, his thinking capacity, and his being able to think, manage, and make sound decisions.

All these factors are to cease as soon as life ceases. Therefore, what makes life stop and end is the departure of the soul that was introduced to the flesh after fertilization took place and after the zygote had been formed.

What is the composition of the soul? Where did the soul come from? Where does it go after a person dies? These are also perplexing questions that may not have one full and complete, satisfactory answer.

Many more questions have been raised: How the soul was introduced into the flesh and how it is taken out from the body are questions that have no direct answer.

After death, where does the soul go? Does the soul visit the deceased person in the grave? How does it come again at the Day of Judgment? How is the flesh to be reborn from the grave? Would the new flesh be composed of the same organic and inorganic matter after the person is resurrected?

More questions have been and will be raised. How could a life in the grave be envisioned when the flesh has been catabolized to its constituents of inorganic matter, silicon, carbon dioxide (CO_2), water, and energy? What type of life would it be in the grave? What type of life in hell and paradise does one expect to have?

All these and many more questions are being raised, and they do need answers. One may not find all the answers in one document or in a series of documents. In this chapter the author has tried to discuss one of the major issues of this life — the process of death, death itself, and the life after. The author has combined his scientific and religious knowledge in presenting these issues. (The rest of these ideas are discussed in his book, *Life, Death, and the Life After.*)

In so doing, the author hopes that readers will contemplate, reflect, think, react, and decide which road to follow in this life. As everyone knows, life is short. No one knows when, where, and how he or she is going to die. Each and every one *is* going to die. All are going to leave behind them everything that they earned in this life. As they came to this world, naked and penniless, they will leave this world in the same way. At the time of death, one should be grateful to God that someone will take care of his or her body and lay it in a casket to be put in the grave with respect.

The religious facts presented in this chapter are reliable ones. They are taken from authentic books such as the *Qur'an,* the sayings of the Prophet, the life history of the Prophet, and the books related to the meanings of the *Qur'an* (*Tafseer*[10]). The scientific information is taken from texts in the fields of biology, biochemistry, anatomy, genetics, heredity, physics, and many others.

Readers should not expect that the author has included everything in this chapter. This is a starting point that needs more research. It is only through research and communication that humanity will improve its knowledge about the essence of this life, the reality of life after death, and the in-between processes that take place.

This chapter will be of benefit to medical doctors, public health officials, clinicians, nurses, legislators, and coroners. It is helpful information for those who work in mortuaries, cemeteries, and hospitals. It is also helpful to non-Muslims who associate with Muslims. Finally, it is informative to professors who teach courses related to cultures, civilizations, religions, customs and habits of different peoples of the world.

The Human Life Cycle

Islam states that our roots as human beings were in Heaven, where Adam and Eve were living. They were the first astronauts who landed on this earth. This landing place was in Makkah, Saudi Arabia. With the help of the Angel Gabriel, they were able to build *Ka'abah*[11] as the first place of worship to God. It is understood that we are their children. We carry the good and the bad traits in the chromosomes of our reproductive cells, namely, the physical, the biological, the chemical, and, to a certain extent, the behavioral traits. The following are the different phases of life that each has to go through before going back to paradise (see figure 5.1).

Phase 1: Life in the Womb

When conception takes place, fertilization produces the zygote of the individual. After forty days, the soul is blown into the flesh to become

Figure 5.1 • Human Life Cycle

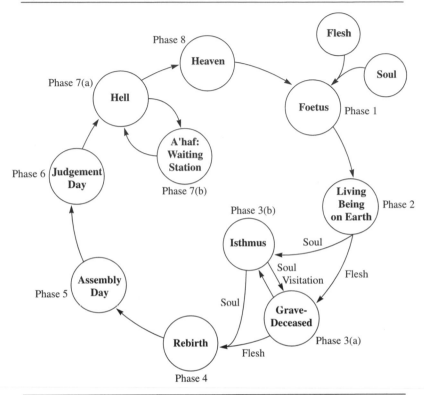

a human being (see figure 5.2). The person has to live about nine months as a fetus in the womb of his or her mother, after which the fetus has to come out as a male or a female. The fetus has no choice about whether to come to this world or not. It has no choice in whether to be born as a boy or as a girl. It cannot choose its parents. It has no chance to decide to be born black, white, brown, or albino. It cannot choose where to be born—in America, Europe, Africa, Asia, or other areas. All of these points and many more are beyond his or her control.

Phase 2: Life on This Planet

After being born, the personality of the individual is affected by genetics, foods, society, and guidance (*hidayah*[12]) from God. He (or she) is given the choice to decide, after the age of puberty, as to which way he wishes to follow. Hence, he will be charged or rewarded accordingly (*Qur'an* 91:7-10).

The person may live a few seconds or as long as 140 years or more. During this phase of his life, the soul and the flesh are working together, staying together except at sleeping, when the soul departs the flesh temporarily or forever. *Qur'an* states emphatically the departure of the soul at sleeping in *Surah*[13] *Al-Zumar* (The Crowds 39:42).

During this phase of life, there are continuous biological processes of life and death. In every cell, organ, and system of organs, life is being produced, and death is being rendered. Allah creates life from death, and He does produce death from life (*Qur'an* 3:27).

Therefore, there are a few hundred thousand enzymatic reactions that take place in the body every fraction of a second, some of which are used in the process of anabolism to build up and to synthesize new materials, while others are being used to catabolize the biological entities of the body. Some of these biochemical reactions are utilized to synthesize living materials, while others are either to synthesize dead materials or to get rid of living materials.

Figure 5.2 • Life in the Womb

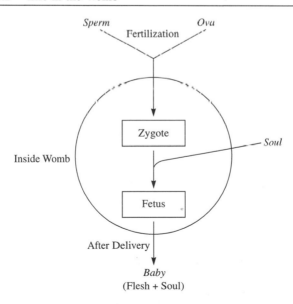

51

This second phase of life will cease completely when the soul is taken away from the flesh. At that time, the person is to go to his third phase of life. He has no choice as to when he is to depart this world or even how to leave it. If he is smart, he plans for himself well in advance. Nothing goes with him. He is to leave everything behind him. The only thing that goes with him are his deeds, preceded by his intention.

Phase 3: Life in the Grave

This phase of life is considered to be life in the grave. This type of life is one where the soul and flesh have been separated completely and are no longer one biological entity. It is understood that the biological entity of the person is to be catabolized, fermented, decayed, autolyzed, degraded, and finally, to become carbon dioxide, water, energy, oxygen, and nitrogen, while the inorganic entity will become silicon, calcium, magnesium, sulfur, sodium, and so on.

There will remain only the seed and its embryo, namely the *'Ajaf*[14] of the sacrum. During the process of dormancy, the seed is to be prepared for the new life to come. Many processes take place, including physiological, physical, metabolic, metamorphic, and others. It stays there until the Day of Judgment.

Since the soul is to stay in Isthmus (*Barzakh*[15]), it will visit the grave regularly for rewards or punishments. One has to recognize that life in the grave is either part of Paradise or a ditch in Hell.

Phase 4: Rebirth

This phase starts with a series of incidents that have to take place in order that the embryos of the seeds of human beings will germinate. Then the new life starts. After dormancy, and at the time of rebirth, Allah instructs Angel Israafeel[16] to blow the trumpet twice. The first one is to shake up every seed to be ready for germination. Water of life is to pour upon the seeds in graves. The soul comes back from Isthmus to join its biological entity. The second blow of the trumpet will help seeds to germinate and to produce every person (*Qur'an* 36:51). They will come out of their graves in a state of shock (*Qur'an* 39:68) and will be unclothed and shoeless.

Phase 5: Assembly Day

Each person is to be brought to a place of Assembly (*Qur'an* 18:99). All will be waiting for the Court of Allah, the Court of Justice, to decide about them. That Day of Assembly is a day of agony and anxiety, and a day of worries. It is a day when everyone is to worry about himself. No one has the time to worry about others.

With the heat of the sun, with the sweating, and with the presence of too many people next to one another, the dilemma is almost too much to be accepted or to be experienced. Each one is worried about what is going to happen to him personally. However, some seven groups of people are to be protected by Allah when He exalts Himself upon them.

Since it is the Assembly Day (*Qur'an* 64:9), each is to be grouped after his leader, prophet, mentor, celebrity, and the like (*Qur'an* 17:71). All will be put in lines waiting for the Court of Allah to take place.

Phase 6: Judgment Day

This is the Day where everyone personally is to be judged by Allah directly, with absolute justice. There will not be any bias or prejudice. Each one will be able to receive his Book in his right or left hand according to his achievements (*Qur'an* 69:19, 25). In that Book he will be able to find out each and every thing he has done from the time of birth until the time of death. The Book includes activities, appearance, and intention. Such a Book could be similar to a video tape which records all these three parameters.

This is the Day when some people are to be happy, excited, surprised, and grateful to God for His Mercy, Blessings, Forgiveness, and Graciousness, because they are accepted by God. This group of people are the ones who are to receive their Books in their right hands (*Qur'an* 17:71; 69:19; 84:7).

The other group of people are those who will be unfortunate. Their faces will express gloom. They will be distressed with anxiety and worries. They will wish that their lives will be generated again on this planet so that they can do good instead of bad things. They are the ones who are to receive their Books in their left hands (*Qur'an* 69:25; 84:10).

Phase 7: Life in Hell

This phase of life is the place where everybody is to go and to be visited (*Qur'an* 19:71). Some people are to be saved from being dumped into Hell (*Qur'an* 19:72). Others are to be taken to another station called *Al-A'raf.*[17] They don't deserve to enter Paradise, and the Mercy of Allah does not allow them to enter Hell. Finally, there is a group of people who deserve to enter Hell. They are either to stay for a short period of time to be purified or to stay forever.

Phase 8: Life in Paradise

This phase of life is the last but not the least. It is the most important phase of life for human beings to go to, to live in, to experience, and

Figure 5.3 • Different Phases of Life

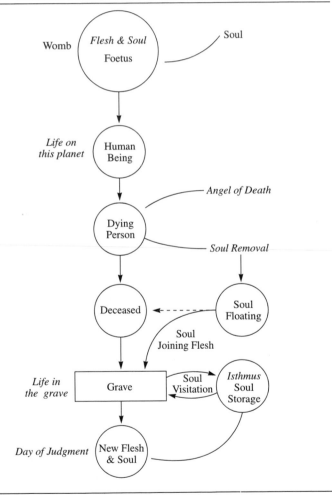

to enjoy. It is the aim and hope of every person to go there. It is the root of life for Adam and Eve; they lived there and enjoyed it.

Life in paradise is an eternal one (*Qur'an* 9:100). It has all the beauties of life to enjoy without being tired or exhausted. It is a life of excitement, peace, happiness, and concord. It is life without hate, jealousy, cheating, lying, or any other vices. It is a place where matrimonial life exists without agony or diseases (*Qur'an* 44:54). It is called The Real and the True Life (*Qur'an* 29:64).

Why Do People Live and Die?

Since we have to die, why therefore do we have to live? It is no fun at all to live a short period of life and then die. There is no value to this life when we strive very hard to earn knowledge, education, property, and wealth, and then all of a sudden we die! When we die, we are to leave everything behind! It is really too awful if life is to end at the time of death!

God created us with love and compassion. He brought us here with His Blessings and Mercy. He brought us to this world in order to help us go back to our roots and our origins — namely, Heaven and Paradise.

He brought us to this planet for a short period of time to prepare us to go to Heaven. He brought us here to this earth through a special system of birth to test us. Who will be rewarded better than others (*Qur'an* 67:2)?

Therefore, the best amongst people is the one who does good and prepares himself for the other life to come. God informs human beings in *Qur'an* that this life is short. It is a life of responsibilities and duties. People's responsibilities are to represent God on this planet as His viceregents. We are to assume our duties as representatives and as ambassadors of God (*Qur'an* 2:30).

We are to live and utilize the facilities of this planet and subjugate its components and utilities for the love of God. Our aim on this planet is, therefore, to promote the concepts of being:

1. Representatives of Allah and of being His viceregents.
2. Obedient to the Creator (*Qur'an* 51:56).
3. Good examples to others, including nonhuman creatures too.
4. Able to utilize our good faculties by assuming our responsibilities.
5. Responsible to establish the Laws of Allah; otherwise, we are to be condemned after being cursed (*Qur'an* 4:47).

6. Capable to utilize the facilities and the other creatures that God created for us in the proper way.
7. Able to inherit this planet directly through us, and indirectly through our progenies and the new generations to come (*Qur'an* 21:105).
8. Willfully ready to leave this world and depart to the other world. It should be stated here that while we are to inherit this planet, and we are to depart willfully without our permission, it is Allah and Allah alone Who is to inherit the planet. After all, this planet and all other planets are His creation, and they are His domain and His property (*Qur'an* 19:40).

All these aims to be achieved are excellent; however, a person also has to have good intentions. He should be sincere, honest, and try to please God. For those who try to please God, He in turn will make them happy, and He will definitely please them (*Qur'an* 98:8).

While life and death are from God, we have to remember that they are to take place with the permission of Allah alone. Each one's life and death are decided by God (*Qur'an* 3:145).

It should be stated here that God makes us die daily at night during sleeping. He makes most of us wake up from our temporary death to praise Him and to worship Him (*Qur'an* 39:42).

Finally, we have to cease functioning on this planet and be decomposed, resynthesized, rejuvenated, reborn, assembled, judged, and finally, go to Paradise (*Qur'an* 22:5). The latter will be our final destination, our final journey, and our true life. We have to accept death as much as we accept the daily sleep. We have to accept death in order to go to Paradise. We are travelers, and we are passing through this life before reaching our other life.

Sickness

Islam looks at sickness from three categories. God tests people with diseases and sickness as a matter of:

1. Purification of the mistakes and sins of the person by God (*Qur'an* 9:120-121).
2. Teaching the sick person patience and perseverance. The reward of patience is Paradise (*Qur'an* 2:155).
3. Elevating the person's position in the Book of God so that he will be on the honor list on the Day of Judgment. At the same time, his faith in this world is to be improved (*Qur'an* 2:177).

56

Some people might be caught by terminal sickness such as cancer, AIDS, or other types of diseases. Such a person's rewards are plenty. Some of these people are considered martyrs. A faithful person who is attacked by terminal sickness is considered as one of the groups of martyrs. His rewards would be the above three categories at one time.

Muslims are asked to visit sick individuals after the third day of their sickness. If they can't visit, at least they should call or send a card or a gift. Otherwise, they will be charged by God on the Day of Judgment for not assuming their responsibility toward their sick friends.

It should be mentioned here that the teachings of Islam state that the prayers and supplications of the sick person are to be accepted by God. Therefore, visitors do request the sick individual to pray for them.

If a Muslim gets sick, he is supposed to seek the help of a doctor. He is to use medicine with the hope of being cured. The healer is God Himself (Qur'an 26:80). God heals, but people are to use the services of a doctor; otherwise, they should not expect miracles to happen to them. While taking medicine, Muslims are to pray to God to heal them and to speed their recovery. In Islamic teachings, for every sickness there is medicine, except for the effects of old age.

If the disease is contagious, Islam legislates quarantine for the sick person. If a plague is in a city, quarantine is to be made on the whole city.

Muslims are not supposed to use illegal or unlawful drugs for medications, such as alcohol (Qur'an 5:90-91). The latter is not lawful for Muslims to use, even for medication.

It is strongly recommended that sick women go to women doctors, while sick men go to men doctors. Moreover, expectant Muslim mothers are asked to find women obstetricians and gynecologists as part of their moral teachings.

Some psychological diseases can be treated spiritually by reading certain verses and/or chapters from the Qur'an. There are also some spiritual diseases that cannot be identified by medical doctors. Some individuals might be haunted by spirits or ghosts. Such individuals can read certain chapters and verses from the Qur'an. This approach is unacceptable to modern scientists and physicians, but it has been applied successfully in many cases.

Death and Dying

The subject of death scares everyone because we don't know too much about it. Moreover, we don't know much about the life in the grave, or even life after death. We do know that we are to die and we are to be buried in the grave, but very few of us want to discuss the details of what type of life is to be there. People are afraid to talk about it because of ignorance and because of the unseen to come, or because they have not prepared themselves for that life to come.

Every one of us is to die, even if we hide ourselves in the world or even if we try to protect ourselves by every possible means. Death is a fact of life. God does send a special Angel (i.e., the Angel of Death) whose nickname is 'Isra-eel to take the soul out of the flesh (Qur'an 32:11).

This angel knows each one of us much better than parents know their own children. He knows where we are, when we are to die, and how we are to die. His main responsibility is extracting or removing the soul out of the flesh and keeping it in the warehouse (i.e., the Isthmus). He can enter any and every place where a person is to die in order to perform his duty. Even if we are hiding ourselves in a fortress, he can penetrate and take care of the person who is to die (Qur'an 4:78).

Every day, the Angel of Death visits each house three times to recognize who's who. Whenever he finds out that someone's life is over and his sustenance is also over, he will take his soul out of his flesh. When the person is dead, his family and relatives come with crying voices as usual. The Angel of Death holds the doors with his hands, saying: "In the name of Allah I never ate up his sustenance; I never stopped his life span, and I never reduced his life. I am supposed to come back to you again and again 'til I finish all of you."

As far as the removal of the soul from the flesh is concerned, the Angel of Death will extract it from good people with ease. For those who are bad, the removal of the soul is difficult. The Qur'anic expression for the removal of the soul from hypocrites and disbelievers is horrifying: More than one angel are to work together; they bare the face and back of the deceased while extracting the soul. Finally, it will come out with difficulty (Qur'an 8:50-51 and 47:27-28).

For those who are good, the Qur'an informs us that the extraction and pulling out of the soul from the flesh is very easy. The dying person will not feel the pain of the removal of the soul from his body. It will be as easy as a piece of hair being removed from dough.

The process of death and dying goes as follows: Angel of Death removes the soul from the flesh. The soul goes first to the upper heaven to be blessed if its person was good, or to be cursed if he was otherwise. The soul comes back and stays floating above the body.

After the body is laid down in the grave, the soul comes back to its body. The person is visited by the two angels, Munkir and Nakeer, for interrogation and cross-examination. Finally, the soul is taken to Isthmus to be stored. However, the soul is to be brought back daily to the grave for reward or punishment. This visitation continues until the Day of Judgment (see figure 5.4).

While the body disintegrates into its biological components, the embryo will remain in its dormancy in its spore form until the Day of Judgment. At that time, it is to germinate. Hence, the grave is a center of transformation, a center of molding, a center of reshaping, a center of preparation, and a place of resynthesis of the body for the individual to be ready for recreation. Therefore, whoever is smart will prepare himself before death comes to him.

Here are some recommendations to be followed when a person is in a state of dying:

1. The face of the dying person is to be directed toward *Ka'abah* in Makkah (*Qiblah*[18]) by turning the person on his side.

Figure 5.4 • Dead Person in the Grave

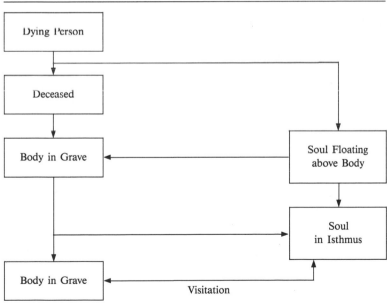

59

2. The people around should recite the pledge of allegiance to God (*kalimah*[19]), encouraging the dying person to recite it also. The Messenger of God said: "Advise the dying person to say, 'There is nothing worthy of worship except Allah,' because a dying Muslim who recites this will be saved from Hell."[20]

3. Loved ones and friends should pray that mercy, forgiveness, and the blessings of Allah be given to the deceased.

4. It is recommended that his friends and relatives should read[21] *Surah Yaseen* (Ch. 36) from the *Qur'an*. Reading such *Surah* will facilitate the removal of the soul from the body.

5. It is advised that people present should talk about the mercy, blessings, and forgiveness of God. The dying person should have a very pleasant feeling toward God, hoping for the best to come for him.

6. The dying person should be able to overcome the fear of death. This can be done when he sees a good number of relatives and friends are still around him. At that period, the dying person enters into a period of strange feelings and acute understanding.

7. The dying person may wish to talk to someone about his experience. The presence of a religious leader may be crucial for a peaceful death. He would feel less lonely and more dignified.

8. The presence of loved ones, friends, and a religious leader may help the dying person to ask forgiveness from them. Hence, he would feel less troubled and more happy than before.

9. Relatives should encourage the dying person to make bequests and perpetual charity (*Sadaqah*[22] *Jariyah*).

10. It is advisable to treat the departing person as a forerunner who is going ahead of us, for we all will join him very soon.

11. Relatives and friends should immediately prepare themselves as to the necessary procedures for his burial.

12. Members of the immediate family are responsible to pay all his debts and loans as soon as possible. These obligations are to be paid before any inheritor receives any of his assets.

13. The inheritors are parents, wife, and children. If the departing person has no children, then the inheritors are parents, wife, brothers, and sisters.

14. Part of the debts could be religious, such as performing pilgrimage to Makkah and fasting the month of *Ramadan*. Both of these items are part of the five pillars of Islam.

15. The departing person has no right to deny any of the inheritors; otherwise, he is committing a sin. He can allocate a maximum

of one-third of his assets to be given to any charitable organization or individual. The rest (two-thirds) has to be distributed according to Islamic laws of inheritance.

Since we are all going to die, it is recommended that each remember death daily. In so doing, he will reduce his mistakes, and at the same time, he will increase his good deeds. It is also recommended that people visit the graveyards as often as they can. By visiting a cemetery, people will remember their final stay under the ground. Such visitations will reduce their distress and their psychological and spiritual problems. They will feel relaxed and will attain peace, tranquility, and concord.

Funeral Practices

The Dead Person

When a person dies, people are to pray for forgiveness. He should be buried as soon as possible, without delay. The idea of embalming is not accepted in Islam unless it is a must. Autopsy is not recommended unless it is absolutely a must. To transfer the body from one city or from one country to another is not part of the teachings of Islam. Prophet Muhammad, the messenger of God, was buried in his own house. Cremation is against the teachings of Islam. Organ donation is accepted by some Muslim jurists. Life support is also accepted by some jurists, but each case is dependent upon the immediate family members to agree or to disagree with it. The deceased has to be honored and to be treated with respect.

When a person dies at home, his family has to prepare for his burial. They do not need to take him to a doctor, to a hospital, or even to a mortuary. They understand that life and death are from Allah. Therefore, they have to accept whatever comes from Allah.

Sometimes when the soul leaves the body, the eyes of the deceased remain open as his sight follows the soul's pathway. Hence it is recommended that someone close the eyes of the deceased immediately. Family members and friends are to be informed of his death. Immediately, and on the same day, the person should be buried. There are rules and regulations as to how to handle the body. There are also customs and habits that might be accepted by Islam. The following are the steps to be followed:

Body Washing.[23] It is obligatory that the body of the deceased be washed. There are ethics in washing the body. Only men are to wash the body of a man, and only women are to wash to body of a woman. Exceptions to this general rule are that a baby can be washed by either male or female; a husband may wash his wife's body and vice versa if the need arises. The private parts, including the areas around them, are to stay covered while washing takes place.

The body is to be washed three times; finally, ablution (*wudu'*) is to be performed. After the body is dried, nonalcoholic perfumes are to be used on the body. Washing can be done at any mosque in the neighborhood or even in the house of the deceased. The body should not be taken to a mortuary or any other place.

Wrapping (kafan). After being washed, the body is to be wrapped with three pieces of cloth (preferably white) for a male and five pieces of cloth for a female. The cloth should not be silk and should be long enough to cover the body totally and to extend beyond it. The body is to be tied with a piece of cloth from the front and the rear in such a way that one can differentiate the position of the head from the legs (see figure 5.5). It is recommended that Muslims prepare their own *kafan* while alive. They should carry it with them wherever they go

Figure 5.5 • Wrapping of the Dead

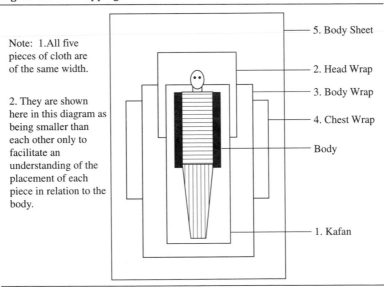

Note: 1. All five pieces of cloth are of the same width.

2. They are shown here in this diagram as being smaller than each other only to facilitate an understanding of the placement of each piece in relation to the body.

5. Body Sheet

2. Head Wrap

3. Body Wrap

4. Chest Wrap

Body

1. Kafan

as a reminder that they may depart this world at any time. Some Muslims wash their *kafan* with blessed water in Makkah, called *water of Zamzam.*

Nonalcoholic perfumes are to be used on the *kafan* as well as on the body. The wrapping should stay over the body. The face is also covered. Nothing is to be exposed to the public. It will stay as such even after burial.

Prayers (*Salat*)

Muslims are to perform a special prayer for the deceased before burial. This can be done at any place — at home, at a mosque, or in the hospital. It cannot be done at the cemetery. This prayer is called *Salatul Janazah*. It is totally different from the regular daily prayer. It is composed of four *Takbeerfs* (i.e., to say God is the Greatest). There is no bowing forward (*Ruku'*) or prostration (*Sujood*).

Those who are praying are to stand in straight lines and offer the prayer with special supplication (*Du'a*).[24] Muslims are to offer such a prayer to every deceased Muslim before burial. It is part of the religious obligation; however, any number of people can offer this prayer. If a person died as a martyr (*Shaheed*[25]), there is no need for washing his body, but the prayer is to be performed for him. In case miscarriage takes place after the fourth month, prayer is to be performed on the fetus after it is given a name and washed as usual.

After the prayer is performed, the religious man (*Imam*), or any qualified person, may give a talk or a sermon (*Khutbah*). He is to remind the audience of their final return to God; that each is going to die; that each should prepare himself to repent and ask forgiveness from people and from God. He is to comfort the relatives and to ask the audience to forgive the deceased before meeting the Lord.

Funeral

During the funeral procession, complete silence is recommended; however, one should ask forgiveness for the deceased as well as for all. Also, one is to remember one's inevitable death and, as such, should be ready to prepare oneself for departure. At the same time, one is to remember God Almighty.

No music is allowed, and no singing is permitted. The outburst of emotions is not recommended. People following the procession should not talk about idle issues. They are to remember the deceased and his good works, activities, nobilities, and good qualities while alive.

Burial

When entering the cemetery, one should recite a special greeting to the deceased ones by saying: "Peace be upon you O people of the graves." One should be silent while reading either from *Qur'an* or remembering God Almighty. As a matter of respect, it is prohibited to step over any grave.

The grave, when dug, is to be made in such a way that the face of the deceased is toward *Ka'abah* at Makkah, in Saudi Arabia. In this country (United States), the graves are dug on a southeast-northwest line. The head of the deceased is to be at the southeast; the face is flipped to his right side so that he will be facing *Ka'abah*. While laying the body, people are to say: "In the name of God, we bury (name) according to the way of the Prophet and Messenger Muhammad of God."

It is recommended not to use a casket unless it is needed; the body is to touch the soil unless otherwise needed. The grave should be dug wide and deep. The body of the deceased is to be lowered slowly and gently. It is recommended that those who are attending the burial each pour three handfuls of soil into the grave. During that process, they should say the following verse from *Qur'an* (20:55): "Out of it We [God] created you . . . and into it We return you . . . and from it We shall take you out once again."

After the body is covered with soil, the religious person is to read certain prayers and supplications for the deceased. He also gives *Talgeen* to the deceased, informing the deceased about his creed and the two angels who will visit him immediately to question him. He also requests friends to ask forgiveness for the deceased, because he is now in the hands of God who has already sent the two angels, Munkir[26] and Nakeer,[27] to interrogate and to question him. Finally, all are to read a special prayer individually and collectively.

The relatives of the deceased are to stand in line while friends shake hands and offer condolences. Men shake hands with men, while women shake hands with women.

After Burial

It is recommended that some relatives or friends cook food and invite the members of the family of the deceased. Friends usually visit the family for a number of days to console them. In some areas, Muslims are invited to the house of the bereaved family and read the whole *Qur'an,* which is composed of 114 chapters, 6,640 verses, and 30 parts. Each person reads one part. After finishing, they make special prayers (supplications) for the deceased. Finally, they all eat together in that house and ask God's forgiveness for the deceased.

Some Muslims feel obliged to visit the grave the second day after burial to pray for the forgiveness of the deceased. Others go daily for the first seven days. Their understanding is that the deceased is to be interrogated by two special angels. Therefore, their presence at the grave is a witness of their moral support for him, and at the same time, they pray for his forgiveness while they are very close to his body and soul. Their visit is a reminder for them that they are next in line, and they wish that someone would visit their graves and pray for their forgiveness.

Widow's Waiting Period

The widow has to wait for a period of four months and ten days before she can marry any other person. *Qur'an* stipulates this injunction in Chapter 2, Verse 234. This waiting period is called *'iddah.* However, if her husband dies while she is expecting, her waiting period is after delivery and after being cleaned from bleeding that comes after delivery. The waiting period for the widow is mainly biological and psychological. Biologically, she has to make sure that she is not pregnant from the first husband. Otherwise, the newly born baby would not know exactly who is his or her real father.

Life in the Grave

Everyone's soul has to depart his or her flesh at the time of death, and everyone has to go to the grave before being ready to go to Hell or Paradise. Inasmuch as everyone has to be in the womb of his or her mother before coming to this world, he or she has to leave this life and assume a new life in the grave (*Qur'an* 20:55).

As soon as the soul leaves the body, it will stay above its flesh until the body is put down in the grave. The soul will continue to be above the deceased body while it is in a hospital or mortuary, in a casket, or being carried by a car in a funeral procession. The soul hears and sees but cannot communicate with the living people.

At the time of laying down the body inside the grave, it is recommended to read a supplication (*Du'a'*) and to give pledge of allegiance to God (*Talgeen*[28]) to the deceased. Someone should speak to the deceased and give encouragement. He is to be informed or to be reminded about the pledge of allegiance and what to say when the two angels come to interrogate him inside the grave.

The soul has to go to its storage place and its warehouse, Isthmus. However, the soul will come back from Isthmus (*Barzakh*) to the flesh in the grave. This means that there is a life in the grave (see figure 5.6.). That life is a life of reward or punishment. Everyone is to be questioned by the two angels Munkir and Nakeer. Their series of questions would be about belief, intention, deeds, actions, God, religion, Prophet, and so on.

The life in the grave is a strange life. The moment the person's body is placed in the grave, he will hear the footsteps of the people leaving him. After the interrogation, the two angels will turn the face of the individual to the right if he is to be rewarded. They will show him his place in Paradise. Otherwise, they will turn his face to the left if he is to be punished for mischief.

While in the grave, the soul is to visit the deceased person who is to be rewarded or to be punished. One day the Prophet visited a cemetery and heard deceased persons being punished in their graves. He informed His companions that those individuals were punished. One was punished for spreading rumors; the other was punished for not cleaning himself from physical impurities, and the third was punished because he found injustice being inflicted on someone and did not do anything about it.

Those who are good on this earth are to be rewarded in their graves. They are assured that Allah will give them strength, felicity, and happiness in the grave as well as in the hereafter. No one can hear what goes on in the graves. The only one who hears is God Himself (*Qur'an* 35:22).

God does not want us to hear what goes on in the graves; otherwise, no one would be willing to bury his loved ones. However, God has allowed the animals, birds, and beasts to hear what goes on inside the graves. Even the neighboring deceased are to hear what goes on around them. Hence, it is strongly recommended that Muslims be buried in a Muslim cemetery. If any Muslim died as a martyr, his neighbors in their graves will receive some of the blessings.

On other occasions, the Prophet informed His companions that punishment in the grave will take place for those who disowned their parents, for tyrant dictators, for those who did not perform their obligatory prayer (*salat*), for those who did not pay their tax for the

Figure 5.6 • Life in the Grave

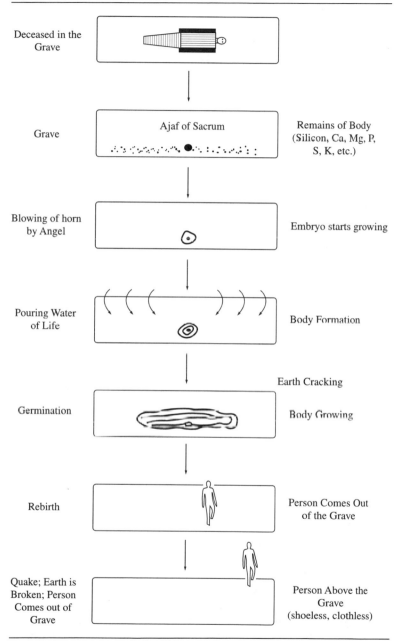

Deceased in the Grave

Grave | Ajaf of Sacrum | Remains of Body (Silicon, Ca, Mg, P, S, K, etc.)

Blowing of horn by Angel | Embryo starts growing

Pouring Water of Life | Body Formation

Earth Cracking

Germination | Body Growing

Rebirth | Person Comes Out of the Grave

Quake; Earth is Broken; Person Comes out of Grave | Person Above the Grave (shoeless, clothless) poor (*zakat*), for those who did not perform pilgrimage (*hajj*), and for those who cheated, lied, stole, and so on. This means that in the grave, there is a temporary life of reward or a temporary life of punishment before the real life comes, that is, the hereafter life.

When deceased people are to be placed in the grave, everything may follow them but nothing will stay with them except their deeds and actions, as well as their faith and intention. In the grave, people cannot do any more good things for themselves. Their deeds and actions will be over. Hence, it is recommended that they do something good while they are alive before they go to the grave.

Since all of us are to die and we have to live inside the grave, it is better that we help one another now and later. The following is a partial list of what Muslims feel they should do for one another:

1. Make supplication of forgiveness and mercy for the deceased.
2. Give charity (*sadaqah*) and *zakat* on behalf of the deceased.
3. Perform pilgrimage (*hajj*) on their behalf.
4. Perform extra prayer (*salat*) on their behalf.
5. Give water to the thirsty people on behalf of the deceased.
6. Fast any number of days outside the month of *Ramadan* for the deceased.
7. Read *Qur'an* on their behalf.
8. Teach *Qur'an* or request someone to teach *Qur'an* on their behalf.
9. Spread knowledge through television, radio, books, and other literature on their behalf.
10. Build schools, mosques, clinics, and hospitals on their behalf.
11. Remember the good deeds of the deceased. Remind yourself about the good achievements of the deceased. We are not to remember or even to mention their mistakes.

All of use are in need of these while we are in our graves. Otherwise, we may be penalized daily. We may cry for help, but in vain. Allah may allow the soul of the deceased to come over in our dreams to remind us of their needs for our supplication (*Du'a'*) and other good deeds on their behalf. We hope and pray that we do something good for the deceased before we ourselves go to our graves.

Method of Rebirth

The method of rebirth of human beings is as simple as the rebirth of a plant from its own seeds. It is a well-known fact that plants carry seeds and have their genetic traits embedded in their embryos. The latter have all the physical traits in their chromosomes. The genes of the chromosomes do, in fact, carry all the necessary information needed to bring the plant back to its shape, height, variety, chemical composition, flavor, aroma, and other characteristics if and when the seed is ready to germinate after dormancy.

To germinate, the embryo of the seed needs to have water, proper temperature, nutrients, and time. If all the factors of life in the embryo are met, it will germinate and give a seedling. The latter will automatically continue to grow up as long as the factors of germination and growth are attained. Finally, it will come back to its parent's shape, size, height, strength, variety, flavor, and chemical composition.

The rebirth of human beings has to take place from their own embryos. Each of the latter is found in the lower part of the sacrum. The embryo is called 'Ajaf-Al-'Uss'uss[29] (the weakest part of the sacrum).

The concept of resurrection of mankind is mentioned many times in the *Qur'an*. It is a simple act of God: "Be and it is." However, Allah explains this act of resurrection (*Nushoor*) from our experience and knowledge in life. He uses the idea of a dead land which is revived to life by pouring water on it (*Qur'an* 35:9 and 43:11).

The idea of a special angel blowing the horn to cause the earth to shake and to open the graves so that each person comes out is explained beautifully in *Qur'an* (50:41-44).

People are to come out of their own graves, scattered in different ways and baffled. This scene is explained in *Surah Al-Qamar* (The Moon). Their eyes are stunned and transfixed, and no one has time to think of anything except to ask: Who has raised us up? (*Qur'an* 54:6-8)

After rebirth takes place, each one is to be called for, to be summoned, and to be brought to a place of Assembly and Congregation so as to be judged.

Final Remarks

It is well realized by the author that this chapter is not a final understanding of the knowledge. Such a study does necessitate more research and more elaboration on certain areas of discussion. More scientists and religious scholars should work hand-in-hand to study the life cycle of human beings. After all, true knowledge cannot be known without a concerted effort of research by a large number of scientists and religious scholars working together as a team.

Special areas of research should be concentrated on the following subjects: (a) life in the grave; (b) the embryo of the seed of the person in grave; (c) life on the other planets; (d) angels; (e) *Jinns* (spirits); (f) life during sleeping; and (g) a comparative study of the subject of this chapter with teachings of other religions.

If humanity concentrates only on industry and business for the benefits of this world, more problems will be created for mankind. Part of the solution to the present world problems could be solved through the scientific and religious studies joined together.

Notes

1. Allah means God; it is the proper name of God.

2. Prophet Muhammad was born in 570 in the city of Makkah, Saudi Arabia.

3. *Qur'an* is the Holy Book of Islam to all creatures that God has created. It is a guide to Muslims, Christians, Jews, Pagans, and Atheists.

4. *Hadith* is the saying of Prophet Muhammad; the plural is *Ahadith.*

5. *Sirah* refers to the writings of the companions of the Prophet about the Prophet himself, his personality, his life history, and his ways of handling different situations.

6. *Salat* means prayer. It is a union between the creature and God.

7. *Sawm* means fasting. Muslims are to fast the whole month of *Ramadan,* which is the ninth lunar month every year. They are to fast from dawn to sunset with total abstinence from food, liquids, matrimonial relationship, as well as from all types of backbiting.

8. *Zakat* is an obligatory payment of money to the poor, needy, etc., starting from 2.5%, 5%, 10%, or 20%, depending upon commodity.

9. *Hajj* means pilgrimage to Makkah and its vicinities at least once in life. It is performed on the first ten days of the last lunar month of *Zul Hijjah.*

10. *Tafseer* means explanation of the *Qur'an,* which should be taken directly from the *Qur'an* itself or directly from the Prophet himself. Personal opinion about the *Qur'an* which is considered as *Tafseer* is rejected by Islam.

11. *Ka'abah* is the first house of worship on this planet. It is cubical in shape and structure. Muslims are to go for pilgrimage to *Ka'abah* in Makkah and its vicinities. It was reconstructed by Prophet Abraham and his son, Ishmael. While praying five times a day, Muslims, wherever they are, face in the direction of *Ka'abah.*

12. *Hidayah* means guidance. In Islam, *hidayah* is from God. However, to be qualified for *hidayah,* a person should be honest, sincere, and seeking the truth from God.

13. *Surah* is a chapter in the *Qur'an.* The latter is composed of 114 chapters (*Surah*).

14. *'Ajaf* or *'Ujb* or *'Ajb* is the weakest portion of the sacrum, located in the lowest part. It is considered to be the embryo from which human beings are going to be re-created on the Day of Judgment.

15. *Barzakh* literally means a place that separates two things from being mixed together. Specifically, it means the place where the souls are to be stored after departure from their own flesh. They will stay there until the Day of Judgment, when they will join the newly born flesh of each individual.

16. Israafeel is a mighty angel whose main responsibility is to blow the trumpet twice for the re-creation of all mankind on the Day of Judgment.

17. *A'raf* is the waiting station for those people who are not qualified to enter Paradise or to be dumped into Hell. They are to stay there until forgiveness is given to them through the Mercy of God (see *Qur'an,* Ch. 7).

18. *Qiblah* means direction. The *Ka'abah* in Makkah is the *Qiblah* for Muslims all over the world. While praying, Muslims direct their faces toward the *Qiblah.*

19. *Kalimah* is the pledge of allegiance and loyalty of a Muslim to God, the Creator. A person is to recite the *kalimah* with understanding. There is no one worthy of worship except God, and Muhammad is the messenger and servant of God.

20. *Fiqhus Sunnah,* Vol. 1, p. 501.

21. *Fiqhus Sunnah,* Vol. 1, p. 501.

22. *Sadaqah* means charity. It is to be given with good intention and without bragging about it. Sadaqah could be money, favor, help, or refraining from doing harm to others.

23. *Ghusi* means taking or giving a bath in a religious, ceremonial way.

24. *Du'a'* means supplication. Muslims are to make *du'a'* directly to God without any intercession. *Du'a'* is the climax of worship.

25. *Shaheed* is a person who dies in the path of God, one who is a martyr. It also means a witness.

26. Munkir is an angel whose responsibility, along with Nakeer, is to interrogate each person after he is laid down in the grave. His eyes are like a pot, his teeth are like horns of a steer, and his voice is like a thunderstorm.

27. Nakeer is the second angel whose main responsibility is to interrogate each deceased person in the grave. His looks are similar to angel Munkir.

28. *Talgeen* refers to helping the dying person to say the pledge of allegiance to God; i.e., to say, "There is no deity but God." It is also said on behalf of the dead.

29. *'Uss'uss* refers to the sacrum. In the lowest part of the sacrum there exists the *Ajaf ('Ajb).* The latter is considered to be the embryo for re-creation on the Day of Judgment.

Recommended Reading

Abdul Baqi, M. F. (1945). *Al-Mu'jam Al-Mufahrass* (Arabic). Cairo, Egypt: Dar Al-Sha'ab.

Ahmed, R. S. (1991). Muslim funeral home. *Pakistan Link Magazine,* Sept., p. 16.

Ahmed, Z. *Islam and the Last Day.* Lomita, CA: Islamic Center of South Bay, Los Angeles.

Al-Abani, M. N. D. (1389 H.). *Sifat Salatun Nabi* (Arabic). 5th ed., p. 125.

Al-Jazeeri. (1970). *Al-Fiqh 'Ala Al-Mazahib Al-Arba'a* (Arabic), pp. 500-535.

Ali, A. Y. (1989). *The Holy Qur'an—Text, Translation and Commentary.* New ed. Brentwood, MD: Amana Corp.

Asad, M. (1980). *The Message of the Qur'an—Translated and Explained.* Gibraltar: Dar Al-Andalus.

Blaiq, E. (1978). *Minhaj Al-Saliheen* (Arabic). Beirut, Lebanon: Dar Al-Fath.

Bukhari, S. A. (1976). *Bukhari. Trans. by M. M. Kahn.* Chicago, IL: Kazi Publications.

Campbell, N. A. (1987). *Biology.* 2nd ed. Redwood City, CA: Benjamin/Cummings Productions.

Cowan, J. M. (1976). *Arabic-English Dictionary.* 3rd ed. Ithaca, NY: Spoken Language Services.

Ezzeddin, I., and Davies, D. J. (1980). *Forty Hadith Qudsi.* Beirut, Lebanon: Dar Al-Koran Al-Kareem.

Ghazali, A. H. *Ihya' Uloom Al-Deen* (Arabic). Vol. 4, p. 468. Beirut, Lebanon: Dar Al-Nadwa Al-Jadida Publications.

Gibb, H. A. R., and Kramers, J. H. (1953). *Shorter Encyclopedia of Islam.* Ithaca, NY: Cornell University Press.

Glasse', C. (1989). *The Concise Encyclopedia of Islam.* San Francisco, CA: Harper & Row.

Hickman, C. P., et al. (1988). *Integrated Principles of Zoology.* 8th Ed. St. Louis, MO: Times Mirror/Mosby.

Hughes, T. P. (1979). *Dictionary of Islam.* Safat, Kuwait: Islamic Book Publishers.

Ibn Katheer, I. (1969). *Tafseer Al-Qur'an* (Arabic). Vol. 1-4. Beirut, Lebanon: Dar Al-Ma'rifah.

Irving, T. B. (1985). *The Qur'an.* Translation and commentary. Brattleboro, VT: Amana Books.

Islam, K. M. (1989) *The Spectacle of Death.* India: Adam Publishers.

Jaza-iree, A. B. (1972). *Minhajul Muslim* (Arabic). Beirut, Lebanon: Dar Al-Fath.

Kamal, A. A. (1982). *Everyday Fiqh.* Vol. 1. Lahore, Pakistan: Islamic Publications.

Khouj, A. (1988). *The End of the Journey.* Washington, DC: Islamic Center.

Moore, K. L. (1983). *The Developing Human.* 3rd ed. Philadelphia, PA: Saunders.

Munziri, Z. D. (1971). *Al-Tarqheeb Wal Tarheeb* (Arabic). Cairo, Egypt: Miktabah Al-Jumhuriyah Al-Arabiyah.

Muslim Community Center of Maryland. *A Guide for the Muslim Funeral.*

Muslim, I. H. (1972). *Sahih Muslim* (Arabic). Vol. 4, ch. 50-52. Beirut, Lebanon: Ihya Turath Arab Publications.

Muslim Students Association of North America. (1977). *Preparation of the Deceased and Janazah Prayers.* Indianapolis, IN: MSANA.

Muslim World League. *Funeral Regulations in Islam.* Cairo Egypt: Dar-al-Kitab Al-Masri.

Nawawi, I. (1979). *Riyadus Saliheen* (Arabic). Beirut, Lebanon: Al-Maktab Al-Islamic Publications. Pp. 360-373.

Pickthall, M. M. (1977). *The Glorious Qur'an* Text and explanatory translation. New York, NY: Muslim World League.

Rana, M. W. Z. (1990). On death and dying. *Nida-Ul-Islam,* Nov.-Dec., p. 12 (San Gabriel, CA, Islamic Center of San Gabriel Valley.)

Robson, J. (1964). *Mishkat Al-Masabih.* Vol. 3, Ch. 7-17. Lahore, Pakistan: Ashraf Publications.

Sakr, A. H. (1991). *Matrimonial Education in Islam.* Lombard, IL: Foundation for Islamic Knowledge.

Shawkani, M. (1973). *Naylul Awtar* (Arabic). Vol. 3. Beirut, Lebanon: Dar Al-Jeel.

Syed, S. (1971). *Fiqus Sunnah* (Arabic). Vol. 1. Beirut, Lebanon: Dar Al-Kitab Al-'Arabi.

Waterval Islamic Institute. *Death and Burial of a Muslim* (No. 49). Johannesburg, South Africa: WII.

CHAPTER SIX

Buddhism, Death, and Dying

Wing Yeung

Death is a universal phenomenon. So is the fear of it. No one can avoid death once being born. People who claim that they have no fear of death won't know for certain until the actual moment arrives.

In order to understand the Buddhist perspective on death and dying, some brief introduction of the Buddha and his teaching relevant to this topic is needed, as Buddhism is not yet a mainstream American religion.

The Buddha

Sakyamuni Buddha, the founder of Buddhism, lived in Northern India in the sixth century B.C. His personal name was Siddhartha, and his family name was Gautama. His father was the ruler of the Kingdom of the Sakayas (in modern Nepal).

He was born a prince. At sixteen, he married a neighboring princess who later bore him a son. Here was a man who seemed to have everything: "heir to the throne, extremely handsome, inspiring trust, stately, and gifted with great beauty of complexion and fine presence," with a wife who was "majestic, cheerful, and full of dignity and grace" and a beautiful son (Dhammananda, 1982).

Despite all this, he felt trapped inside the luxurious palaces. During a visit to the city one day, he saw what is known as the "Four Passing Sights," namely, an old man, a sick man, a dead man, and a holy recluse (Smith, 1986). He had never seen these before inside the palaces. When he saw these sights he realized, "Life is subject to age and death."

He asked, "Where is the realm of life in which there is neither age nor death?"

With these unanswered questions, he determined to leave home to find the cure, not for himself only, but for all mankind. At the age of twenty-nine, he left his kingdom and became an ascetic in search of enlightenment.

For six years he wandered about the valley of the Ganges, studying under famous religious teachers and submitting himself to rigorous ascetic practices. He did not feel fulfilled, so he abandoned those methods and went his own way. In one evening, seated under a tree near Gaya (in modern Bihar), at the age of thirty-five, he attained Enlightenment, after which he was known as the Buddha, "The Enlightened One," or "The Awakened."

After his Enlightenment, the Buddha, for forty-five years, taught all classes of men and women — kings and peasants, Brahmins and outcasts, bankers and beggars, holy men and robbers — without making the slightest distinction between them. At the age of eighty, the Buddha passed away at Kusinara (Rahula, 1962; Narada, 1973).

The Buddha's Teaching

Buddhism today is divided, broadly speaking, into the Southern school, the *Hinayana,* or *Theravada,* "the Teaching of the Elders," including Ceylon, parts of India and Southeast Asia; and the Northern School, or *Mahayana,* which covers China, Tibet, Japan, Mongolia, and Korea. Even though the practices are different in all those countries, the basic teaching of the Four Noble Truths remains the same.

The Four Noble Truths are very important concepts. The Buddhas have said that it is because we fail to understand them that we have continued in the cycle of birth and death. The Four Noble Truths are: (a) *Duhkha,* (b) the cause of *Duhkha,* (c) the cessation of *Duhkha,* and (d) the way leading to the cessation of *Duhkha.*

Besides meaning suffering, *Duhkha* also includes imperfection, pain, disharmony, and impermanence. *Duhkha* includes the physical and mental suffering of birth, aging, illness, and death. Even during moments of joy there is a *Duhkha,* because those moments are all impermanent. Therefore, the truth of *Duhkha* encompasses the whole of existence, in our happiness and sorrow, in every aspect of our lives. Because of impermanence, we suffer. Therefore, while there is reason to feel glad when one experiences happiness, one should not be attached to these happy states and forget about working one's way to complete liberation. As long as we live, we are profoundly subjected to this truth.

In order to cure ourselves from suffering, we must first identify the cause. According to the Buddha, craving and ignorance is the cause. This is the Second Noble Truth.

Knowing the cause of suffering, we are then in a position to eliminate its roots by the removal of craving in the mind. This is the Third Noble Truth. The state where craving ceases is known as *Nirvana*. This state is so sublime that no human language can express it. It has to be realized by the individual.

The Fourth Noble Truth is the Eightfold Path, which consists of eight groups of the finest possible codes for a happy life. It can be practiced by every understanding person, irrespective of his or her religious beliefs.

Reincarnation

As we can see from the above, the essential teachings of the Four Noble Truths is about the origin and extinction of rebirth and death, commonly known to the West as reincarnation, although it is not exclusively a Buddhist concept.

Belief in reincarnation is one of the biggest cultural differences between Western and Eastern thought. Recently, the mass media seem to be paying more attention to this issue. Movies (e.g., *Dead Again* and *Defending Your Life*) and talk shows (e.g., *Oprah Winfrey*, Dec. 25, 1991) have presented the phenomena of reincarnation but without explanations. A recent article by KlinKenborg (1992) described the incidence of near-death experiences which may be an indicator of life after death.

Studies on reincarnation vary from a report on individual clinical treatment under hypnosis (Weiss, 1988), life-before-birth experiences revealed under hypnosis (Wambach, 1979), and long-term case studies of people who could remember their past-life events (Stevenson, 1977; Story, 1975), to the compilation of numerous data and perspectives on the possibility of reincarnation (Fisher, 1985; Willson, 1987).

However, according to Buddhist teaching, reincarnation is part of life. Buddhists believe there are at least five planes of life; the Heavenly Beings, Humans, Ghosts, Animals, and Hells, with *Asuras* existing among them. All beings in these five or six classes continue in the cycle of rebirth and death until they can be liberated. They also can "transmigrate" from one class to another, from one life to another. The law that maps their destinies is *Karma.*

Karma

Karma is motivation and motivatedness (sGam-po-pa, 1986). Literally it means action, whether it is physical, verbal, or mental. When there is an action, there will be a consequence that follows. This is the concept of cause and effect: "You reap what you sowed." Good deeds bring good effects, and bad deeds will bring bad consequences. However, the time span between cause and effect varies from this life to the next life or even the life after that, depending on the magnitude of the deed.

The concept of *Karma* is not quite so straightforward as this, however, because it is also influenced by various factors or conditions. An analogy is growing something from a seed (cause) to the maturation of the fruit (effect). In between, the conditions of weather, the soil, the caretaker, and so on, all can affect the outcome. Therefore, what we are now is not just the result of acts from past lives. What we do now can make a significant impact to change the course of our lives. So the concept of *Karma* is not fatalistic at all.

Buddhist View of Death

Buddhists look at death as part of the endless life cycle. Before the attachment of *Nirvana,* no one can avoid it. It is one of the eight sufferings in life. However, sometimes sickness and death can be a blessing in disguise, as illustrated in the following story:

A man in China was born crippled. However, he was very kind and helpful to others. He was also a filial son.

One rainy day he came across, in the street, a statue of an immortal God which was flipped over as a stepping stone in the muddied rainwater by a woman. He saw that and put it back in the proper place.

That night after he went home, his eyes started to hurt and later he became blind. Soon afterwards, he was killed by lightning.

A rich young man living across the street knew all this and was disgusted, because he felt it was unfair for that crippled man to be so good and yet having such a bad ending. So he went to the mountains. Suddenly, out of nowhere, he saw a sedan being carried by four men with a band of musicians. The crippled man was sitting inside the sedan. The rich man was puzzled. Instantly, the vision disappeared, but a note was left by his feet. It explained that the crippled man was supposed to have three lives of suffering: one life to be crippled, one life to be blind, and one life to be killed by lightning. Because he had done so much good in this life, all the three lives of suffering were condensed to one brief time. He was on his way to be born into a rich family.

Such a tale serves to illustrate the Buddhist's view of the intricate systems of *Karma* and reincarnation.

Fear of Death

No Fear

Mahayana Buddhists place emphasis on attaining Buddhahood through *Bodhisattva* acts, namely, to save all suffering sentient beings. An enlightened Mahayana Buddhist chooses to come back to this world to continue the task of helping others after he dies rather than entering *Nirvana*. With such strong compassion and vows, these people have no fear of death. The reincarnation of the Dalai Lama is an example of this.

Hinayana Buddhists emphasize self-salvation. Such enlightened persons will be in *Nirvana* when the worldly life comes to an end. There will be no more rebirth and death. For these people, fear of death does not exist either.

For lay people, if they are strong believers they need not have fear, because without death there is no rebirth. Someone who wants to come back as a human with a better next life or to be born as a Heavenly Being can keep the Five Precepts and the Ten Good Deeds.

Buddhist View of Medical Care

During the Buddha's time, one of the four kinds of offerings of monastic people were medicines. There were many herbal formulas as medical treatments recorded in Buddhist sutras. So it is obvious that the Buddha encouraged people to seek medical treatment when they were sick.

However, some people misunderstand Buddhism as fatalism, believing *Karma* cannot be changed. They suffer without doing anything when they are sick, not knowing a fruit comes from a seed but also contains new seeds for the future. Another group of people surrender themselves to the erroneous belief or imagining that evil spirits are the only cause of their illnesses. They do not seek proper medical treatments.

In fact, the Buddha has advised, "Whenever you are physically sick, don't allow your mind also to be sick" (Dhammananda, 1968). Based on this advice, we should be guided by our intelligence and common sense to get proper medical treatment for our illnesses.

On the other hand, there have been many recorded cases of a "miracle cure" for severe illnesses with utmost sincere prayers and chantings throughout the Buddhist history. However, those were unusual cases and not day-to-day happenings.

Therefore, besides seeking normal medical treatment, it is advisable to invite monks to perform some special blessing service for the patient. "Such blessings would tend to infuse a considerable spiritual and psychological influence on the patient, thus accelerating his recovery" (Dhammananda, 1968).

The Moment of Dying

Buddhists believe there is an "intermediate body" between death and the next birth, which the Tibetans call Bardo (the gap). Thus it is important to guide that being to the right path of rebirth.

For the Mahayana Pure Land Sect (Conze, 1975) or the Jodo Sect in Japan (Suzuki, 1990), when a person is dying, family members and friends gather around and chant the name of the Amitabha Buddha. This is to stabilize the mind of the dying person and to help him or her chant. They believe that if the person chants the name of the Amitabha Buddha with absolute sincerity, it is enough to bring the dying person into the most connection with the Buddha; that is, salvation or a rebirth in the Pure Land is assured. Therefore, many Buddhists prefer to die at home because it is usually not acceptable to hospitals to have chanting by so many people in the patient's room. According to the *Tibetan Book of the Dead* (*Karma-glin-pa*, 1987) and the *Bardo Guide Book* (Nyima, 1991), the encounter that comes after death ranges over a symbolic forty-nine days, from blissful envelopment in "Clear Light" to the most horrifying hallucinations. This "Clear Light" experience is quite similar to the reported near-death experience in many studies (KlinKenborg, 1992). At this point, direct communication to the dying person that he or she is actually dying is important.

Death is no longer a myth. They recite the *Book of the Dead* into the ears of the dying and of the deceased, hoping to steer the liberated spirit across the "dangerous ambush" and away from the necessity of rebirth. This helps the dying to let go, to alleviate the pain of leaving the physical body, and to protect the *Bardo* from fear.

Immediately after Death

According to the Mahayana Buddhist belief, the spirit or consciousness of the dead takes about twelve hours to leave the corpse. Therefore, it is so important that it should not be disturbed, because the physical contact may generate some unpleasant vibrations that may drag the spirit to a deviant path of rebirth. Touching, cleaning, changing clothes, and wrapping of the dead body should be delayed, which is difficult to achieve in a hospital. During those hours, there should be no weeping or crying. Instead, chanting of the Amitabha Buddha's name should be continued, according to the Pure Land Sect.

However, nowadays, many compassionate Buddhists pay no attention to such practice because they want to donate their organs to needy patients immediately after they die. The Venerable Master Shing Yun of Taiwan has set an example by signing such a release to authorize the removal of his body parts for transplant when he dies.

Buddhist Funeral Rites

As pointed out by the Venerable Master Sir Dhammananda, "A real Buddhist funeral is a simple, solemn and dignified ceremony." However, people of different countries have incorporated oral traditions and customs into their ceremonies. This has resulted in many unnecessary, wasteful, and superstitious practices. It is unfortunate that a bad impression has been created that Buddhism encourages people to do such debased practices, like burning special paper "money," paper houses, and paper cars for the dead. These may have some comforting meaning for the family or friends of the dead but have nothing to do with Buddhism.

In the book *Questions on Buddhism,* the Venerable Master Shang Yen (1991) says that a proper Buddhist funeral should primarily have recitation of sutras for the dead by monks and/or nuns. Family members, relatives, and friends can participate in the recitation. Then the monk in charge of the ceremony will give a brief introduction of the dead and tell about his or her life and the good deeds he or she has done. Also, the monk will give a brief talk so as to help the dead to be unattached to this world of suffering and to comfort and advise the family and friends of the dead. This is almost like a session of brief psychotherapy for the beings of the two worlds, the alive and the dead. The whole process takes around an hour.

Crying during the ceremony is not encouraged in the Buddhist tradition, although it is such a natural thing to do. As discussed earlier, when one understands the meaning of death from the Buddhist perspective, there is no need to cry. However, human emotional response cannot be intellectualized. When the Buddha passed away, all his disciples cried except those who were enlightened.

Buddhists are not very particular about the burial or cremation of the dead. The Buddha's body was cremated, after which thousands of relics of different colors were found in the ashes. It was regarded as a sign of the Buddha's utmost pure cultivation. So, in many Buddhist countries, cremation is customary. Other than highly cultivated monastic people, laymen can have relics after they are cremated, although the number is usually much less.

In China, cremation is still not a popular practice among Buddhists because of the influence of Confucianism and Taoism. "To have peace in the soil" is a common Chinese saying, which means they prefer burial.

In Tibet, there is a practice called "Heaven Burial." The dead body is left out in the open on a hill for the eagles to dispose of so as to enable the dead person to be reborn in heaven.

After the funeral, particularly in the Mahayana Buddhist practice, continuation of reciting sutras for the dead in the next forty-nine days is encouraged. According to the Earth-store Bodhisattva sutra, the merits of chanting by family members with a cultivated monastic person, giving alms to the monks, and helping needy people can be transferred to the dead before rebirth takes place. If the family cannot do it every day, they can do it every seventh day. This is a very comforting practice for the family, because the dead person may be able to avoid the destiny of being born as an animal, a ghost, or in hell with the additional merits.

Therefore, no matter how different the rituals are, Buddhist funeral rites have the primary purpose of enabling the dead to be reborn in a better next life, whether it is in this world, in heaven, or in Buddha's Pure Land.

Grief of Death

Death is a great sorrow that we are compelled to face in this world. In the Buddhist practice, expressing grief openly is not encouraged. However, the destructive energy of grief can be transformed into continuous chanting with vigor and sincerity for the dead. This belief of transferring merits to the dead helps to decrease some guilt and grief feelings of the survivors. During the forty-nine days of doing repentance ceremonies and changing sutras, the interactions between monks and family members also may help to decrease grief. The participation of relatives and friends has a strong supportive element in alleviating the family's grief as well. Grief of death can also be illustrated by a case handled by the Buddha.

A woman named Kisa Gotamis lost her only infant, and she became extremely distraught. She carried her dead son's body to the Buddha. She wanted the Buddha to revive her son. She was beyond reason. Seeing the woman in such overwhelming grief, the Buddha agreed to help if she would bring back some mustard seeds. She was so happy to hear that. However, the Buddha told her that the seeds had to be from a household where no one had died. Without hesitation, she set forth to look for the seeds from village to village. After a long and exhausting search, she found no such seeds, but she found out the nature of life (Narada, 1972). When she went back to see the Buddha, she was calm and peaceful.

Buddhists look at death as part of life. People have to actually realize it, like Kisa Gotami. Words of condolence or intellectualization will not resolve the grief that comes with the death of a loved one.

Conclusion

The Buddhist perspective on death and dying is quite different from the mainstream American practices and values. Buddhists look at death as part of the life process. As long as one maintains one's desires, hatred, and ignorance, the cycle of rebirth and death goes on. The karmic force behind this does not die until one is able to get out of that cycle by studying and practicing what the Buddha has taught. When one is enlightened, all the suffering, including death, ultimately stops.

It is dangerous to look at Buddhism as cold and detached; it is just the opposite. With compassion and wisdom, the Buddha has told us the truth of life as it is and how to be liberated.

A quotation of a Chinese Zen poem may serve to end this chapter as a stimulus for further thoughts on this topic:

Flowers fall without raining,
willow catkins fly without the wind.

CHAPTER SEVEN

Death, Dying, and Religion among Dominican Immigrants

Ana M. Paulino

Death as a social phenomenon is considered and accepted by Dominican families as part of one's life. In the Dominican Republic, for example, this process stimulates emotions and activities among family members that are different from those seen in an Anglo-American family. Aguilar and Wood (1976) describe the Anglo-American situation as follows:

> American culture, confronting death, has attempted to cope by disguising it, pretending that it is not a basic condition of life. . . . The unhappy result, all too often, is that the dying patient is left to die emotionally and spiritually alone. We do not even permit him to say goodbye. . . . (P. 50)

In the Dominican Republic, the concept of death and the ceremonies that follow are viewed in a way similar to the description given by Kübler-Ross (1969) in her book *On Death and Dying*. Kübler-Ross recalls:

> A farmer who asked simply to die at home . . . called his daughters into the bedroom and spoke with each one of them alone for a few moments. . . . He asked his friends to visit him once more, to bid goodbye to them. . . . When he did die, he was at home, in his own beloved home . . . among his friends and neighbors. (P. 5)

This example illustrates how death is accepted as a natural outcome of one's life cycle. The home environment allows the dying person a place in which he or she feels in charge of the separation process.

This chapter identifies and discusses cultural characteristics exhibited by Dominican families residing in the United States who participated in an ethnographic research project designed to examine what people do when a family member develops a catastrophic illness.

Mr. R. R., age seventy-two, Catholic, died at home in the company of his relatives and close friends in the Dominican Republic. He had stomach cancer and was unable to eat. Consequently, he lost a great deal of weight even before he became very ill. Following surgery, it was learned that he did not have much time to live. The family was informed about his prognosis, and he was taken home to be with them in a familiar surrounding. During the time of his death, late in the evening, he was home with his family. They had just finished an offering of prayers. The family arranged a few hours for the viewing of his body. There was no embalming and no face makeup to pretend sleep. The burial took place the following day.

In the Dominican Republic, wakes are held occasionally in funeral parlors; however, they are expensive, and most people are unable to afford them. It is customary for the family to participate in a wake that is held in the home of the deceased. Traditionally, there is someone who is knowledgeable of what needs to be done from the moment the person dies and thereafter. Following the wake, there is a period of mourning called *los nueve dias* or *novenas* (nine days). During the *nueve dias*, family members gather in a semi-dark room to pray and to reminisce about the dead person. There is also reminiscing about previous losses. People from the community come to pay their respects and to provide support to the family during this period. A formal prayer including the holy rosary is said daily for nine days, chaired by someone whose main role is to help the mourners to gain emotional and spiritual support from others. The group process involved in this religious activity can be intense and powerful. During this period of nine days, close relatives of the deceased dress in either white or black. No red is allowed; it is considered inappropriate for the occasion.

It is not unusual for a family member to become "possessed" or to have an "attack" (*ataque*) resembling an epileptic seizure while reminiscing about the deceased. Garrison (1977b) refers to this concept of *ataque* as the "Puerto Rican Syndrome." The *ataques* are culturally approved and sometimes even prescribed reactions under certain stressful circumstances; for example, for a mourner to claim to be

85

possessed by a spirit during these religious activities is seen as culturally syntonic. An *ataque* is a defense mechanism for releasing intense
feelings in a physical form. *Ataques* are generally characterized by a
transient state of partial loss of consciousness, convulsive movements,
hyperventilation, moaning, groaning, profuse salivation, and some
aggressive physical gestures. They are of sudden onset and termination.

The focus of this chapter is the family's reaction to death, dying,
and the role of religion in handling this type of crisis, particular attention is given to children's reactions to the death of a significant other.

Dominican Immigrants in the United States

It is estimated that over 1 million Dominicans reside in the United
States. Dominicans comprise the second largest Latino group in New
York City after Puerto Ricans. Currently, Dominicans represent the
largest number of Immigrant Naturalization Service–registered aliens
in New York (U.S. Bureau of the Census, 1991).

In spite of the significant number of Dominicans residing in the
United States, the relevant literature suggests that mental health practitioners are not effective with this ethnic group, as represented by their
high dropout rates in treatment (Acosta, 1980; Baekeland and Lundwall, 1975; Lefley, 1984; Sue, 1977). The cases discussed in this chapter demonstrate that Dominicans, as other immigrant groups, have
found comfort in natural and informal healers and religious beliefs
that they utilize during times of stress. Many ethnic groups support
alternative providers of mental health care who may be used prior to,
in conjunction with, or following the mainstream services; for example, herbalists among Chinese Americans (Hessler, Nolan, and Ogbru,
1975), bonesetters among French Canadians (Lacourciere, 1976),
remede-mans among Louisiana Cajuns (Brandon, 1976), *curanderos*
among Mexican Americans (Kiev, 1968), *espiritistas* among Puerto
Ricans (Garrison, 1977a), and various healers among urban Blacks
(Snow, 1974) are just a few of the ethnic curers who have been described
in the literature.

The Bereavement Process: Issues to Consider

Although death and bereavement issues have generated increased
professional interest in the past decades, many gaps still remain in the

literature. Considerable work has focused on the dying person, how adults cope with the death of a spouse or child, and diverse aspects of grieving. Few studies have explored the bereavement process among children. The gaps in the literature underscore a need for continued research on childhood bereavement.

At present, there is no generally accepted model, or "profile," of a bereaved child or how bereavement is manifested in children, whether directly or symptomatically. It is suggested by Anthony (1972) and Deutsch (1937) that it is not until the age of seven or after that a child is emotionally and cognitively ready to define death as the negation of living. Before the age of seven, these authors consider that even when children witness the event, they cannot fully imagine their primary caretaker as dead.

Within the Latino culture, and to a certain extent within the Dominican community, death is seen not as an end to one's existence but, rather, as an opportunity to enter another dimension within the cosmological world. This is consistent with the definition of spiritism provided by Delgado (1988): "Spiritism is the belief that the visible world is surrounded by the invisible world inhabited by good and evil spirits who influence human behavior" (p. 36). Death is approached as a spiritual event in which the individual is given another opportunity to "serve God." When people are faced with the fact that they are mortal (Patton, 1966; Joseph, 1988), they start searching for ways to allay the feelings of fear and anxiety that the idea of death produces. Joseph (1988) suggests that research data reflect "the prominence of God and religion in times of illness and crises" (p. 448). Ghalis (1977) adds that within the Latino culture there are values or belief systems — such as the family network consisting of the extended family members, co-parents, friends, and informal social network including *espiritista, santero,* or priest — which are readily available to Latino families during times of stress. Garrison (1977) identifies *espiritismo* and *santeria* as forms of alternative (folk) healing systems utilized by Latinos in times of stress. *Espiritismo* and *santeria* are considered adaptive coping indigenous beliefs which are utilized by many Latinos in their efforts to manage "events" in life (Sandoval, 1977; Rogler and Hollingshead, 1961; Harwood, 1977; Comas-Diaz, 1981; Delgado, 1988). Given that religion and spiritual activities play a central role in people's lives, especially during times of stress, it is critical for mental health professionals to address them in their therapeutic work.

The following case examples illustrate cross-cultural issues reflective of Dominican families who utilize traditional and nontraditional healing methods for coping with stresses related to death and dying.

Carlos, a nine-year-old boy of Dominican ethnicity, lost his father to AIDS two years ago. His mother was dying of the same illness. She was hospitalized and was suffering from full-blown AIDS. She had approximately three months to live. Carlos was brought to my attention by a clinician who had been providing ongoing treatment for him. He was initially referred to her based on his poor academic performance and depressive moods. Carlos was described as withdrawn in class; he cried often, made demands for constant attention, and lacked concentration in achieving daily tasks. Developmentally, he was not industrious. For the past two years, Carlos had been living with his paternal grandmother. Prior to that, he lived with a maternal aunt for eleven months. Carlos was removed from his mother's home and placed in his aunt's custody by the public child welfare agency staff because of his mother's drug use and alleged neglect. Carlos had two older half-brothers who lived in another part of the city and whom he never saw. He had a younger sister who resided in Puerto Rico. No contact was reported between these siblings either.

The Use of Community Systems:
Church, Family, and Friends

Therapeutic work with Carlos was slow and painful. Carlos's grandmother, Mrs. S., was reluctant to tell him the true nature of his mother's illness. He was told that his mother was sick because she smoked too much. The word *AIDS* was not used. When asked by Carlos if his mother was going to die, his grandmother responded, "Everyone eventually goes to heaven." In addition, she assumed that he had "gotten over" his father's death. Carlos was an extremely affectionate, friendly child who was able to articulate his feelings clearly and was well liked by his peers. He began school late and had been placed in a special education class and was diagnosed as learning disabled.

According to Bowman (1959), children's responses to the loss of loved ones are different, at least in the mode of expression, from those of adults and are, therefore, frequently misunderstood. Deutsch (1937) also discusses how children express, or fail to express, this reaction about the death of a loved one. It is believed that one reason why children under the age of seven react in a different manner may be the fact that intellectually they are unable to grasp the reality and meaning of death.

The mechanism of narcissism is believed to be used by children to protect themselves from dealing with the problems of separation. Most professionals are in agreement that when a child undergoes this experience, there is a need to support and provide assistance so that they do not feel alone.

> It is of the utmost importance that the surviving parent or other members of the family help the child at his level and in his way to insure that the world is a secure one in which to live, that life is worth the living in the finest possible way. (Bowman, 1959, p. 171)

Bowen (1978) and Bowlby (1960) also discussed the importance of recognizing the loss of the object. The child needs to successfully work through issues of separation from the lost object before he or she can reattach to future ones.

Rosen (1991) identifies six factors that have bearing on grief reactions for children and adolescents: (a) the relationship of the child to the deceased, (b) the availability of a substitute object; (c) how the surviving family members respond to the loss; (d) the developmental level of the child; (e) the child's understanding of death; and (f) characteristics of children's mourning process. Specifically, in Carlos's situation, his involvement in his mother's process of dying might complete his unresolved grief from the loss of his father, loss of his siblings, and other previous losses.

It was suggested to Carlos's social worker that the grandmother needed to be central in Carlos's therapeutic treatment. Since group work was not available in the clinic where Carlos was in treatment, it was recommended that he and his grandmother be seen as a family unit in addition to individual sessions.

Mrs. S. was able to provide a stable, supportive environment for Carlos, although she was also depressed and had not allowed herself to fully mourn her son's death.

Mrs. S. was a fifty-one-year-old Dominican woman. She was well educated, held a professional civil service position, and was an observant Roman Catholic. Mrs. S. was the mother of Carlos's father, who had died two years ago. She described herself as being emotionally, physically, and mentally overwhelmed. She had undertaken the role of actively participating mother and grandmother; she had a demanding and very stressful job; and she invested a lot of energy in her church and local political organizations. She had high blood pressure and was

89

overweight and when combined with symptoms of depression, lack of sleep, overeating, and increased cigarette smoking, it was a problem. Emotionally, Mrs. S. was "burnt out"—she was known in her family as "Sarge" on account of the type of support and assistance she provided to the family. She appeared to be the family member to whom the others turned if they were having financial, emotional, or other problems.

During ongoing treatment, it became evident that the grandmother was involved with religious groups in her community. Indeed, Mrs. S. and the worker discussed her use of that network. Boyd-Franklin (1982) notes that religion has long been recognized as an extremely important institution utilized by many families. This area of Mrs. S.'s network was underutilized by the worker, who was not familiar with its therapeutic value for Latino families, who rely on these systems of support in times of crisis.

As the treatment progressed, Mrs. S. was able to recognize the need for Carlos to have accurate information concerning the inevitability of his mother's death but said that she was unable to give him this information. She asked the worker to do so. As Mrs. S. worked through her unresolved mourning, she would be more in tune with her grandchild's need to mourn the impending loss of his dying mother.

Fulmer's (1983) conceptualization of unresolved grief suggests that the grandmother's depression is considered as a special problem in the treatment of family members who are experiencing an impending loss. Mrs. S.'s inability to resolve her own mourning for her son interfered with Carlos achieving an accurate perception of what was really going on with his mother. Carlos needed validation and reassurance that his feelings were real.

Burnell and Burnell (1989) say that loss of a parent is more devastating to a child than to an adult; thus, people with early loss of parents might be more prone to depressive disorders as adults.

Carlos's depression may be seen as resulting from unresolved mourning that is maintained by the family system. Some techniques of structural family therapy are proposed in a specific order to facilitate mourning in such families.

Following Minuchin and Fishman's (1981) model of structural family therapy, Fulmer demonstrates the following techniques, which are effective in working with families to facilitate and promote their working through unresolved mourning. These techniques were used successfully in the case of Carlos and his grandmother.

Change the rules of the system so that mourning can be promoted:

1. *Joining:* The clinician's initial efforts will be to develop an atmosphere in which the family can have a sense of trust. The grandmother will be allowed to merge with the clinician so that a therapeutic alliance may be formed. By doing this, the clinician will bond more closely with the grandmother so that she will not have to rely so much on Carlos for support.

2. *Framing and Reframing:* The clinician will make an effort to universalize mourning as a normal process following the loss of a loved one. Sometimes family members feel relieved to hear the clinician identifying such an issue and feelings as normal.

3. *Transformation Through Enactment:* The clinician will work on the client's maladaptive pattern of behavior and the explicit rules of the family system (i.e., Mother cannot cry, so she acts out her feelings to cover or to avoid expressing painful feelings; consequently, she will distract herself from expressing mourning). In this stage, which is labeled "construction of a mourning ritual," the grandmother is allowed to verbalize her fear, fantasies, guilt, and pain regarding the loss via death, divorce, or desertion of her beloved object (e.g., her son), and for Carlos, his father and possibly his mother, siblings, and others.

4. *Drawing Boundaries:* The clinician will reinforce rules that allow mourning. The clinician must intervene so that family members will not reassure themselves prematurely. The clinician will continue to encourage the grandmother to mourn, recognizing, at times, that different family members might have different abilities in working through the mourning process.

5. *Restructuring.* The clinician will help family members to become more involved with peers. In a transitional structure, the clinician can be the peer. The following suggestions can be included as part of this family's treatment goals: (a) to help grandmother to mourn apart from Carlos; (b) to reassure Carlos that his grandmother is okay even though she is sad; (c) to arrange for the family to visit Carlos's dying mother at the hospital; and (d) to increase peer support for Mrs. S. and Carlos. Mrs. S. is already making use of community systems.

Canino and Canino (1982) contend that any family therapy approach is more effective than individual or group therapies in treating Puerto Rican families. They explain "Hispanic familism," which includes "the perception of illness as a family problem rather than an individual problem." Family therapy is the treatment of choice for family members who are experiencing bereavement issues, especially family members exhibiting the "deep sense of family commitment, obligation, and responsibility" which Garcia-Preto (1989) refers to as a hallmark of Puerto Rican families. Mrs. S. and Carlos are not Puerto Rican, but given the common cultural heritage shared by Dominicans and Puerto Ricans, Dominican families will also respond positively to a system-oriented family approach.

The "E." Case

E. had overcome many life stressors, but nothing prepared her for the death of her three-month-old son, D., who was admitted to a community hospital intensive care unit with a diagnosis of meningitis (Group B Streptococcus). E. was a nineteen-year-old single mother of Dominican descent, who lived with her parents. The baby's father, A., was also Dominican, a recent immigrant, age twenty. He provided minimum support to this young mother and their dying son.

Apparently, D. was born with no complications. His feeding was reported to be within the norm; he was alert and had no fever. Two months later, he developed a seizure disorder; his eyes rolled, and he developed convulsions and "turned blue." E. rushed him to the emergency room located in the hospital where D. was born. The infant was admitted and appropriate medications were administered, and he was maintained on a respirator. His head was shaved to facilitate some medical procedures, and there were many tubes and monitors connected to him. D.'s convulsions would not stop, and he did not respond well to the various medications administered. Instead, his condition progressively worsened. A few days after his hospitalization, E. was informed that D. had suffered a massive stroke, which destroyed major brain cells and left him lifeless. A "Do Not Resuscitate" (DNR) order was then discussed with E., to be implemented in the event that D. went into cardiac arrest or developed further complications. From the time of D.'s sudden illness leading to his anticipated death, E. consulted community folk healers hoping to clarify what was going on with her son and to enlist the spiritist to assist the medical staff to save her son.

An *espiritista* (spiritist) was consulted by E. and her family to rule out *mal de ojo*. In the Latino community, it is felt that babies are susceptible to *mal de ojo*. Babies are oftentimes taken to a *santiguador* or spiritist to get proper protection for them against evil eye. The act of *mal de ojo* can be either intentionally or unintentionally done, even by looking at a child or by wishing bad thoughts. Sometimes these thoughts do not have to be directed to the child. It is believed that "cross-eyed" individuals are likely to cause *mal de ojo* even without their awareness. Mothers are warned to protect their children from these individuals and/or those who praise children without blessing them. Some mothers are advised to buy *azabaches* or *reguardos* (amulet fetish made of black coral and prepared, spiritually). An *azabache* is used to protect children against evil eye. The child wears the *azabache* on his or her wrist, or it could be attached to his or her underwear. If the *azabache* is shattered, this is an indication that someone has tried to do *mal de ojo* to the child and did not succeed because the child was protected (Harwood, 1977). In D.'s case, he was not wearing an *azabache,* although his aunt had given one to him, but it was not yet blessed or *santiguado.* (A *santiguador* is a folk healer primarily known for his knowledge about herbs and their treatment connection to some physiological disorders; the *santiguador's* role is similar to that of a medicine man or a general practitioner.) A Catholic priest may also bless the *azabache* with holy water and prayers.

If the infant has suffered a *mal de ojo,* it is believed that an individual untrained in spiritism might not be able to properly diagnose the child. Spiritists are trained individuals who are able to make this type of diagnosis and prescribe treatment plans accordingly. The spiritists would work in conjunction with the physicians by using their spiritual "power." The spiritists may also perform tasks such as going to the hospital and providing a spiritual cleansing, called *despojo,* to the ill individual. In this case, one can see how some Latino families combine both healing systems — the traditional medical establishment and the spiritual indigenous one.

When E. went to visit the spiritist, she was accompanied by her mother, who also had a "spiritual consult" with the spiritist. E. was told by the spiritist that the baby contracted a disease associated with a "bad air." She refuted the possibility of a *mal de ojo* based on the symptoms that the baby was exhibiting. She added that D. was an angel passing by; his time as a living angel was brief. It seems that both E. and her mother were satisfied with the spiritist's assessment of the situation. The spiritist was very sad; she wrote the infant's name on a piece of paper. She mumbled something inaudible and proceeded to her alter, where she placed the piece of paper underneath Saint Michael's picture. She stated that she would pray to God and her spirits for guidance. She would not promise anything, but she wanted E. to know that she was praying also for the living, for her. She was the one who needed strength, faith, and hope. The spiritist was very concerned about E., fearing that she was not strong enough to endure the possible loss of her son. The spiritist prescribed some remedies for E. so that she would gain the necessary strengths and faith.

Frank (1961) states: "The spiritist as a socially sanctioned expert, healer, and as a member of the clients' reference group is able to mobilize forces sufficiently powerful to produce beneficial changes in them" (p. 45).

Around this time E. was also encouraged by some friends to talk to a woman from the community, Mrs. L., whose area of specialization was to do a series of prayers in the form of *novenas* for people who are seriously ill and/or facing death. Mrs. L. visited D. in the hospital and provided ongoing *oraciones* (prayers). Mrs. L. gave E. a booklet of prayer, a rosary, and a *medalla del Santo Nino de Antocha* (a small picture of a saint who is supposed to protect children). The saint's picture was taped on the baby's crib. Mrs. L. instructed E. about what needed to be performed, explaining that God operates in strange ways; in other words, E. was to pray for a miracle to happen if God so desires it would happen. Since the baby was not baptized, a Catholic priest was requested, a *madrina* was chosen, and the christening ceremony was performed. The hospital social worker also started to meet with E. to discuss alternate plans for D., for example, possible placement in a nursing home.

The nurses were patient and supportive of E. One Latino nurse, in particular, provided clarification about religious and cultural rituals done for babies in preparation for funeral arrangements. For instance, she stated that babies do not require a regular mass as adults do. The rationale is that they are little angels. Instead, they get *una misa de angelitos* (a mass for little angels). The formal prayers that are performed for adults for nine days after the burial of the dead individual are not needed in the case of a baby. The rationale is that they are innocent angels. There is nothing to forgive them for. Babies are buried dressed in white to symbolize the religious tradition of "purity" and "innocence." E. expressed an interest in burying D. with a hat especially made for him. Even though this hat was light green, her wish was honored.

Initially E. was hesitant about the helping process offered by the hospital social worker. The service of a social worker was offered at the time that an alternate plan of medical care was being considered by the medical staff. It was felt, given D.'s condition and his lack of progress, that he needed to eventually be transferred to a skilled nursing home for continuous care and management. Around this time,

E.'s reluctance, or "resistance" (Nelson, 1975), was seen within the hospital context and the stresses that E. was experiencing. The social environment of the hospital added to E.'s stress, which, of course, impacted on the worker's ability to establish a relationship with her, as she was seen as a hospital representative. However, with persistence in conveying interest, acceptance, and empathy, E. was able to establish a positive therapeutic alliance with the social worker. In the process of the work with E., D. died. He developed some intestinal obstruction. E. was formally referred for consultation regarding appropriate determination for further counseling services.

E. discussed how, since her son's death, she had been spending almost all of her time with friends and relatives and had plans with someone almost every day:

> WORKER: What do you mean by getting your life in order?
> E.: I am tired of constantly having plans, and not living the way I used to live my life when D. was alive.

She talked about the time she was pregnant, the baby's movements in her uterus, all the tests done, and all her plans and dreams. Later in the session, E. described the month before her son died as one in which she was entirely absorbed in caring for him day and night. She disclosed information about her experience with the spiritist and other religious activities. E. later talked about the depth of her grief:

> E.: . . . I feel like my heart has completely crumbled, and I don't know if I will ever recover. At first I was completely numb and didn't believe that D. was gone. Now some days I manage fine, and other days I feel like I am going to collapse. I don't sleep at night, or I want to sleep constantly. I wonder if it's ever going to end.
> WORKER: The feelings of pain that you are expressing are quite similar to those expressed by other people who have lost a spouse or a loved one. Grief is both an individual and a universal experience. Your feelings about losing your son are not like anyone else's. But the numbness and the mood swings you describe are all experiences that affect people who are grieving the loss of a loved one. It's important to give yourself time to grieve and understand that you will carry the grief with you for a long time. The pain may diminish, but it probably will never completely go away.

The interventions in these transactions were geared to normalizing E.'s feelings of grief so she wouldn't feel, as she described herself

95

at times, like she was going "crazy." The therapeutic sessions were focused on providing her with a safe environment in which she could express her grief without feeling judged. Efforts were made to demystify the grief process and to normalize the grieving experience as a healthy process.

During the ninth session, E. started to talk more about the changes in her identity now that she was no longer a mother and was not involved with D.'s father. She was struggling to find a comfortable place for herself. She mentioned the day-to-day life changes and how she felt she had many decisions to make. She also raised fears about a mass that she was preparing for her son now that the tombstone had arrived. This event was to be held in two weeks.

> E.: I am terrified.
>
> WORKER: Could you clue me in as to what are the feelings aroused in you by the experience of this event? What exactly will you expect to happen?
>
> E.: It will be so difficult for me to go again to the cemetery with everyone else around and not be able to have a private moment with D. I also don't know if I will be able to handle sharing anyone else's pain.
>
> WORKER: . . . This is going to be an emotionally difficult day for you. We have over two weeks until this event, so if you like, we can work together on identifying ways that will help you make it through the day.
>
> E.: That will be helpful

E. asked if she could be seen twice a week for the next two weeks before the upcoming event, as she felt it would be helpful.

Through the preparation for the placing of her son's tombstone, E. finally gave herself permission to express her feelings of grief publicly, which was a big step for a person who had stoically faced her son's death. E. also began to discuss, later in the session, her new role as a single woman and how odd she felt not holding her baby. Again memories about her pregnancy with D. were salient here. She felt proud to say that since the birth of her son, she never separated from him. She talked about the decisions she felt she needed to make regarding her future. She planned to re-enter college, but prior to this she said she wanted to go to the Dominican Republic to spend some time with relatives. She said she might stay there and continue her education.

> WORKER: Given all that you have been through over the past couple of months when your son was sick, perhaps you should take some

> time to make major decisions. Moving to the Dominican Republic sounds like a big step, and it doesn't sound to me like you are under any pressure to move or make this decision now. What else is going on?
>
> E.: It is true . . . there is no hurry . . . perhaps I just need some time away from where my baby died. I need to make a distance for a while. It's just been difficult to be in the house without D. I will wait.

It was important to assist E. in understanding that she had been through extreme stresses and trauma. She did not need to add to this by making big decisions regarding the future. E. was encouraged to put off the decision of returning to the Dominican Republic by helping her prioritize.

E. talked quite openly about how she used her religion to provide guidance and to answer questions that are often too easily answered by religion; however, religion can be important in working with terminal illness and death, and it can be used in a very powerful and positive way. It was important to address E.'s discussion regarding her visits to the spiritist and other religious activities in its own framework and not to deny its potent meaning; indeed, doing so resulted in her sharing some other spiritual experiences, which served to help understand her sense of self and cosmological belief.

E. realized that the grieving process would go on for a long time—that while her feelings of grief for D. might diminish over time, they would never completely go away. After her visit to the cemetery and her attendance at the mass, which had spiritual as well as personal significance, E. began to see a shift in her life and in therapy. This realization assisted her in moving forward in the therapeutic relationship and in her grieving process. E. felt supported by family members. She began to focus on her needs as a single woman who wished to re-enter college to prepare for her career in business administration.

The "J." Case

The use of religious beliefs and cultural factors is also evident during the following therapeutic session which took place while J. was hospitalized in a not-for-profit Roman Catholic medical center.

J. was a thirty-seven-year-old, Dominican, gay male with AIDS who was hospitalized for complications related to the illness. J. requested social work intervention in his efforts to deal with his family, who refused his desire for a DNR order. Family members were

97

at a different level of accepting the dying person's request. J. stated that his parents wanted him to fight his illness at any cost and not to give up. J. was stressed out by the family's demand to fight and continue to live. The family did not want to face the future reality of J.'s death and the possible implications of not having a DNR order and a Living Will. It was also evident that J.'s parents were still struggling to accept his homosexuality and the way he contracted AIDS. The siblings were comfortable with J.'s wishes, and because of their very close relationship, each had worked out their issues with homosexuality.

J. was the third child of a family consisting of six children, a mother, and a father. He had two older brothers, a younger brother, and two younger sisters. J.'s parents had been married for forty-one years. His father was sixty-two years old, and his mother was fifty-seven. They were born and raised in the Dominican Republic and immigrated to the United States twenty-eight years ago. Both parents came from very traditional and strongly religious Catholic backgrounds. Both parents came from a small farming village on the island and described their parents as being very hard working, religious, and dedicated individuals. Both were civil service employees. The father spoke fairly good English; the mother made herself understood in English but struggled with the language. They stated their reason for coming to the United States was to explore a better life and opportunities for their children. They reported that moving to the United States was very difficult for them, especially because of the poor housing conditions in which they lived, the discrimination they experienced, and the lonely moments they went through without their families.

The couple raised their six children in a very strong family and religious environment. The family was able to stay together and cope with the neighborhood external environmental stresses of crime, drugs, poverty, and racism. All of their children graduated from college and had good jobs and careers. One of the sons became involved with drugs but managed to seek help and to recover.

J. was seen three times alone for the purpose of gathering appropriate information to determine further need for social work intervention. Upon J.'s request, the worker explored ways to approach his family in order to allow each member to express his or her view of the situation and to hopefully arrive at a plan satisfactory to all. The worker met twice with J. and his family, and then with J. alone to help him express his concern and goals based on the outcome of the family meetings. What follows is an account of a family meeting from which J. requested to be excused:

Members present: F = J.'s father
M = J.'s mother
W = worker
R = oldest brother
P = youngest brother
L = youngest sister

During the family session, the father began to intellectualize and spiritualize. The mother was dealing with her stress by somatizing her pain and resorting to faith for a miracle. The siblings were dealing with the stress of J.'s illness and also with the stress the parents were causing by not facing reality and putting demands on J.

F: I don't understand why he has to get that disease. I wish I could change things.

L: Dad, J. has been through a lot. He was and he is the best as a brother and as a person. Please don't start again about changing him. He has enough pain in his life.

R: . . . J. wants to give up and—(He stops and there is silence. The mother's eyes are filled with tears, the father looks like he is holding back his tears, the sister is silently crying, and the youngest brother has a blank look—almost frozen.)

W: You want J. to live no matter what?

M: I believe in miracles. When I was five years old, my mother was very sick with high fevers and she wasn't expected to live. I remember kneeling all night in my room and praying to Jesus and to Mary. She was cured, and the next day she began to feel better. God has done many miracles in my life and other people's lives. I believe that there is still hope and that J. will get better.

As the meeting progressed, it became evident that the father felt guilt and anger toward J.'s homosexuality and AIDS. He had a hard time trying to reconcile his religious beliefs and convictions with J.'s homosexuality:

F: I wish I could understand how you can be gay. I have a hard time understanding the homosexual life. You know about the Bible and what the Church says . . . I don't want J. to suffer. I want him to live too. He was the hope of my life. I remember having a lot of dreams about J. He was a very good boy. He was always obedient. He worked very hard. I am sorry that I was hard on him.

R: Dad, tell him that. Sometimes I feel that you punished him too much. What can he do? He was born that way. He is such a good person.

The time you did not talk to him, I felt so bad. Having the holidays without him was very hard.

L: Yes, I agree with Robert. Let's change things now. Let's give him some happiness and peace.

M: Well, I guess whatever God's will is, it will happen.

L: Mom, God's will is to love J.—don't you understand that?

P: (The youngest brother is silent. He looks frozen, with a sense of sadness.)

W: You look pensive. (Referring to P.) I am curious to know what you are thinking about. What is going on here?

P: I guess I don't want to accept it either. I don't want to think that J. is going to die. He is so good to me. He helped me a lot when I was going through my drug problem. He spent days and nights talking to me. He is like my father. I am sorry Dad, but that it is how I feel. That does not mean I don't love you. J. is so special. I don't understand either about the gay life. It's so easy to be labeled. I don't know, I guess I am selfish and want J. to live. If we love J., we have to make him happy. I pray every day that he would be cured but I have to be realistic.

Monat and Lazarus (1991) state that extensive research shows that stress and coping may contribute to physical illness. Lazarus and Folkman (1984) state that definitions of coping must include efforts to manage the stressful demands, regardless of the outcome. This was manifested not only in J. but also in his parents, who suffered from stress-related physical ailments. This stress was also evident in J.'s emotional life. The concept of coping is very important in looking at how the family handles the stress of a catastrophic and stigmatized illness.

Social Work Values and Ethical Dilemmas

For the social worker in the situation, it was important to recognize the stability of the father's belief system and background and to be careful not to disrupt those. Yet, it was also important to the son's situation to get the father to accept the pain of the son and to accept the father's feelings for the son and the son's need for the father to let go and allow the son to die.

There is an ethical dilemma in how one approaches the family on the homophobia/religiosity issues. It was important not to condemn the father for his beliefs and for his insensitivity to his son, and it was also important not to encourage the father's homophobia. It was hoped that with continuous work with the family, they might be

100

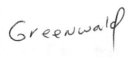
Greenwald

able to arrive at a better fit between their religious and cultural beliefs and their son's situation. Social workers who are knowledgeable and sensitive to these issues can certainly function as cultural brokers for these families.

The culture broker is the individual who negotiates the challenges posed by living in an ethnically diverse, sometimes hostile society. The mental health professional carries out this role during daily routines with the client and the agency. The concept of the culture broker refers to the notion of relationship, interaction, and linkage between the individual within the family, and between the family and the broader social environment.

Conclusion

The clinical cases presented in this chapter illustrate cross-cultural issues reflective of Dominican families who utilize traditional and nontraditional healing methods of coping with stresses related to death and dying, and their religious beliefs. This study illustrates how some Dominican families cope with the intrapsychic as well as the environmental stresses affecting them and their ill family members. These families indicate that religion and religious activities provided them with a sense of spiritual comfort. Canda and Phaobtong (1992) and Cornett (1992) support the need to incorporate the spiritual component of the client's belief system into the overall assessment and treatment plan. They suggest that the time "has come for social work to broaden its perspective, to include the spiritual aspects of the physical, phenomenological individual in her or his environment" (Cornett, 1992, p. 101). Educators who teach content on cross-cultural work need to include information related to religious and spiritual beliefs and the importance of these beliefs to the delivery of social and related services.

Mexican-American Women: Death and Dying

Juliette S. Silva

A few years ago, I had the distinction of appearing on a program with Dr. Elizabeth Kübler-Ross about understanding the dying woman and her family. My presentation, entitled "Cultural Attitudes toward Death among Mexican-Americans," was a beginning effort to distinguish between American and Mexican-American attitudes, beliefs, and values surrounding death. More than anything, it raised a multiplicity of questions about culturally expressed death-and-dying beliefs and practices.

The experience and knowledge for this chapter developed from life in the Southwest in a culturally traditional American border town in Arizona; the metropolis of Los Angeles, where multilevels of cultural development are found; and the medium to large cities of Denver, Colorado, and San Jose, California, which reflected changing and modern cultural styles. The observations, investigation, and study of those experiences helped to develop my interest in the field of cross-cultural social work. This chapter puts forth a formulation and conceptualization from practice wisdom and university-level teaching of social work into the understanding of the Mexican-American woman's experience with death and dying.

The woman's role within the culture can best be understood by reviewing historically evolved traditions and their changes, which, in time, account for cultural patterns in transition. A profile of the Mexican-American people identifies four major cultural eras giving rise to death-and-dying practices and rituals, religion, and spirituality. They are: the Meso-American Indian era, the Spanish era, the Mexican era, and the American era.

Historical Evolution of Death-and-Dying Practices

At the time of the Spanish conquest of Mexico, the Aztec civilization flourished. Other Indian groups, including the Otomi, Huaxtecs, and Totonacs to the north, and the Mixtecs, Zapotecs, and Mayas to the south, also contributed to a Mesoamerican Indian cultural definition of life and death. Aztec religion, which dominated, joined Quetzalcoatl, the giver of life and peace, with Huitzilopochtl, the blood-thirsty warrior—two diametrically opposed deities. Quetzalcoatl promoted love and peace for all humanity and asked "man" to take care of the earth and himself, and as such, he could never condone human sacrifice; flowers, fruits, and poems would suffice for him. Huitzilopochtl represented death by human sacrifice, which was the warrior's legacy, along with a belief in death as an inescapable part of life (Del Castillo, 1977). These values were carried forward and integrated into the cultures that followed.

After the conquest, the Spanish era began. The Spaniards brought Roman Catholicism and a European history of death observances. They also brought death in the form of plagues and epidemics, such as small pox, to indigenous people who had no immunity to European diseases. The Catholic church was male dominated and European. Both of these elements locked into place a new interpretation of death in the New World. It also locked out of power the indigenous cultures and the female population, who proceeded to acculturate the observances of death and dying.

The Catholic church played a major role in designing the role of women in Mexican society. It directed women to accept the concept of *marianismo*—the veneration of the Virgin Mary—which defined the role of woman as virgin, as wife, and as mother (Asuncion-Lande, 1979).

Furthering the understanding of the role men play in the maintenance of the woman's submissive expectations, another Chicano writer examines the paradoxical attitude of masculinity, in *machismo*, and an attempt to be sensitive:

> Mexican men have conflicting images of women as either virgins or mother figures epitomized by the Virgin of Guadalupe or as prostitutes or traitors, represented by La Malinche. Neither image offers the authority role which supposedly only men are capable of commanding. This conflict poses a singular situation for the Chicano male caught between two cultures and two value systems

in that it is more difficult to explain or understand the origins
of his feelings. (Gonzales, 1977, p. 70)

In the Mexican era, Mexico's culture became a blend of the
Indian-Mesoamerican and the Spanish-European cultures, in which
rituals of death, dying, and religion brought together a mosaic of practices. In a continuity of Indianness, the Day of the Dead combines
Roman Catholic religious observances of All Saints Day with Aztec
rituals and symbols using food, flowers, music, and incense. Death
is affirmed as an important aspect of life, creating a *mestizo* (mixed)
fusion of death beliefs and practices.

The Mexican writer and philosopher Octavio Paz (1951) describes
traditional and symbolic beliefs of Mexico's relationship with death:

> The word *death* is not pronounced in New York, in Paris, in Lon-
> don, because it burns the lips. The Mexican, in contrast, is familiar
> with death, jokes about it, caresses it, sleeps with it, celebrates
> it; it is one of his favorite toys and his most steadfast love. True,
> there is perhaps as much fear in his attitude as in that of others,
> but at least death is not hidden away: he looks at it face to face,
> with impatience, disdain or irony. As in a popular folk song, if
> they are going to kill me tomorrow, let them kill me right away.

Application of this philosophy is not made specific for women!

Two female figures are prominent in the Mexican era: La
Malinche and La Virgen De Guadalupe. Del Castillo's (1977) enlight-
ening research into the life of La Malinche recognizes the historical
forces shaping fundamental perceptions of women and the political,
religious and social structures that maintain them. La Malinche is held
responsible for the conquest and destruction of Mexico by her role
as traitress, the interpreter and concubine of Cortes. Simultaneously,
she is the woman who gave life to the *mestizo* child—a new people:
la raza cosmica.

La Virgen De Guadalupe is the patron saint of Mexico, the Virgin
Mary, whose virtues are held as expectations for Mexican woman.
Blea's (1992) account of religion, spirituality, and acculturation ampli-
fies the systematic evidence of oppression in the role of women.

The American era brought new death-and-dying practices. In
American dealings with death, death is present, but death is feared,
denied, guarded against, and avoided. In his Pulitzer Prize–winning
book, Becker (1973) documents the denial-of-death dynamics in this
rare coverage of women:

The woman as a source of new life, part of a nature, can find it easy to willingly submit herself to the procreative role in marriage, as a natural fulfillment of the Agape motive. At the same time, however, it becomes self-negating or masochistic when she sacrifices her individual personality and gifts by making the man and his achievement into her immortality-symbol. . . . The reason that women have such trouble disentangling the problems of their distinctive individualities is that these things are intricately confused. The line between natural self-surrender, in wanting to be a part of something larger, and masochistic or self-negating surrender is thin indeed, as Rank would say. The problem is further complicated by something that women — like everyone else — are loathe to admit: their own natural inability to stand alone in freedom. This is why almost everyone consents to earn his immortality in the popular ways mapped out by societies everywhere, in the beyonds of others and not their own.

The Mexicans' seeming preoccupation with death is exaggerated by the Americans' vehement rejection and denial of death. This perhaps accounts for the paucity of data on Mexican Americans, especially data related to death and dying. Mortality rates are sparse, inconsistent, or speculative (Cuellar, 1990).

This backdrop of culture and history helps us to understand the Mexican-American woman as someone who is linked to history by the shared beliefs and practices built around the idea of natural and supernatural forces that link the individual to a much greater power (Blea, 1992).

The Mexican-American Woman

The caring role of a Mexican-American woman for the terminally ill person is a continuation of the caring role she has occupied in the family. This is influenced, shaped, and modified by an adaptive process. The adaptation is across a continuum of role changes from (a) traditional role, (b) transitional role, to (c) acculturated role, further explicated by class differences and adaptations to modernization and time.

It is important to remember that women don't fall neatly into these categories, since they are defining and adapting their own identity as women as they proceed through the stages of life. Mexican-American women may be traditional in some attitudes, behaviors, and roles, transitional in others, and acculturated in still others. A modern woman may concurrently demonstrate traditional values related to her early socialization. The diversity of Chicanas is illustrated by identifying three age groups — old, middle-age, and young — who are of Spanish, Indian, and Mexican cultural roots. Some trace their origins back hundreds of years to Europe and the Moorish influence on Spain, while others are more recent immigrant women from Mexico, Central America, and South America. They are all ages, sizes, body types, ideologies, educational levels, and economic levels, and they bring with them a variety of experiences. Among the several things they have in common is the Spanish language and their inheritance of the Chicano colonial experience, as well as their endurance of its discrimination.

In a collection of oral histories of Mexican-American women of New Mexico which Blea (1992) discusses, Elsasser, MacKenzie, Tixier, and Vigil (1980) identify four categories of women by age cohorts who call themselves Mexicans, Hispanics, and Chicanas.

The first cohort, the *Elder Generation,* is characterized as over seventy. They are from rural and isolated areas and endured four American wars, grew up in a *traditional* culture at the turn of the century, experienced hard physical labor, and speak Spanish. Caring for the physical and emotional needs of their families was a common responsibility. They also were characterized by a fierce connectedness and bonding with their communities. This cohort of women had little access to modern medicine or services and occupied many traditional practitioner roles in folk medicine (*curanderismo*), such as healers (*curanderas*) who work with physical, emotional, and spiritual ills. These women worked with the dying and often experienced the deaths of their own children.

This system of folk medicine has been documented historically and written about in the social science and social work literature, such as Saunders (1954) and Clark (1959).

The system of *curanderismo* is a traditional folk medicine health/mental health delivery of services especially used by rural and urban poor and traditional people to fill the gap of nonexisting services or to substitute for services unavailable because of discrimination and lack of access to modern medicine. *Curanderismo,* as a system of care, has undergone tremendous cultural change recently, and its use and credibility in both Mexico and the United States for Mexican Americans is an unknown. A study of older people in Texas by Alegria, Guerra, Martinez, and Meyer (1977) reveals an active practice by older folk medicine providers who provide a spiritual base of practice, including Catholic practices, but not restricted to them. Their future, though, was reported as unclear. Two studies concluded that in spite of long tradition, the importance of *curanderismo* has greatly diminished (Edgerton, Karno, and Fernandez, 1977; Cuellar, 1990). In a survey conducted in San Jose, California (in Santa Clara County), findings revealed that *curanderos* and other folk medicine providers were no longer highly utilized or highly trusted. In contrast, 78 percent of women chose pharmacies as their entry point into the health care system (Manzanedo, Walters, and Lorig, 1980). This is an area that would benefit from further empirical research. Acceleration to modernity may be due to the impact of television, both English and Spanish, all over Latin America and the United States.

The *Older Women,* the second cohort, tended to be Catholic, and expected to be married and taken care of by their husbands. When they were widowed, they were poor, and they mostly lived in urban cities. They retained their culture by story telling (*cuentos*), preparing ethnic food, gardening, and dancing. Some attended senior citizen centers.

A third cohort, the *Contemporary Women,* had work experience outside the home but were still mothers and homemakers, relating to family and their neighborhood and serving in community activities. Their work experience occupied most of their lives.

The fourth cohort consisted of *Young Women,* the first generation to complete high school and attend college. Although the family was still considered their focal point, careers and other activities were part of their lives as well.

This is typical of the diversity increasingly apparent in the Mexican-American culture and in its women. The factor of diversity very clearly and dramatically affects roles pertaining to the care of dying members of the family and the rituals and ceremonies connected to death. The way Mexican-American women carry out their roles is dependent on other factors as well: social class; poverty; immigration; degree of acculturation and assimilation; proximity to their homeland, Mexico; and gender roles for males and females—*machismo* (male dominance and male role), *hembrismo* (the female role), and *marianismo* (the veneration of the Virgin Mary defining women's roles as virgin, wife, and mother).

Role Adaptation

For this chapter, the age and identity cohorts found by Ellasser et al. (1980) would be categorized in the following way: The elder women, cohort one, are *traditional* women; both categories—the older women, cohort two, and contemporary women, cohort three—would be designated *transitional* women; and finally, the young women, cohort four, are *acculturated* women.

Table 8.1 illustrates the factors included in Mexican-American women's role adaptations.

Role Experience Variables with Death and Dying

If one could assume that role adaptation explains the prescription of tasks, rituals, and ceremonies in death- and dying-related roles, everything would be simple. But the fact remains that not all women anywhere, and specifically in the Mexican-American culture, have the same experience with death and dying. There are differential levels of exposure to the ceremony, ritual tradition, and practices impacting learned behavior and roles to express respect toward a dying person, from the mere discussion of death, to attending wakes, funerals, and burials, and to caring for the needs of the dying person and the surviving family. Furthermore, many Mexican-American women have never experienced a *Dia de los Muertos* celebration.

To understand death- and dying-related experiences for individual Mexican-American women, it is necessary to determine the degree to which a woman has role experience related to the following:

1. *Socialization:* how she was socialized to take on roles related to death and dying which required her to know rituals, participate in rituals, and even provide active leadership or supportive roles in rituals, observances, and practices.

2. *Interest and calling:* the degree to which a woman chooses not to participate and to defer to others or feels she has a special interest and skill in leadership for rituals and observances.

3. *Empathy:* the ability to carry out roles which require dealing with the issues of death and dying, working with grieving families, and imparting empathy to others.

4. *Exposure to death and dying rituals, roles, and expectations:* the degree to which a woman has had to deal with death and dying

Table 8.1 • Mexican-American Women and Role Adaptation

Women's Roles	Culture	Culture Change Transmission	Modernization	Time
Traditional Mexican traditional roles; values, beliefs, and behavior rooted in the Mexican culture.	*Monocultural* Mexican	*Enculturation* Transmission of culture from one's own family; person is Mexican.	Technology, Science, Medicine, Pharmacology. Epidemiology, Law, and their effects on culture. Both Mexican and American cultures are adapting and changing due to impact of modernization. Regardless of the role—whether she is traditional, transitional, or acculturated—a woman's role will be affected by the modernization of culture.	Traditional role change over time. Roles in 1930 vs. 1990 vary for a traditional woman.
Transitional Values, beliefs, and behavior in transition in both Mexican and American culture and lives in two worlds.	*Bi-cultural* A mixture of two cultures but not necessarily equal. Mexican-American role dimensions are held in varying degrees.	*Enculturation* Person receives transmission of culture from family/culture. *Acculturation* From dominant American culture.		Transitional roles respond to time and differential expectations.
Acculturated Values, beliefs, and behavior rooted in the American culture	*Monocultural* American	*Acculturation* *Enculturation* Person is more American than Mexican in cultural traditions.		Acculturated roles are affected by the era in which women live.

Roles are not static but dynamic and in flux. The pattern of roles from traditional to transitional to acculturated is a continuum—a moving and changing adaptation of the woman's role through culture change, modernization and time.

and has collected an experience due to participation in activities related to death and dying.

Table 8.2 illustrates the role experience with death-and-dying variables and the role experience that differentiates the many areas concerned with participating in death and dying rituals, observances, practices, and roles.

Traditional Death and Dying Rituals

Tradition

Kalish and Reynolds' (1976) study of death and ethnicity found that it is the women who hold the culture together with bonds of service and affection and who interweave the ties between family and the church. And as might be expected, it was the Mexican-American woman who was the most apt to turn to extended family, friends, and church for practical and emotional support.

The Mexican-American woman's identity is defined by the image of the Virgin Mary within the Roman Catholic religion. As a mother, she is expected to be self-sacrificing and forbearing (Madsen, 1964; Saunders, 1954). The structure of roles within the family is often prescribed. Men and boys work outside the home, while women and girls are caregivers and do the domestic work within the home (Saunders, 1954; Clark, 1959).

Interactions and communications among family members are more open than in Anglo families when dealing with death. Often cultural norms will predict the process of mourning. Those closest to the dead person are expected to openly grieve and are provided the comfort and support of extended family and friends. However, death and grieving for the Mexican family also takes place in a larger social context that can alter centuries-old traditions. For example, the wake (*velorio*) is traditionally held in the home, where the body is viewed in an open casket. Open grieving is expected, and events around the dead person's life are shared. Life in a new country, like the United States, does not allow for this custom because of Health Department laws, but such wakes are still held.

Death is very much a family event for the Mexican American. A death may pull together geographically separated family members both physically and psychologically as no other event can. Mexican Americans say that (a) if they had six months to live, they would focus

Table 8.2 • Mexican-American Women's Role Variables Related to Dying and Death

	Continuum of women's roles:		
	Traditional	Transitional	Acculturated
A. Familiarity and exposure to death or dying, whether it is real or symbolic.			
B. Role experience and learning *Participant observer role:* Woman experiences the drama of a family death or burial (real) or the celebration of El Dia de los Muertos (symbolic) but has no firsthand experience with it or caring for a terminally ill person. *Active role:* Woman is personally affected by caring for or attending to a death or dying of a significant person and has participated in the death and dying rituals. *Leadership role:* Woman has had responsibility for planning and carrying out of care and healing of a terminally ill person; has tended needs of family of a dying member; or administered death tasks and rituals of family. *Supportive role:* Woman has knowledge of the death and dying tasks and works to help others carrying them out.			

C. Ascribed vs. assumed roles as a:
Caretaker—mother, wife
Nurse—trained professionally
Medicas—lay practitioner
Comadre—in-law
Madrina—godmother
Senora—wise woman
Curandera—healer
Yerbera—herbalist
Sobadora—lay chiropractor
Church role—officiates church
   services, leads prayers
Organizadora—organizer: in charge
   of church rituals			

D. Woman's role achieved via: Self-learning Mentoring by another experienced person in that role "Calling"			

111

their concern on others and be with loved ones; (b) they would encourage their family to visit even if it was somewhat inconvenient for family members; (c) they would want funerals with lots of friends and acquaintances; (d) they would like to be buried where loved ones are buried; and (e) they would like to have a wake preceding their funeral service (Kalish and Reynolds, 1976).

The Day of the Dead

The celebration called Day of the Dead originated in Europe in the ninth century and was introduced by Spaniards after the Conquest. The Mexicans' blend of this ritual incorporates a uniquely Mexican expression of their relationship with death as a constant fact of life. Every year, *El Dia de los Muertos* (the Day of the Dead) is celebrated from October 31 to November 2. In a combination of Indian and Spanish beliefs in the spiritual world, the souls of departed loved ones are thought to return home in a joyful reunion with the living.

Art forms abound as women create special home altars, prepare flowers for graveyards, make special bread, and bake pastries and sweets in the form of skulls, skeletons, coffins, and bones. They enlist the family in the care and cleaning of their family grave sites, while the men paint and repaint family crypts and dig new graves. Women cook for relatives and visitors and prepare food for the grave sites to welcome visiting souls. It is both a solemn and happy occasion, with music and dancing (Franz, 1979). The Day of the Dead is observed by segments of the Mexican-American population. San Francisco, for example, has a city-wide observance calendared every year in its predominantly Spanish-speaking Mission District.

Culture exerts a significant influence on the way loss is perceived and experienced and how idioms for articulating personal and family distress give meaning to bereavement.

Velorio

The wake (*el velorio*) is the collective sharing of grief and mourning for the dead. Family, friends, neighbors, and other members of the community pay their respects and offer condolences. Wakes are also opportunities for reminiscing—for expressions of other losses of people, of possessions, and of homeland and the changes that accompany them.

Women play a combination of roles in attendance by leading prayers, officiating at the informal part of the service, preparing family members to attend, preparing food and drink for after the wake, and grieving openly in a manner that symbolically includes males, who cannot, by tradition, express their grief openly.

A social role may be viewed as the link between the individual and society. An individual's social role combines many separate roles, at one time including age, sex, family, occupational, friendships, and so on. These roles may be clearly defined or vague and confused, congruent and conflicting (Stein and Cloward, 1958). Women's roles in the Mexican-American tradition carry multiple demands for the woman, who is a wife, mother, and the "heart" of the culture (Paz, 1951).

Funeral

Unlike the *Dia de los Muertos* or the Day of the Dead, which is characterized by festive celebration acknowledging the place of death in life and symbolic remembrances of dead members of the family, the funeral is a sad occasion. Death has come very close, and the family feels its presence and the loss of one of its members.

The funeral brings the family together from many different locations. Family members make special efforts to attend to represent their branch of family relatedness to the dead person. The family hopes for a "large funeral" not only to demonstrate how much the person was revered, but also to show, in the presence of the entire extended family, how strong the family is in life, perhaps against death. Women are particularly aware of the numerical attendance of family, as it represents their collective offspring: *Mira quien vino a dar sus despedidas* (Look who came to pay their respects). The funeral is a time for family members to make statements about their own impending death; this atmosphere of understanding and sympathetic empathy seems like an appropriate time and place to do future planning, to state their wishes for a similar funeral or ceremony. This informal planning is then a daughter's or sister's responsibility to remember and carry out when the time comes. Responsibilities are continued in this way, with the transfer of roles, tasks, and memories from one generation to another.

The funeral procession entering the church or the mortuary and cemetery gives deference to the women in the family. The matriarch or the eldest women enter first and are assisted by other women in the family, followed by the men. Traditional women educate the family about funeral traditions as the family moves through the ritual. The

113

transitional, modern, and acculturated women are respectful of tradition but tend to follow their own interpretations and apply the customs to their own and their family's needs, translating the ritual step-by-step to their children and explaining what the older and more traditional family members have to do which differs from their own modern versions. The funeral is a time when all family disagreements and differences are held at bay while the family uses the opportunity to bring people together.

Care-Giver Role of Women

In the Mexican-American family, a female — usually the mother or wife or daughter (in the case of parents' illness) of a dying person — carries out the role of care giver. The care-giver role is designated a woman's role and is seen as an obligation to the family. The obligation is part of the role carried by the woman as the wife of a dying or deceased person, or the mother, daughter, sister, or daughter-in-law. In an extended family, cousins may also be expected to help out.

If a sick person is at home, the tasks are many, as the woman occupies a role as "healer." She is expected, in her role, to have been socialized to take care of her family in health and sickness. As a mother and wife, she is supposed to provide relief, remedies, care, and nurturing to all family members (Manzanedo et al., 1980). The degree to which this role is adopted by women depends on class, acculturation, and also personal choice. However, woman-to-woman advice networks exist to assist women in their roles. Women consult their mothers, their godmothers or *madrinas,* older women in the neighborhoods, and their *comadres* or in-laws. In times when immigration or migration from one region or state to another makes it impossible to get advice from their own network, women seek an equivalent in their new surroundings (Manzanedo et al., 1980).

In its broadest sense, social support refers to optimum personal and social integration and may include the following elements: (a) supportive religious and other social rituals, (b) supportive values and beliefs by which individuals and families are comforted; (c) supportive shared norms that provide "meaning;" (d) social networks that supply supportive needs; (e) the fit between the role(s) of the bereaved and the meeting of acute dependency needs at death and recovery time; (f) the availability and supply of nurturant others; (g) the availability of support that "protects" the self; (h) the function of self-supports in terms of the ability to seek and get support; (i) the availability of supportive others who "permit" or elicit emotional release; and (j) structural supports such as community, work, and the like (Kaplan, Cassell, and Gore, 1977).

Acculturation

Immigration from one country to another generally involves separation from extended family. Initially isolated, the family experiences considerable stress, which is especially true for the woman, who usually is not engaged in a social role outside the family upon relocation.

With migration comes the loss of extended family and the disruption of the family's homeostasis and ability to cope. Yet, there is a tendency among Mexicans in the United States to reconstitute the extended family in order to gain help and control. There is a tendency to also establish an extended kinship system of *compadrasgo* as a continuing support system by having *padrinos, padrinas, madrinos,* and *madrinas* to guide children.

Different stages of acculturation have been identified within the Mexican-American family. Mother and grandparents may be at the beginning stage, the father at an intermediate level, while children may be at an advanced stage of acculturation. The different stages of acculturation may result in familial conflicts over expectations and norms within and outside the family system.

Repeated contact with the new values over a prolonged period of time changes the family's outlook on such issues as child rearing, sex roles, and philosophy of life.

Family values may act to impede or facilitate the acculturation process. Values of interdependence can mediate the effects of discrimination. On the other hand, the dominant role of the extended family may interfere with reliance on alternate support systems, that is, school and social service agencies.

Traditionally, women in the Mexican-American society were content to be passive. Their cultural tradition expected them to be patient, submissive, and dependent upon men. But the struggle to define a new role for themselves within the American society has caused women to define a new role for themselves within the Mexican-American culture. In a society which often has been viewed as sexist, Mexican-American women are becoming more assertive in communicating both their ethnic and their social identity (Asuncion-Lande, 1979).

What is the context in which Mexican-American cultural practices prevail is an empirically based question calling for research. The extent to which Aztec- or Mayan-specific, Spanish- or Mexican-based philosophies of death and life and symbolism still exist in the heritage of the culture is unknown. The structure of the family is undergoing continuous change, as are the gender roles of females and males. The significance of death and dying, its rituals, ceremonies, tasks, and continuities, are in dynamic change, and the role of women in the reshaping work, the role of care giver, provider of nurturance, and tender of the ill, dying, and dead will need to be examined.

CHAPTER NINE

Spirituality and Death and Dying from a Gay Perspective

David A. Housel

By their very nature, the topics of spirituality, death and dying, and gayness evoke such a vast array of interpretation, emotional and otherwise, that clarifying definitions, for the purposes of this chapter, must be offered from the onset. By "spiritual," I do not necessarily mean identification with a particular organized or institutionalized religious belief system or dogma. Rather, like Fortunato (1987), I feel that spiritual refers "to the aura around all of our lives that gives what we do meaning, the human striving toward meaning, the search for a sense of belonging," and spiritual need refers to "the need for grounding, some deep sense of belonging in a cosmic context" (p. 8). Each of us, over the course of our life, develops a spiritual or philosophical framework that informs and ensures our daily survival and enables us to cope with adversity and various forms of oppression.

As Becker asserts in *The Denial of Death* (1973), the strongest motivating factor in human psychology is not sex (as proposed in Freudian psychoanalytic theory) but, rather, the terror of death and the fear of our own mortality. In the United States, fear of dying makes us ostracize those who are terminally ill, disabled, or elderly and lends itself to the reverence of youth and beauty. Although gay men can die in a variety of ways—from heart disease to cancer to bias-related murder—I will focus my discussion on AIDS, given its disproportionate impact upon the gay male community.

For me, "gayness" transcends the object of one's sexual, erotic, and affectational desire or preference; "gayness" is a personal identification

117

that influences one's perception of, and interface with, the world. Unlike one's racial/ethnic background or biological gender, sexual orientation does not have identifiable physical characteristics. Consequently, one can be "in the closet" and not share this aspect of him- or herself with others. "Being closeted" *might* protect one from harassment, discrimination, and ostracism on the community level; however, one is imprisoned within oneself, unable to express his or her true nature in authentic ways to others. Many men and women will have same-sex sexual contact but not identify themselves as lesbian, gay, or bisexual. This discussion will focus on self-acknowledged and self-identified gay men who live their lives with varying degrees of openness around their sexual orientation and who have some connection to the organized gay male community. I feel that the patriarchy and institutionalized sexism found within organized religion, not to mention the pernicious, ubiquitous gender bias in our society at large, makes the spiritual journey and psychic realities for lesbians fundamentally different from gay men, meriting separate discussion by a lesbian author.

The perspective/bias that I bring as the author is one of a thirty-one-year-old, openly gay, white, European-American man, raised in the Midwest but currently living and working in New York City. I am from working-class roots but am now middle class and free of disability and HIV infection (to the best of my knowledge). My religious upbringing is in the Judeo-Christian tradition (specifically, Roman Catholicism). I have formal education as a social worker (M.S.W.) and have been doing AIDS-specific work for six years. For the past four years, I have worked as an inpatient social worker at an AIDS-designated hospital center, assisting patients, their families, and significant others with discharge planning and psychosocial adjustment to the AIDS diagnosis and its impact on their lives. I am also an educator/trainer/activist who has done anti-oppression and multicultural work on the community level. This chapter flows forth from this personal and professional life experience.

Overview

From my perspective, one of the most powerful forces perpetuating homophobia (the fear and subsequent oppression of lesbian, gay, and bisexual people) is the overriding sex phobia that pervades this country and that has been institutionalized in Judeo-Christian religious dogma and the medical model. As Bullough (1975) asserts, "Most of our vested medical interests in sexuality were formed in the nineteenth century and are associated with Victorianism—what happened is that a new age of science had given its *imprimatur* to explanations which tended to reconfirm the old religious truths" (p. 291). Ultimately, "the effect was to incorporate traditional Christian prejudice about sex into a system of medicine" (p. 292). Each new scientific discovery seemingly seized the opportunity to inculcate fears of sexuality; for example, cunnilingus and fellatio were said to cause cancer, menstruation was claimed to be a source of male gonorrhea, and, of course, venereal disease in general was proof positive of the pathological nature of most sexual activity (Bullough, 1975, pp. 295-97). Bullough continues, "As the public became more aware of the medical 'dangers' of sexuality, they were willing to put more limits on sexual expression, and most states enacted penal codes designed to curtail sexual activity" (p. 300). The laws used to criminalize and entrap gay men are the sodomy laws (still in effect in nearly half of the states in this country). The influence of this medical model also empowered the American Psychiatric Association to categorize homosexuality as a pathological illness until 1974.

As Clark, Brown, and Hochstein (1989) state:

A homophobic or heterosexist bias permeates twentieth century Western culture and society so thoroughly as to make separating social attitudes from their roots in religious belief systems virtually impossible. . . . The insistence upon separating sexual orientation from sexual fulfillment, upon "loving the sinner" but "hating the sin," belies a fundamental homophobia. . . . Gay/lesbian individuals within a majority of religious denominations consequently encounter religious as well as social obstacles to the process of developing self-acceptance and self-esteem. . . . Religious doctrine thus exacerbates the tensions and alienation already potentially present between gay people and their families. (P. 267)

Historically, organized religion has been a place where people gain solace and comfort from the harsh realities of the world and affirm a spirituality that gives them the strength to persevere and survive with a degree of integrity. But, as the above quote illustrates, gay men are denied this access in mainstream congregations, which, in fact, make little effort to provide them with the support and relief lacking in law and society and, in some cases, officially preach condemnation

119

and judgment of their "life-style." Undaunted, gay men who are invested in practicing their religion in traditional ways have formed groups within virtually every Christian denomination (e.g., Dignity, Integrity, Affirmation, etc.) and have even established their own denomination of churches (the Universal Fellowship of the Metropolitan Community Churches) and a loose federation of synagogues (the World Congress of Gay and Lesbian Jewish Organizations) (Clark et al., 1989).

In traditional Native American cultures, "two spirits," since they are equally male and female, were seen as bridges and often served their nations/tribes as emissaries and diplomats. Their dual nature was seen as special in a spiritual sense, and many became powerful shamans, soothsayers, and medicine people. They had respected and revered places in their communities (Roscoe, 1988; Williams, 1986). Nelson (1981-82) asserts that Christian churches need the healing power of gay men and lesbians in a similar way; he claims that we call "into question the dominance-submission patterns of any patriarchal society as well as the myths of super-masculinism by which that society lives" and [we demand] "release from dehumanizing sex-role stereotypes and liberation from fears about the continuum of sexual feelings within the self" (p. 174). In a sense, traditional congregations need us as much as we need the benefits of inclusion in their spiritual communities.

Many gay men choose their spiritual journey outside of traditional religious paths. Some do individual studies of philosophy, meditation, and yoga, while others throw themselves into social change and gay liberation community activism (e.g., ACT-UP, Queer Nation, etc.). Their efforts to nurture gay culture and to raise issues germane to the gay community (including AIDS and health care) are attempts to heal their own internalized homophobia and hopefully to eradicate the social stigma surrounding homosexuality that fosters feelings of self-loathing, isolation, and aloneness. Gay men in drug, alcohol, and other types of recovery have embraced the twelve-step program philosophy as their guiding principle in life, while others have found strength and meaning in "new age" approaches, from Louise Hay to crystals to psychic healing.

The concept of a "gay male community" is not a monolithic one. Self-identified gay men are found in every racial/cultural/ethnic background, religious/spiritual tradition, socioeconomic class, gender identification, occupation, position in society, age, geographical location, national origin, and ability. To represent such a diverse reality is impossible, and the oppressive forces that plague our society—racism, sexism, homophobia, classism, anti-Semitism, ageism, ableism, and so on—are also present in the organized gay male community. The attempt to "mainstream" the gay liberation movement has often left people of color, women, working class and poor people, folks with disabilities, and youth and older people on the periphery of the movement, denied access to the real power structure/decision-making process. As can be seen, the gay community, like the larger society, must do tremendous healing before true equality and justice will be realized.

Lastly, being "gay" is a quality that one may not share with anyone else in one's family of origin. For example, as I was growing up, my family was unable to share my gay culture with me, nor did they affirm or role model pride in my gayness. In contrast, people of color and women at least have people surrounding them who can validate their struggles toward self-acceptance in the face of an oppressive society and lend coping strategies and a sense of belonging in ways that are denied a gay person. In fact, when a gay person "comes out" to his family, he risks rejection and ostracism from the very system that is supposed to be supporting him. Often, he is exiled and forced to forge a life of his own, creating another "family" of supportive friends who accept and love him in his totality.

Illness and Medical Care

The Protestant work ethic, the notion of rugged individualism, the concept of "survival of the fittest," and male conditioning/machismo have also filtered into the consciousness of gay men. Therefore, illness, disability, and inability to work are all seen as weaknesses and failures that are counter to independence and self-sufficiency, the cornerstones of being "male." Seeking help or medical treatment might prove difficult, particularly when the illness is potentially life threatening (like AIDS).

Most people in our society attribute a magical, omnipotent power to physicians and hospitals. They expect modern medicine to cure them of all ills, and when these establishments fail to do so, anger and resentment are displaced onto them. In many ways, modern medicine has disappointed people living with AIDS (PLWA's), and they have sought so-called "alternative treatments/therapies," including acupuncture, herbs, and nontraditional healers in attempts to "cure" themselves and to prolong the quality of their lives. Clearly, those who are proactive and involved in their medical treatment tend to survive longer, with less psychic pain, because their anxiety and fear of death is abated by a feeling of taking control of their situations (Weitz, 1989).

With AIDS, gay men deal with the stigma of a sexually transmitted disease in the context of a homophobic world — an illness that can kill them in the "prime of life." A diagnosis of AIDS might expose their homosexuality for the first time, as well as a nonmonogamous sexual life that lies counter to the Victorian sexual morality that underlies social customs, law, and the medical model in the United States. In many cases, gay men blame themselves for their illness and internalize the shame and guilt thrown at them by society. These feelings make dealing with the illness in positive, life-affirming ways problematic and seeking help from medical facilities to home care to friends/family all the more troublesome.

Young men dying goes counter to the mythology that people are to live a long life and die painlessly (in their sleep) in old age. Dying young shatters this myth that protects us from confronting our own mortality and death phobia and forces us, on some level, to integrate sick and often disfigured people into our lives. All of the above breed feelings of awkwardness and discomfort that further stigmatize and alienate the PLWA.

Credence in mainstream medical care among gay men varies based upon their historical access to and experience with the medical institution. White, middle-class people, overall, have had access and positive experiences with mainstream medicine and thus have more faith and trust in it. People of color and poor people have had to deal with the racism and classism in these institutions and may distrust and place less faith and credibility in modern medicine. Western medical practitioners may also devalue and dismiss healing practices and rituals found in Asian, Pacific Islander, African, Caribbean, and Native American cultures and insult the people who embrace these traditions, which, in turn, keeps them from accessing conventional medical treatment in the future. In many cultures, going to the hospital or to a physician outside one's community is the course of last resort out of fear of "losing face" or bringing shame upon the family, particularly when AIDS is the diagnosis.

Overall, my experience in the hospital suggests that PLWA's balance Western medicine with other approaches as they develop unique strategies in coping with their illnesses. They learn to overcome their fear of questioning and challenging the "god-doctor" and become

122

informed consumers and participants in their own medical management. They create a multifactorial approach (medical, emotional, psychosocial, and spiritual) to deal with their illness on a day-to-day basis.

Death and Dying

Like mainstream American society, the gay male community generally views death as an evil to be avoided at all costs: "Physical appearance, youth and beauty, is highly valued in our culture, especially in the gay sub-culture" (Andersen and MacElveen-Hoehn, 1988). This reality makes the physically wasting and disfiguring elements of AIDS particularly stigmatizing and damaging to one's sense of self and value in the world. PLWA's

> face the vulnerability of a terminal illness from a disease that is greatly feared by the culture in which they live. The person with AIDS also experiences in varying degrees isolation, rejection, and alienation from their community due in large part to their sexual orientation [or drug addiction, prostitution, etc.]. (Andersen and MacElveen-Hoehn, 1988, p. 54)

Many of my patients have articulated that they are less afraid of death (which, for many, is a relief from pain and suffering) than of how they are going to die. Will they be in uncontrollable pain? Will they be an emotional and care-giving burden to their loved ones? Will they be actively involved in their care until the end, or will they lapse into coma or suffer from dementia?

The degree of openness in discussing a person's AIDS diagnosis or impending death varies widely among gay men, based on their own level of acknowledgment and acceptance of what is happening, their significant other's degree of comfort with AIDS and death, the patient's historical relationship with those surrounding him, the patient's physical and mental capacity to engage in dialogue toward the end of his illness, the patient's cultural heritage and religious background, and so on. The very diagnosis of AIDS demands an often rapid spiritual readjustment and alteration in the person's way of being in the world; his health and care management becomes a top and pressing priority. He must rely on a collective wisdom that comes from a community that has experienced other AIDS deaths and, in so doing, has developed a life philosophy that will inform and provide comfort and support to what the PLWA is now confronting (Andersen and MacElveen-Hoehn, 1988, p. 51).

As men, we are rarely given permission, in a sexist society, to display emotion other than anger in often violent ways. Internalized sexism can be powerful among gay men because, in a heterosexit model, we are like women in that we desire and are attracted to men. As a consequence, many gay men avoid any behavior or emotional expression that might be construed as "feminine." They will dress in hypermasculine ways and present a "macho-bravado" facade that is void of any so-called "tenderness." Crying or expressing feelings of shame, guilt, helplessness, or inadequacy is seen as weakness, vulnerability, and passivity. "Being a victim" to his own emotions or being unable to exact control is damaging to a gay man's sense of himself as a man and may prohibit open discussion that could prove healing with those surrounding him. He may need to "tough things out" on his own.

With an AIDS diagnosis, the person may wish to reconcile with the church of his childhood

> but not wish to disown his sexual identity, his lover, or his gay world. The family may be helped to locate clergy or rabbis who will be understanding, non-judgmental, and willing to work with persons with AIDS and their families to approach the spiritual dimension of the illness. . . . Acceptance by a religious or spiritual community can do much to counter the attribution of sin and guilt often associated with the disease. (Tibier, Walker, and Rolland, 1989, p. 93).

The support of a comforting religious/spiritual presence may, therefore, act as a catalyst to a discussion between the PLWA and his significant others that promotes healing, places closure on their time together, and enables both to say "goodbye."

Fear of contagion or a feeling of being overwhelmed by caregiving responsibilities may keep the PLWA's from dying in their own home or that of a loved one. Most die in hospitals or hospices where pain management and comfort measures can be secured in the presence of trained medical and mental health professionals. Some, however, do insist that the loved one die in his home, in an environment that feels familiar to all involved. Clearly, these decisions lie in the hands of the PLWA and his significant others and will be influenced by the availability of needed concrete and supporting resources (which is often a byproduct of insurance coverage, financial resources, and socio-economic class).

The stigma and misunderstanding surrounding AIDS may disconnect survivors from traditional mechanisms of bereavement support. Family members may misrepresent their loved one's cause of death out of fear of negative repercussions from their communities or religious congregations. This deception may only exacerbate the pain, guilt, and shame that the survivors are feeling and will only complicate an already complex mourning and bereavement process. Tibier et al. (1989) assert that seeking compassionate and culturally sensitive family treatment during the time of anticipatory grief and subsequent bereavement will enhance current family functioning and impact positively on future generations.

Funeral Practices

Funeral practices and memorial services are socially sanctioned rituals to assist the survivors in working through their feelings of loss and grief, to put a sense of closure on their relationships with the dead person, and to celebrate the deceased's life. Oftentimes, prior to his death, the PLWA articulates (via a will or more informally) his wishes for the disposition of his remains (burial, cremation, etc.) and his preference for service. These decisions will be influenced by his religious belief systems that will determine place (church, synagogue, etc.) and method (cremation is unacceptable in certain religious belief systems). Sometimes the survivors, out of their own needs, disregard and disrespect the person's wishes and formulate their own funeral plans. In my experience, most gay men tend to either have a closed casket or are cremated (secondary to the debilitating and disfiguring aspects of end-stage AIDS) and have a service either in a secular or religious institution (depending upon religious beliefs). In either case, there is usually a place for testimonials that allow the survivors to publicly bear witness to the person's death and what impact/meaning the person had on their lives. These testimonials and being surrounded by others who loved the dead person often prove healing as the survivor passes through the complicated maze of the grief/mourning/bereavement process. In the case of cremation, there is usually a photograph of the person displayed and specific instructions regarding where the ashes are to be kept or scattered. For many people, in lieu of flowers, they will suggest donations to be sent in their name to a favorite charity. The degree to which the person's biological family has accepted their loved one's AIDS diagnosis and homosexuality will determine whether his lover and friends will be incorporated into the funeral planning process. Socioeconomic class and financial empowerment will also impact upon the nature of the funeral/memorial service arranged.

Grief/Mourning/Bereavement

In my conceptualization, I see grief as the immediate initial response to a loved one's death (ranging from shock and numbness to relief); mourning is the process, begun with the funeral/memorial service, where one puts a degree of resolution and closure on his or her loss and is eventually able to reenter life and society more fully; and bereavement is a life-long endeavor where memories of the dead person reemerge and an acute process of mourning is reactivated (e.g., anniversaries of the death, holidays in general, favorite songs and places of the deceased, etc.) but is quickly resolved.

Prior to AIDS, loss was still prominent in the lives of gay men as they dealt with "coming out" (i.e., losing a sense of who they were for a new, more authentic identity; losing a heterosexual future that was more secure and societally less oppressive; losing connection, sometimes, with traditional mechanisms of support, etc.). AIDS has introduced additional complications, including a sense of survivor's guilt—"the survivor's belief that a disaster has an allotted number of victims and, if one remains alive, it is because others died in her/his place . . . the conflict between mourning the lost object while simultaneously feeling relief that one has survived" (Boykin, 1991, p. 249). Survivors somehow try to blame themselves for the death of a loved one and therefore feel guilt about still being alive. These feelings of guilt accumulate with every subsequent AIDS death, which can lead to a certain psychic numbing—a phenomenon in which the survivor's psyche closes itself off so as not to feel the onslaught of emotions that occurs as a result of so many deaths (Lifton, as cited in Boykin, 1991, p. 250).

According to Biller and Rice (1990), AIDS grief and multiple loss is made more difficult for gay men because of

> society's inability and unwillingness to accept the gay identity, the importance of the loss of a gay significant other, and the

consequent legitimate sense of loss the individual feels when a significant other dies of AIDS. The second factor relates to the exacerbation of grief induced by repetitive loss over a brief period of time. (P. 284)

Eventually, the person may suffer from "bereavement overload" (Kastenbaum as cited in Biller and Rice, 1990, p. 285).

Studies suggest that bereavement is more intense for survivors below age forty-five than for those who are older (Lovejoy, 1989, p. 308), which includes many gay men affected by AIDS. AIDS bereavement is also complicated by the disease process itself. As cited in Biller and Rice (1990), "Survivors [of AIDS] have to deal with varied memories of a rapidly changing person; in many cases, the person that died was not the same person the survivor formed a relationship with" (p. 289). In the larger community, survivors are too often forced to be silent; denying one's grief leads to guilt and shame over the loss, the relationship, and oneself (p. 289).

Studies have indicated that "gay men who could express their grief to their entire support system — co-workers, family, and friends — were able to have a more positive grief resolution than those with fewer supports" (Boykin, 1991, p. 251). For gay men who have endured numerous losses, their historic support group of friends may no longer exist secondary to AIDS deaths or current debilitating illness. Consequently, these survivors either must create new support systems for themselves (which is no easy task given the cumulative grief response) or must avail themselves of AIDS-specific bereavement support groups (Biller and Rice, 1990, p. 289).

In addition to AIDS specific bereavement groups, the gay male community has created other rituals by which to deal with the current holocaust we are facing. The NAMES PROJECT, the international AIDS Quilt, was founded by Clive Jones, a gay activist from San Francisco. The intent of the AIDS Quilt is for survivors to construct panels memorializing those whom they have lost to AIDS, to be joined with other similar panels, like a quilt. The process of making the panel will hopefully help survivors move through the mourning process. The Quilt itself reminds people that they are not alone in their feelings of pain and loss and serves as a powerful testimony and education tool for the larger society. World AIDS Day, A Day Without Art, AIDS Vigils, and moments of silence in annual lesbian/gay-pride celebrations are also ways in which survivors have public, community-sanctioned spaces to acknowledge and work through their feelings of loss, grief, and mourning. Some carry photos or placards with them for those they have survived as they march in the parade. In these forums, open displays of emotion and grief are welcomed.

Case Examples

The following case examples are meant to illustrate some of the points made previously as specific individuals and their significant others reacted to their AIDS diagnosis and subsequent deaths.

John was a gay white man who was raised in the rural South but who, as an adult, relocated to New York City to pursue professional opportunities and to live openly as a gay man. His relationship with his family, who are fundamentalist Christians, was tenuous at best. When he was diagnosed with AIDS, he decided to reconnect and share his gayness and AIDS diagnosis with them. After a rather emotional phone call, John began receiving fundamentalist Christian literature from his mother encouraging him to "repent his evil ways" and decrying his AIDS diagnosis as "God's retribution for his sins." As John grew sicker, his mother came to New York City to visit him. She would not touch him, and she was emotionally distant. As a Christian, she could not disown her son and would be present during his time of need, but she could not forgive him of his "sin." She would not discuss John's diagnosis of impending death; she would only talk about the "Lord's will" and the perversity of the "homosexual life-style" and pray at his bedside.

Gerald, an African-American gay man, was brought up in a strict Baptist tradition. He, too, relocated to New York City but was never comfortable with his gayness. He was sexually active but was otherwise very closeted about his sexual orientation. When he was diagnosed with AIDS, he converted and became a practicing Jehovah's Witness in the hopes of repenting for his "sins" and reconnecting to a religious belief system that would provide him with solace during his trying time. His "family" (he was long estranged from his biological family) became the other members of his church. Their presence provided him with tremendous emotional comfort, but his new religion prohibited blood transfusions and certain other medical procedures. His illness progressed rapidly, and he refused certain kinds of pain medication (in "penance for his sins"). He would not discuss his past or his death, but he did die according to his own wishes, surrounded by his newfound "family."

Steve, a gay man of African-American and Panamanian descent, was raised in the Baptist tradition in the Midwest. He moved to New York City to pursue a performing arts career and remained close to his family, who knew of his sexual orientation and who supported his long-term relationship with his lover, Donald. When Donald was diagnosed with AIDS and Steve acted as his primary caregiver, Steve's family, especially his mother, rallied around him throughout Donald's illness and subsequent death. When Steve began noticing AIDS-related symptoms himself, he discounted them and finally went in for treatment in advanced stages of illness. Throughout his rapid decline, his mother was at his bedside. As death approached, Steve, a practicing Buddhist, shared his belief in reincarnation and acceptance of death with his mother and helped her to come to terms with, and eventually accept, his imminent death. Once she was able to let go of him and articulate such, Steve discontinued all treatment and was dead in twenty-four hours. He was cremated, and the memorial service that celebrated his life was jointly planned by his biological family and concerned New York City friends.

Summary

The gay male community, despite all of its variety, is still influenced by the death practices of America and the Judeo-Christian tradition. Overall, gay men have internalized societally sanctioned belief systems concerning death and dying, funeral practices, and grief/mourning/bereavement. Gay men's total acceptance into mainstream America, however, is obstructed by homophobia, AIDS-phobia, and, in many cases, racism and classism. Society's refusal to acknowledge gay men, their sexuality, and their relationships as valid denies gay men access to traditional mechanisms of support to deal with the death and subsequent mourning of a loved one. Criminalization of homosexuality, oppression from most institutionalized religions, and fear of sexually transmitted diseases and AIDS have "legitimated" persecution and violence against gay men by their families of origin, employers, and society at large. The horrific AIDS pandemic and the psychic pain of mourning is thus made more stressful for gay men because of their systematic oppression for who they are and the belief that their sexual orientation is a willful choice. Consequently, special outreach efforts, in culturally sensitive and competent ways, must be made to assist gay men as they deal with the multiple losses surrounding death and dying. Efforts must also be made to eradicate homophobic policies and practices wherever they exist.

Additional Reading

Boswell, J. E. (1980). *Christianity, Social Tolerance, and Homosexuality: Gay People in Western Europe from the Beginning of the Christian Era to the Fourteenth Century.* Chicago: University of Chicago Press.

Fortunato, J. E. (1982). *Embracing the Exile: Healing Journeys of Gay Christians.* San Francisco: Harper & Row.

Gamson, J. (1989). Silence, death, and the invisible enemy: AIDS activism and social movement "newness." *Social Problems, 36*(4), 351-367.

Kimmel, D. C. (1979-80). Life history interviews of aging gay men. *International Journal of Aging and Human Development, 10*(3), 239-248.

McNeill, J. J. (1976). *The Church and the Homosexual.* Kansas City, Mo.: Andrews and McMeel.

The Lesbian Perspective on Death and Dying

Idella M. Evans and Julie Carter

The inclusion of lesbians as an ethnic minority may be somewhat controversial, but the trend in recent years has been to encourage this invisible minority to become more visible and thereby better understood. It is commonly accepted that approximately 10 percent of women are lesbians and that a much higher percentage of women have experienced homosexual behavior, according to the major large-scale studies of human sexual behavior by Kinsey et al. (1953) and Hite (1976). Social workers, psychologists, and others in the helping professions are agreed that ethnic and minority group clients are entitled to competent professional services and that insensitivity to cultural differences in clients defeats the purposes of the helping professions.

This chapter presents the lesbian cultural perspective first, then takes a look at death, dying, and religion from such a viewpoint.

The Invisible Minority

Historically, the term *homosexuality* has related to sexual activity rather than to a general way of relating and living. Homosexuality has been associated with sinful or criminal behavior, deviance, and mental illness. These associations tend to perpetuate negative stereotypes. The term is often assumed to refer exclusively to men, rendering lesbians invisible.

Prior to 1962, sexual behavior between persons of the same sex was a criminal act in all fifty states. However, laws against homosexual behavior between women were seldom enforced, and this selective enforcement of laws has contributed to lesbians being fearful and closeted. The last thirty years have seen changes in the penal codes of most states, but the legal status of lesbians in this country is still determined on a state-by-state basis.

The criminalization of sexual behavior not only affects those apprehended or charged but also legitimizes discrimination by other sectors of society. For many years, the federal government justified its employment discrimination against lesbians and gay men on the grounds that since they were criminals subject to arrest, they were susceptible to blackmail and thus were poor security risks.

Currently, the terms *lesbian* and *gay* are used to refer to identities and the modern culture and communities that have developed among people who share these identities. Some people have sexual relations with others of their own gender but do not consider themselves to be lesbian or gay. The essence of lesbianism is a more all-encompassing life-style than mere sexual preference. Lesbians have rejected the social role that our society considers appropriate for females in the traditional patriarchal family. As an alternative to accepting the traditional feminine role or the masculine role as defined by our socially accepted standards, they promote androgyny, taking the more desirable traits of both sex roles and seeing equality as the ideal basis for interpersonal relationships.

Emergence of a Subculture

In the last half century or so, a subculture has emerged that is concerned with civil rights and political representation for lesbians. During the Depression years of the 1930s, only a few lesbians were able to find each other because of their limited means and society's restrictions on them. As this country mobilized for the Second World War, women made unprecedented strides toward independence, both economically and socially, leaving their small towns and rural settings to take up employment in the war industries and to take over men's non-combat jobs in the military services.

Women who joined the military establishment were soon made aware of the fact that lesbians were considered undesirable and were being discharged as unsuitable for military service. Since 1940, all branches of military service have had strong policies prohibiting homosexual behavior and punishing offenders. At the present time, known lesbians are denied entrance into military service, and they are being discharged upon discovery. Since 1975, a coalition of mental health professionals has been actively involved in attempting to influence the Department of Defense (DOD) to rescind its policy, to no avail. Each year a resolution has been introduced into the House and the Senate calling for the president to rescind the DOD policy, and each year it gains a few co-sponsors. In 1992, President Clinton indicated his intention to rescind the ban against gays and lesbians in the military, and it will be done in due time.

At the end of World War II, women were encouraged to return to civilian life and to resume traditional gender roles. Many lesbians who married during and after the war waited until their children were grown or their husbands died to resume a lesbian life-style. Others remained part of a lesbian circle of friends, and some maintained spasmodic contact with lesbian friends throughout their married lives. Those unmarried women who chose to remain in the military, and those who joined the services after the war, were immediately suspected of being lesbians and were subjected to harassment and antilesbian witch hunts.

Alice and Ruth met when they were stationed together in the navy during World War II. They planned to live together and attend college after the war, but Ruth's parents influenced her to change, to live at home until she married, a view supported by Jehovah's Witnesses. Ruth lived with her parents for several years, but she kept in touch with Alice, who finished college and took a job in another state. Ruth married a friend of her family and had two children. Alice and Ruth kept in touch with each other and saw each other whenever they could arrange it. When both her children were grown, Ruth told her husband that she had always been in love with Alice and that she wanted to live with her. After a stormy divorce, Ruth was finally free to live with Alice, and she was fortunate that she and her partner were both accepted by her grown children.

The postwar years were dominated by political oppression, and within a short time, the federal homosexual policies had spread from the military to nearly all levels of employment in this country. One area of employment in which homophobia remains widespread is that of public school teaching. Most lesbians who are teachers are closeted for fear of losing their jobs. Closeted lesbians in academia developed an unspoken understanding of their commonality, but they tended to treat it as if it were some unspeakable affliction they shared but never mentioned (Cruikshank, 1982). Until very recently, any hint

133

or suggestion of lesbian relationships was grounds for dismissal from teaching positions. While it may no longer be possible to fire teachers because of lesbianism, it is still common practice to avoid hiring known lesbians and to consider them less than desirable.

The fear of disclosure and its consequences caused many lesbians to pass as heterosexual or asexual, thus adapting by becoming invisible. Many went so far as the engage in a "front" marriage with a gay man, primarily to win the approval and acceptance of family and to be able to "pass as normal." Educators in colleges and universities in some states are protected from discrimination, but at this time only three states (Hawaii, Massachusetts, and Wisconsin) have enacted civil rights legislation to prohibit discrimination against lesbians and gay men. California has twice passed laws against sexual preference discrimination, only to have those laws vetoed by two successive governors.

The decades of the 1950s and 1960s saw the development of an underground subculture in which gay bars became popular meeting places for lesbians and gay men, although the bars were mainly illegal and subject to being raided by local police. The first lesbian rights organization was founded in San Francisco in 1955 as an alternative to the bar scene (Martin and Lyon, 1991). Daughters of Bilitis (DOB), with their newsletter *The Ladder*, was instrumental in organizing chapters of DOB in cities across the country. This organization served as a rudimentary base of the lesbian counterculture during the fifteen years when it was considered unsafe and unpopular to be known as a lesbian.

The Gay Liberation Movement was initially a male-dominated movement that began with the 1969 riots in response to a routine police raid of the Stonewall Inn, a gay bar in New York's Greenwich Village. Our patriarchal society has always considered that whatever men do is more important than anything women do; therefore, male homosexuality has been punished legally, socially, and economically to a greater extent than female homosexuality. The public demonstrations and demands for gay rights kept lesbians invisible until the decade of the 1980s, when organizations began to use the names "Lesbian" and "Gay."

The Women's Liberation Movement initially preferred to have lesbians remain an invisible minority, and those who were unwilling to do so graciously were subjected to discrimination and rejection. The National Organization for Women (NOW) was fearful of a takeover by "The Lavender Menace" in the early 1970s, and it was not until the National Women's Conference in Houston in 1977 that NOW approved the right of women to choose their sexual life-style. Since then, NOW has been actively promoting the rights of lesbians and gay men along with other issues of importance to lesbians and other feminists.

At the March on Washington in 1987, when 500,000 demonstrators assembled for lesbian and gay civil rights, their demands included the following: (a) having domestic partners entitled to the same rights as heterosexual couples with regard to taxes, insurance, medical care, and survivor benefits; (b) foster care, adoption, child custody, and visitation rights; and (c) recognition of same-sex unions by religious organizations (Martin and Lyon, 1991).

Later, in 1987, the Lesbian Agenda for Action (LAFA) held a conference of five hundred women to devise strategies for making the government more responsive to the issues of domestic partners, child care, reproductive freedom, violence prevention, overcoming poverty and racism, and advancement in the workplace. The main thrust of the LAFA conference demonstrated that public visibility is an indispensable tool for creating change. The dilemma facing lesbians living in a homophobic society is that until they are known as lesbians, it is easy to pass as heterosexual and avoid the issue of discrimination—but unless they do come out in large numbers, they will be unable to change public attitudes and laws to prevent discrimination.

National Coming-Out Day, started in 1988, was so successful on the Oprah Winfrey show on television that she has continued to observe it each year since then. The past two decades have been important times for lesbian musicians, writers, playwrights, film and video makers, artists, sports figures, and entertainers. They have come out of their closets in large numbers and have been promoting greater visibility, but not without some problems. The religious right has directed attacks on women's studies programs, sexuality courses, and any program suspected of endorsing lesbianism.

Levels of Visibility

The "closet" has been defined as "a system of lies, denials, disguises, and double entendres" by Berube (1989). Many lesbians have spent their lives being closeted and passing as heterosexual. These women were vulnerable to external and internal homophobia, to guilt and

135

self-hatred, and to distrust of each other. Many of today's lesbian elders are coming out of their closets, having retired from professional positions and feeling free of the need to hide. Many others have adjusted so well to their closets and to passing that it has become a way of life they are unable or unwilling to abandon.

The process of "coming out" is a gradual and difficult one for most lesbians. The conscious or unconscious need to falsify one's true self and pass as something else is detrimental to a person's self-esteem and overall health, yet the denied or hidden self may be a source of danger in a homophobic society. For many lesbians, the potential dangers outweigh the possible rewards.

Coleman (1982) has described five developmental stages of the coming-out process as follows:

1. Pre-coming-out: feeling different, alienated, and alone
2. Coming-out: facing lesbian feelings, self-acceptance, and disclosure to others
3. Exploration: experimenting with the new sexual identity
4. First relationships
5. Integration: incorporating private and public identity into one's self-image

Social workers and others in the helping professions should be able to accept the lesbian client as she is, at whatever level of visibility she can handle. Sometimes the woman may simply need to confide in someone that she is a lesbian, but she can go no further because of her own guilt and fear.

To come out as a lesbian, a woman must face her own feelings of being different and somewhat alienated from mainstream society. When she has rejected the traditional role of wife and has accepted her unconventional feelings of preference for a partner of her own gender, she must reconcile her feelings about homosexuality and resolve her guilt for failure to accept the commonly held values and traditions of her family, her church, and society at large. At this stage, she may not confront her own homophobia, and she may internalize the fear and hatred generated by a hostile environment.

The lesbian who has accepted herself can reach out to make contact with other closeted lesbians and will develop a social group that is supportive of her life-style. She may socialize with co-workers and/or professional colleagues with whom she feels safe and protected, or she may limit her social activities to participation in groups with common interests; but in the process of coming-out, most lesbians establish a few close personal friendships that often endure throughout their lives.

The most difficult step for lesbians is coming out to family members. Siblings are usually the first to know, then children of lesbian mothers, and finally, the lesbian's parents. Many older lesbians have never come out to family members and have no intention of ever doing so. Even when the lesbian has never married, has lived with a "woman companion" for many years, and has never dated men, she may fear disclosure to her family members. This fear of disclosure to family can cause severe anxiety in lesbians facing terminal illness and may cause problems for the helping professionals who are there to assist the person in coping with death.

Maria and Lisa are a lesbian couple, both in their early fifties, who have in common Catholic family backgrounds and careers as elementary school teachers. They have been each other's primary relationship for the past twenty years, although they have chosen to live in separate apartments for fear that their intimacy would be discovered and would result in damage to their careers and rejection by their families. Their internalized homophobia has been reinforced by their religious beliefs that their relationship has been denounced as an immoral and unnatural life-style. They live more than a thousand miles from their families, and they have avoided any close association with other lesbians.

Maria has been diagnosed with terminal ovarian cancer, and her family has arrived to take care of funeral arrangements, putting Lisa in the position of a casual friend. In this time of crisis, both Maria and Lisa lack any lesbian support system, and they feel powerless in any decision making. Their internalized homophobia is heightened by their fear of disclosure by possible homophobic hospital staff or other professional personnel with whom they are now closely attached.

In contrast, the lesbian who has accepted herself, been accepted by friends, and has achieved a comfortable tolerance, if not total acceptance, by her family, may come out to anyone who asks. She may affiliate with lesbian groups and support lesbian causes, or she may find it necessary to continue passing for fear of losing her job or jeopardizing her professional career. Lesbians in this situation frequently become active in feminist groups where it is not necessary to make their sexual orientation known.

The final step is to become involved in public life as lesbian-identified persons, politically active in promoting greater visibility and acceptance of lesbians. These people are involved in confronting homophobia in religion, health care, the teaching profession, the judicial system, and society in general. Those who have taken this final step are able to achieve integration by incorporating their private, religious, and public identities into their self-image.

Ollenburger and Moore (1992) found that older lesbians experience a triple jeopardy: as an older person, as a woman, and as a lesbian. This makes it particularly difficult for those who are coming out in their later years and need the same social, medical, and legal support systems as other people, but are fearful of rejection.

Lesbian Family Issues

Alternative family structures are usually developed by lesbians, primarily because their minority status is not shared with other members of their biological families, as is the case with ethnic minority groups. These social networks of close friendships often provide a means for meeting their needs for unqualified acceptance, recognition, belonging, and protection from the discrimination of a homophobic environment. Some who have not actually been rejected by their families have distanced themselves physically and emotionally from their families because they fear the rejection they would face if their families knew they were lesbians. These fears may be realistic if the family is intensely involved with certain religions. Lesbians generally make a supreme effort to sustain meaningful relationships with former partners and long-term lesbian friends, many of whom are closer than their biological sisters.

Social workers and others in the helping professions are finding an increasing need to deal with alternative family groupings as they see traditional patriarchal families declining in number. Lesbians may be seen as single-parent families, as adoptive or foster parents, as parents of two sets of children being raised together, or as unmarried couples with or without children.

Slater and Mencher (1991) have identified the challenges and coping mechanisms of the lesbian experience and have outlined a systems theory approach. Systems theory holds that family boundaries must be intact and flexible to promote functional family dynamics. The withholding of relational status by family and society, or the lack of any validation of the relationship, creates an ongoing central stress that is a major distinction between heterosexual and lesbian families. Confrontation with internalized homophobia may plague the lesbian family

138

throughout the life cycle, particularly at such rituals of passage as registering a child at school, buying a home together, writing wills, making medical or financial decisions for one's partner, and choosing a nursing home. The negotiation of roles provides additional flexibility which both liberates and complicates family functioning for lesbians.

Religious Beliefs and Practices

Many lesbians have rejected organized religion, while others have actively worked for church reforms. Some have become atheists or agnostics, and some have rationalized the negative aspects of their churches and continued to follow the faith of their early religious teachings. Some have joined together in metaphysical groups that offer spiritual meaning, and nearly all have recognized the need for some philosophical understanding of the nature and significance of the individual.

Dignity, USA, is a nationwide organization of similar-faith communities which has ministered to Catholic lesbians and gays since 1969. According to its printed brochures, its chapters promote a three-fold purpose as follows:

> 1. To individual lesbian and gay Catholics: to reinforce their self-acceptance and sense of dignity and to help them become more active members of the Church and society.
> 2. To society: to work for justice and social acceptance through education, political, and legal action.
> 3. To the Church: to develop its sexual theology and the acceptance of lesbians and gay persons as full and equal members of the one Christ.

The Universal Fellowship of Metropolitan Community Churches (MCC), founded in 1969, now has over two hundred congregations worldwide, with lesbians and gay men serving as ministers and elders. In 1991, MCC was endorsed for membership in the National Council of Churches by unanimous vote of the membership committee, but it must have final approval from two-thirds of the member denominations, and this has brought out some strong opinions both pro and con. Whether MCC will succeed in its struggle for acceptance among Protestant church leaders is yet to be determined, but it has become a well-established and growing force in lesbian and gay communities.

Some Jewish lesbians have rejected the patriarchal aspects of Judaism while continuing to identify with the Jewish ethnic culture by revising the rituals to provide a gender-neutral stance affirming women as equal persons. The three main branches of Judaism, with more than a million members each, are Orthodox, Conservative, and Reformed. Reconstructionism is a fifty-year-old movement involving 50,000 members of seventy congregations, which considers itself a leader in adapting faith to the modern world. All except Orthodox branches ordain women, and in 1990, both Reconstructionist and Reformed Judaism approved admitting homosexuals as rabbis. The Reconstructionists, in opposition to all other branches of Judaism, have come out in favor of sanctioning same-sex unions. The board of directors of the Federation of Reconstructionist Congregations and Havurot said, "Jewish sexual ethics apply regardless of sexual orientation. As we celebrate the love between heterosexual couples, so too do we celebrate the love between gay and lesbian Jews." Their "committed relationships" are to be affirmed in Jewish ritual "with the value of *kedushah,* holiness," the board said (Cornell, 1992).

Native American lesbians have taken a more positive view of themselves compared with most ethnic groups in that they consider themselves *Berdaches,* or extraordinary people, because of their androgyny. Grahn (1984) has described the traditional and honorable roles reserved for lesbians and gay men in the ancient cultures of more than eighty of North America's Indian nations. They were picked by tribes for the tasks of naming, healing, prediction, leadership, and teaching because they displayed characteristics that were both masculine and feminine.

Many feminist lesbians have turned away from patriarchal religions toward a goddess worship or spiritual sisterhood which has spread across the country since its founding in 1971. It is difficult to ascertain how widespread or popular this alternative religion has become, but it is known to be alive and well, if not well publicized.

Medical Care and Concerns

One important factor in keeping lesbians invisible was the attitude of the medical profession toward them. Historically, when a woman's lesbianism became a part of her medical history, she was stigmatized as having a mental illness and referred to a psychiatrist. In 1952, the American Psychiatric Association (APA) developed the first *Diagnostic and Statistical Manual of Mental Disorders* (DSM-I) based on the Association's experience with military psychiatry. With that volume, homosexuality was classified as a sociopathic personality disorder.

In 1969, the American Sociological Association passed a resolution preventing discrimination based on sexual preference. The National Association for Mental Health followed in 1970, and in 1972, the National Association of Social Workers rejected homosexuality as a mental illness. In 1973, the Association of Lesbian and Gay Psychologists became involved in the broader agenda of advancing the civil rights of lesbians and gay men. Finally, in late 1973, the APA removed homosexuality from its official list of mental disorders, but at that time it retained a diagnostic category of ego-dystonic homosexuality for those who wished to become heterosexual. Since 1976, mental health professionals have been actively working to remove the stigma of mental illness that has been associated with lesbian and gay sexual orientations and to promote changes in the attitudes of health professionals. It was not until 1987 that homosexuality as a diagnostic category was removed from *DSM-III, Revised.* In 1990, Congress removed the long-standing exclusion of "sexual deviate" from the immigration statute and passed the Americans with Disabilities Act, which made it clear that same-gender sexual orientation does not constitute a disability.

The concept of lesbian health care has focussed more on mental health than on physical health, but in those few places where lesbian health clinics have been established, the response has been overwhelming. A 1979 study of lesbian health needs in San Francisco found that because of social, institutional, and medical prejudice, lesbians were much less likely to seek medical intervention than were non-lesbian women (Martin and Lyon, 1991).

The National Association for Lesbian and Gay Gerontology (NALGG), founded in 1978, advocates the development of health and welfare services responsive to the needs of aging lesbians and gay men. It also provides factual and technical assistance to program planners and others interested in addressing lesbian/gay issues.

> Among the concerns of the terminally ill lesbian are the following: whether "exposure" as a lesbian will negatively affect the quality of care administered by medical and other health personnel; whether her definition of family will be respected when it involves hospital visitation and health care decision making; and whether there will be any kind of social and/or psychological support provided for her and others significant to her. (Potter, 1985)

Lesbians are being advised to have their attorneys draw up a "Durable Power of Attorney" designating a specific person as the one chosen to make decisions for them when they are unable to decide or to make their decisions known, because of disability. This is an important step for older lesbians who may have lived in a committed relationship for many years and, at a time of crisis, may be at the mercy of relatives who take over and consider the lesbian's partner to be an unrelated person.

Karen and Sharon had lived together in a committed but closeted relationship for four years when Sharon was critically injured in an auto accident that left her brain-damaged and quadriplegic. Karen, a professor of physical education trained in rehabilitation techniques, was able to help Sharon regain basic life skills, as she was the only one to whom Sharon responded. Doctors acknowledged that Karen was the key to Sharon's progress, but Sharon's father was named her guardian by the court. He denied his daughter was a lesbian and claimed that she was in danger of being sexually abused by Karen, so he moved her to a nursing home and forbade Karen to have contact with her. Sharon begged to be with Karen, but her father and the court succeeded in circumventing her wishes.

Karen had spent four years hiding her lesbianism, but when she disclosed it and attempted to prove her relationship with Sharon, she found she had no legal rights. Karen embarked on a national crusade to bring Sharon home by appealing for emotional and financial support from lesbian and gay groups, and government and health agencies across the country. She collaborated on a book entitled *Why Can't Sharon Kowalski Come Home?* and finally succeeded in getting Sharon transferred to a rehabilitation center where she was allowed to visit whomever she chose.

Sharon's father kept Karen defeated by legal battles over custody for eight years before the court of appeals finally decided that Karen and Sharon make up a "family of affinity" and awarded Sharon's guardianship to Karen. Karen felt strongly that this would not have happened if she and Sharon had been in a legally recognized relationship like marriage, and she is now an activist and advocate for the rights of the disabled and lesbian/gay domestic partners.

Coping with Death

Lesbians facing terminal illness and death generally prefer to be cared for at home if it is not too great a burden on the family. The services

142

of social workers, home health aides, hospice workers, and volunteers can usually be obtained, making home care more flexible and personal than hospital care. No one wants to die alone, and any person needs the comfort of having understanding and supportive people with them in their final hours. Some need the support of their minister, priest, or rabbi, but all need someone to help them let go of this life with comfort, dignity, and companionship.

An assessment and intervention model appropriate for anyone facing terminal illness and coping with death must be based on the physical, emotional, spiritual, interpersonal, and legal-financial needs of the individual. In the case of lesbians, some additional factors that should be taken into account are level of visibility with which she is comfortable, her extended family and support groups, and her problems of confronting homophobia in herself, her therapist, and the health-care system. We need to determine the strength of family ties and cultural bonds and how these impact on the lesbian relationship in times of crisis. We should find out what social support network the person has, and how this network will respond to terminal illness, death, and the needs of the surviving partner.

A surviving partner who has to deal with final arrangements while not being recognized as a legal spouse or family member faces stressful times. There may be a conflict of values or plans for rituals, ceremonies, and final disposition between the surviving partner and relatives of the deceased partner. The family of the surviving partner may be supportive or critical or denying of the importance of the relationship, and thus may create additional stress for the survivor.

Many formal and informal lesbian groups and organizations offer supportive help to terminally ill lesbians, their partners, and close friends or extended families. If the lesbian in crisis does not have a support group and is not part of an ongoing lesbian network, she may be helped by referral to an appropriate professional, agency, or organization. Women's bookstores, general bookstores with a women's studies section, and most public libraries have a selection of guidebooks or directories of services for lesbians. An example of what began as a listing of gay bars around the world in the 1960s and now consists of over one thousand listings in two hundred different categories is *Gaia's Guide* (Horn, 1991). Information that can be found in many of the lesbian travel guides will include addresses and phone numbers of national, state, city, and local organizations, events, publications, health clinics, religious groups, special-interest groups, and referral services, as well as the listings of commercial establishments that cater to lesbian clientele.

Bibliography

Adelman, M. (1980). Adjustment to aging and style of being gay: A study of older gay men and lesbians. Ph.D. diss., Wright University, Berkeley, CA.

Adelman, M. (Ed.). (1986). *Long Time Passing: Lives of Older Lesbians.* Boston, MA: Alyson Publications.

American Psychological Association, Committee on Lesbian and Gay Concerns. (1991). Avoiding heterosexual bias in language. *American Psychologist, 46,* 973-974.

Beck, E. (Ed.). (1982). *Nice Jewish Girls: A Lesbian Anthology.* Watertown, MA: Persephone Press.

Doress, P. B., and Siogal, D. L., and The Midlife and Older Women's Book Project. (1987). *Ourselves Growing Older.* New York: Simon and Schuster.

Garnets, L., and Kimmel, D. (1991). Lesbian and gay male dimensions in the psychological study of human diversity. In J. Goodchilds (Ed.), *Psychological Perspectives on Human Diversity in America* (pp. 137-192). Washington, DC: American Psychological Association.

Gonsiorek, J. C., and Weinrich, J. D. (Eds.). (1991). *Homosexuality: Research Implications for Public Policy.* Newbury Park, CA: Sage.

Kehoe, M. (1989). *Lesbians over Sixty Speak for Themselves.* New York: Harrington Park Press.

Messing, A., Schoenberg, R., and Stephens, R. (1984). Confronting homophobia in health care settings: Guidelines for social work practice. *Journal of Social Work and Human Sexuality, 2,* 65-74.

Parry, J. K. (1990). *Social Work Practice with the Terminally Ill: The Transcultural Perspective.* Springfield, IL: Charles C. Thomas.

Raphael, S. M., and Robinson, M. K. (1980). The older lesbian: Love relationships and friendship patterns. *Alternative Lifestyles, 3*(2), 207-230.

Steinem, G. (1992). *Revolution from Within.* Boston, MA: Little, Brown.

Guinea across the Water: The African-American Approach to Death and Dying

John L. Bolling

The cultural world view of a particular group of people determines how that people see reality and view the major issues of life and death. America and the Western European world tend to perceive and react to African Americans as if they had no world view outside the American mainstream world view. African Americans possess their own unique value system and world view. This unique world view is a synthesis of the African and American aspects of their collective character development. The aspect of collective character related to one's African background will be referred to in this chapter as the Africentric world view. This cultural world view of African Americans is a legacy from Mother Africa that antedates slavery. This soul-centered world view governs the everyday interactions with the visible and invisible worlds. It governs one's relationships with music, food, the elements, rhythm, the seasons, and other aspects of the nonhuman world. In the human world, it governs parent-child, husband-wife, and male-female relationships, and interactions with the ancestral invisible world.

The American aspect of African-American character development will be referred to as the Eurocentric aspect. W. E. B. Dubois made the observation that Black folks are forever dual in their belief systems, their realities—two souls trapped in one dark body, often warring against each other. This dual approach to reality extends throughout life and affects how African Americans approach and handle the major themes of development and maturation. This dual approach to reality is often most pronounced during the final stage of maturation, the final rites of passage—death.

One of the central themes of the African aspect of identity, and of Soul Culture, is that death is a continuation of life. For people of African descent, whether they be African North American, African Caribbean, African South American, or others, the underlying unifying thread of identity is the Culture of Soul. Soul Culture, as described by W. E. B. Dubois, is an ancient unbreakable set of beliefs and moral practices that govern the interaction of a group of people in their source. Soul Culture consists of a unified and systematized inner constellation of archetypal Symbols/Imagoes. This organized inner system of Symbols/Imagoes has been given various names in African-American tradition such as Soul Forces, Orishas, Obosum, Deities, Neters, Gods, Ancestors. In Africentric belief, these organized systems of invisible forces govern and regulate the everyday interactions and relationships between the material world and the spiritual world, between the living and the dead. These organized systems of invisible forces guide and direct one's rite of passage at the various stages of growth, maturation, and transition, including death.

Death as a Rite of Passage

Death, viewed from an Africentric perspective, is a rite of passage wherein the soul passes into but yet another phase of continuous existence. The soul leaves the material world and crosses over into the spiritual world.

Traditionally, the soul of the dying person is helped in its preparations before and long after this death transition. The Eurocentric aspect of the African-American character development in many ways prohibits this preparation of the soul before and after its final transition from the material realm. Nonetheless, the Africentric aspect of the African-American character development often compensates for this prohibition by the usage of traditional belief systems that are overtly and/or covertly practiced and interwoven into current American religious belief systems and ritual practices.

The Eurocentric aspect of the African-American identity (the religious-materialistic-logical aspect) tends to view death as final. With the arrival of modern Christianity, the spiritual belief systems of the African world view were suppressed, denied, disowned, and repressed.

146

These beliefs became banished into the dark, unconscious mind as evil, sinister, voodoo, demonic, and a host of other negative associations. Therefore, the Eurocentric aspect of one's African-American identity leaves one in a rather fatalistic and final approach to death. This approach views death as an end to life until some later time when "Gabriel blows the horn in the sky" and the souls wake up for the final judgment. The recent research findings of such people as Dr. Elizabeth Kübler-Ross, Raymond Moody, and others serve as the scientific salvation from the fatalistic/finalistic Eurocentric approach to death. These research findings and writings help us integrate the reality of death as a continuous aspect of life. The finality of death in the Eurocentric aspect of our identity structures tends to hamper the mourning, loss, and grief process and turns the death experience often into a frightening and morbid experience.

The Approach of Death

The approach to sharing feelings and discussion around the issues of dying and death varies greatly in different cultures of Africa and among various groups of African Americans. Again, no matter how the approaches differ, there is usually an underlying belief in the continuity of the soul and life of the spirit after death; therefore, silence around these issues does not always connote the same fear and denial that may be present in the Eurocentric world view. In certain African cultures, the traditional approach to death is not to discuss death openly or call it by that name, especially concerning certain persons such as kings, queens, dignitaries, and infants. In some cultures, the living cannot speak the names of the dead. Yet, in all African cultures, veneration, respect, and communication with the deceased are integral parts of everyday life. Ritual forms surrounding dying and death serve as the format to express feelings surrounding these events in a symbolic manner. These ritual-symbolic practices of Africentric culture rely upon the underlying belief in continuity of life and reincarnation of the soul. Traditionally, when any of the above-named persons die, it is said that they have gone to their Village. In the case of a child, it is said that the child has gone on a journey because it is believed that the child will soon reincarnate in the family.

Some of the old cultural beliefs of Africa still influence the unconscious and conscious behavior of African Americans today. These beliefs influence and direct African Americans in their approach to death. In many instances, the role of religion and the church serves as the outer format in which death is handled, but African spirituality is central to the inner format of the death/dying experience. While the traditional Black church encouraged an open mourning and grieving process, the more Eurocentric, modern Black church often does not encourage this, and therefore, in many instances, cuts people off from their feelings and beliefs in the continuity of the soul. Even though there often seems to be a conspiracy of silence in some African-American communities around the issues of death and dying, it is not always because of the acculturation of Eurocentric values. Rather, there often is an underlying continuous symbolic-spiritual communication before, during, and after the passage of the soul of the beloved one.

Going Down to the River

A host of metaphorical experiences often accompanies the experience of dying in the African-American community that allow for this symbolic-spiritual communication to take place among the living and with the departed. These metaphorical experiences serve as a context in which some discussion and preparation can, and often does, take place between the dying person and the family. During the days of slavery in America, the metaphor of "Going Home to Guinea" was popular in certain parts of the South. Guinea was a name that was synonymous with Mother Africa as the navel source of humanity. It was believed, not so unlike modern psychology, that all human beings must ultimately "return to the Mother." More recent in African-American tradition is the usage of the metaphors of the "River" and "Water." These metaphors often serve as underlying themes of the dying and death experience in the African-American community.

Water often is used symbolically to pay respect to the deceased, and it is used frequently in other ways in reference to the deceased. When a member of the family, usually an elder, makes the statement that it is time to go down to the river or cross the water, it is understood that death is approaching. Within this context, the family is given time to discuss and help the dying member with preparations.

Cultural Approaches to Dealing with Dying and Death

The ways African Americans deal with a dying member vary widely according to religious and spiritual beliefs, the personality and tem-

perament of the dying, the personality and temperament of the significant caregiver in the home, the resources of the family, and a variety
of other factors. Traditionally in Africentric culture, due to culture values,
economics, and availability of institutions, the dying member was usually
kept in the home. African Americans traditionally have expressed puz-
zlement in regard to the practice by some White Americans of placing
the elderly and the dying in nursing homes. With more American-
Eurocentric acculturation of the African American, the values and practices in regard to aging, the sickly, the elderly, and the dying began to
change. In general, at least in my practice, it would be safe to say that
those families that have made conscious attempts to hold onto and practice the old cultural traditions are the ones most likely to make every
effort to make sure that the dying person is returned to the familiar
environment of home and family to spend the last days.

In regard to the place and process of dying, often the role of
the more Eurocentric Black church is focussed more on the burial
ceremony than the dying process and the post-death experiences and
adjustment of the family. Especially in regard to the AIDS issue, many
families have expressed a sense of frustration and disappointment in
the Black church in what they perceived as failed leadership and lack
of empathy and outright condemnation for those with AIDS. In other
cases of prolonged terminal illness, the responses of the family, and
often members of the church congregation, range from self-sacrifice
to saintly endurance with statements such as, "His comfort is our
primary concern, and whatever we can do at this time to make it easy
for him, we will do." In other cases, the caregiver feels put upon, bur-
dened, and taken advantage of. In such cases, overt anger and vindic-
tiveness may be the reaction of the caregiver, with such statements as,
"I wish you would die today," "I wish you would go and jump into
the grave tomorrow," or "Sometimes I feel that I am being used right
down to the last moment."

One such example of the enduring and supportive family is the
case of the family of W. D., a thirty-three-year-old African-American
male who was married but later divorced, and he had a twelve-year-
old daughter. I had formerly seen this young man during his late teens
and early twenties in therapy. I had been out of touch with him for
a number of years until his mother called. She stated that her son had
been diagnosed and treated for AIDS over the past couple of years.
He was now in his terminal days, and she felt that it would be helpful
if I would visit him. His mother had honored her son's request to return
home for the final days of his dying and death process. She had turned

149

to the church and had coaxed her son to turn to the church in these final days of his life. She expressed disappointment and dismay that she and her son received nothing but silence, avoidance of the issue, and sometimes outright condemnation because of his illness. The mother had helped her son prepare for his death but was seeking other support. Because of my busy schedule I did not go to visit right away. But a few weeks later, as I was leaving an Africentric rites-of-passage ceremony for young females, I had an intuition to go to visit this young man because I had a strong feeling that he was ready to go through his final rites of passage, and if I didn't see him now, I would miss the opportunity to greet him and say goodbye.

On arriving at his bedside, I was still wearing the African Kinte cloth strip from the ceremony that I had just left. He was on a morphine machine to help control his pain. Between states of wakefulness and sleeping, he told me of his readiness for death and that he felt at peace with himself. He felt that his experience had brought him closer to most of the members of his family. His father, who had recently moved back into the home to help his son and the family through this period, could not move past the sedation that the TV in the living room offered. The father-son bond was one area that the son and family felt was not in the process of healing through this occasion. During one of his periods of sleeping, I had an optical experience of seeing him raise up slightly to a sitting position, even though logically I knew that he was still lying flat in the bed. I followed a strong intuition and took the African Kinte cloth strip from around my neck and placed it around his neck and told him to be at peace, and that the woven fabric was symbolic that his soul was getting ready to be woven back into the great fabric of the universe. Later, I told his mother that I sensed that death was imminent and that he probably would be making his transition within three days. She agreed that she sensed the same thing. On the third day, she called to say that he had been rushed to the hospital where he died peacefully with his Kinte cloth strip around his neck. She later buried him in the Kinte cloth strip, and I joined the family and close friends a week later in an Africentric celebration of his transition into the spiritual world of the ancestors.

Considerations of Preparations for This Stage

One of the biggest tests during this stage of the dying process is how to help the person maintain hope, faith, and a creative-fighting spirit, as well as prepare him or her for the inevitable. Here the crucial difference between the American-religious approach and the African-spiritual approach to death is important. One gives the picture of finality, and the other gives the picture of continuity, life everlasting, and survival of the soul. Since the soul survives, there is a picture of a continuous growth and consequences according to one's life process up until the final moment of death and transition into the spiritual world.

The Lonely Soul Coming to Terms with Aging and Dying

Many times, single elderly persons with no family find themselves experiencing the metaphors of death in the form of dreams, "visions," or "visitations from the ancestors." During these times, they often express the wish for someone with whom they can discuss their encounter with the spiritual, aging, and dying. Some have made statements like "I wouldn't talk to my minister about things like this because he is young and shows interest in the young members of the church. I don't want to burden him with my problems." Others have made statements such as, "I wouldn't even know how to begin to talk to my minister about this kind of thing; he probably wouldn't let me get it out."

A variety of metaphoric-intuitive experiences begin to manifest themselves with the individual and family when death is approaching. Such symbolic-metaphoric experiences as visions, dreams, and inner intuitive voices of guidance and visitations from the ancestors begin to happen. Within my family, certain of the elderly females usually predict the approach of death when they have dreams or visions of "Muddy Water," "washing clothes in muddy water," "crossing over muddy water," "gathering of the Ancestors," or "Ancestor coming to get someone." Other dreams and symbolic, intuitive experiences associated with the dying, death, and mourning process are dreams or visions of wedding scenes; teeth falling out; birds that fly to the window sill or fly into the house, especially the blackbird; gusts of wind; and others. There are various other symbolic experiences that may be specific to that person or general in the cultural belief system of a region or of the majority of the culture in general.

Another Africentric belief of Soul Culture is that there is no respect for distance or time in the soul or spiritual world. These intuitive metaphoric experiences cut across time, distance, and religious, cultural, and ethnic boundaries. One elderly Black domestic worker had a vision of a gathering of ancestors of her White employers, which she relayed to them. Within the week, one of the married sons fell from the roof and died. The family felt that the shock did not have the same impact that it would have had if they had not been somewhat prepared by the warning.

Often the spiritual belief system of a family is a sustaining support in addition to, or as an alternative to, the church and Eurocentric religious belief systems. In the following case example, a forty-two-year-old female attempted to comfort her first cousin with the Africentric cultural belief system of the ancestors and spirits. Her maternal aunt died the week before she came to therapy. She stated, "My aunt died last week. I had a dream that all of my front teeth had dropped out a couple of nights before this incidence. When you dream of your front teeth dropping out, that is a sign of death, and I knew it would be a close family member.

"My cousin was very upset and really taking it very hard. She wasn't eating or sleeping. I told her that her mother was spiritual and that she just didn't die. She says that her mother's spirit is still there with her. When my mother died, I could still feel her spirit. I worried too, and wouldn't eat or do nothing until my mother came to me. I was laying in the bed about 1:00 P.M. in the afternoon. I heard the door open and my dog's ears perked up, and she came in just as plain as day. She came in the exact same clothes that she was buried in. She came right up to the bed in the casket and took out her false teeth and started talking. She asked me if I wanted to go with her, and I said, 'Who would take care of my children?' She said, 'Well done' and backed out of the room, casket and all, and I could see her as she went out of the front door. The dog came to the bed and looked very confused as if he just couldn't get himself together. She [her cousin] has been talking to her minister, but she didn't seem to have any relief, so I told her that if she didn't get herself together, my aunt would be coming back for her. She said she wasn't ready to go but wanted her mother to come back to her. I told her to light her candle and put out a glass of water for her mother, and her mother would probably come back to her."

There are cultural rituals that help the grieving family member to mourn and let go of the pain of loss of the family member. This is demonstrated in the advice of the same lady to her grieving cousin. She advised her cousin to begin to let go of the soul of the deceased:

"I told my cousin, 'If you grieve too hard, you hold the spirit back in its development. Do you want to hold your mother back in her development? You must start giving away all of your mother's clothes and personal items. You should put any photos of her away for a couple of years. You must light a white candle, put out a glass of water, and offer white flowers in her name and say prayers for her weekly."

When the archetype of death is approaching, a variety of metaphoric experiences begins to happen in the soul of the individual, as well as in the soul of the collective. A few years ago, I had a young cousin who was living in New York and who died of AIDS. This was before the medication AZT was on the market, so the course of the disease was relatively short from the time of diagnosis to the time of demise. The week before he died, his mother began to have a series of dreams in which I had placed an urgent call to her to come to New York because her son was dying. She later saw me, in the vision, accompanying the casket back to our home town in Virginia. This young man was not known to have any illnesses.

A week later, these same events happened almost exactly as in his mother's dreams, which she revealed to me a couple of weeks after his death. He announced that he was sick with a possible diagnosis of AIDS and that he would have to go into the hospital. We talked about how he felt about having the illness and what he understood about the course of the disease. We expressed our love for each other and our spiritual attraction to each other. We discussed his desires and wishes in case of emergencies, and we affirmed that no matter what the future held in store, we would always be tuned in to each other through whatever symbolic-intuitive modes of communication allowed to us.

One experience we shared with each other prior to his death was hunting Indian arrowheads in the field across the street from his home. On the day of his burial in Virginia, I went into the field with a group of relatives and friends as a commemoration of this experience that bonded us. I said a silent prayer for him and asked to be shown a memento to remember him by. Of the group of seven or eight people searching for Indian arrowheads on that day, I was the only one to find a stone. Of the two dozen stones that I have found in this field, this stone was the largest and the most perfect in cut. I found this significant and had the stone framed in gold and put on a chain. I wear this stone around my neck daily to remind me of my spiritual bond to my cousin.

Funeral Practices

Often funeral services have a great attraction in the African-American community and tend to serve as a time of group and community catharsis, which is often afforded by the soul-touching music and preaching. In the more traditional Black churches, open and full expression of the emotions of grief and loss was encouraged. This cathartic aspect of old African-American funerals was, and often still is, facilitated through cadences of the preacher's voice, the soulful music, and the symbolic selection of the songs. Opinions do vary in regard to the effects of the funeral in attenuating the sense of loss. Some of my clients have expressed that they don't feel that the funeral service helped them. They feel that the approach of the funeral tended to accentuate the loss in the "need to hurry and get it over with," or "they don't deal with the spirit of the person; they just deal with the physical aspect of the person." This latter sentiment is often more commonly expressed by African Americans who have some knowledge and experience of the more Africentric beliefs and practices, which tend to deal with the spirit and its guidance into the spiritual world.

In the more Africentric approaches to death and funerals, there is often what could be interpreted as the jubilant element of dance, drink, and celebration. It was not uncommon in the old South for the family and friends to go to the home of the deceased after burial for food and drink. This postburial ritual also often included music and dance. In other areas of the African-American community, most noticeably New Orleans, this celebrant aspect of the funeral rites of passage is still a central and unique aspect of African-American funeral practices. With the increasing disenchantment of young and educated African Americans with traditional Eurocentric religious beliefs and practices, the dominant sentiment often is, "People are looking more and more to what we used to do and what our ancestors used to do."

In general, it is felt throughout the African-American community that funerals do attenuate the sense of loss on behalf of the family. The sense of lessening of the pain of loss comes in feeling that one's loved one has had a proper funeral and burial. Traditionally, in most religious and funeral practices within the African-American community, the "proper burial" is considered a below-the-ground burial. Cremation has traditionally not been a widely accepted practice, and some who oppose it offer the religiously tinged opposition that it is "like burning in the hell fires."

Medical Model versus Traditional Healing Model

Sometimes, even after the metaphors of dying and death are introduced by the medical doctor or the dying member, denial sets in on the part of the family. This denial and conspiracy of silence often are overtly and/or covertly encouraged by the Eurocentric medical establishment. Such denial and avoidance of the reality of dying and death prevent a realistic handling of the issues with the dying member. Such statements and actions as the following on behalf of the Eurocentric medical establishment foster denial and avoidance of the dying-death issue:

1. "Don't worry about anything. We are going to give you this treatment and you could live until you are old and gray."
2. "You may tell your relative if you want to, but how can you tell a person that she is dying? Why not let them live out the rest of their lives as happily as possible?"
3. "This treatment will shrink your tumor and you will be fine."
4. "This treatment will make your tumor go away." (What is most frequently omitted in these communications where malignancy is involved is that there is a high expectancy that the tumor will recur and that it will be more resistant to treatment, if not fatal.)

There often is anger and resentment against the medical establishment after the death and burial of the loved one on the part of families who listened to such advice. There often is a sense of betrayal of trust, a sense of having been misinformed and misguided. There is often a sense of having been robbed of the opportunity to help in the preparation of the soul of the deceased. There is a feeling of having been robbed of the chance to spend the last moments saying farewell and other last things. There often is anger that the deceased was not allowed time to make preparations for death and to settle business affairs that would have made it easier on family members after his or her death.

Natural roots and potions as adjuncts to the healing phenomenon are not far from our collective consciousness as a people. While first-line credence and trust is often given to mainstream medical care, many African Americans of all classes supplement medical care with a visit to the cultural healer and the usage of herbs, potions, and prayers. With the increased disaffection with the mainstream medical model, there is more of a blending of treatment of the ill and dying with both traditional and medical models. Often the more Africentric

155

families will bring their traditional healers as consultants even into the hospital setting to collaborate and treat the family member, often unbeknownst to the medical staff. The more Eurocentric African-American families tend to hold on tenaciously to the mainstream medical model but will more readily consider and embrace alternative approaches, if and when failures accrue within this medical approach.

The age of the dying person is often important, and the funeral ritual often differs slightly for two groups. In both groups, the reactions and approaches to dying and death tend to vary with the cause of death. The first group is that of infants or very young children. The death of a child is sometimes handled in a questioning and blaming fashion, again depending on cause of death. The surviving members of the family may ask the question, "Why did he have to be taken so young?" Generally, the death of an infant or very young child is handled in a less grave manner, especially in regard to the funeral services, than the death of one who has lived a long and productive life. A part of this less grave reaction is attributable to religious-spiritual underpinnings that are carried over from the African ancestry and which have been discussed previously. The religious traditions of the American background also contribute to this reaction in that it is often felt that the "child is gone to heaven before it had a chance to sin." A Puerto Rican colleague told me about traditional funeral practices for children in old Puerto Rico: "Somebody would come to the house and create jokes and laughter to symbolize the innocence of the child, the joy and frivolity of the child, the jokester and trickster nature of the child. The service would end with everyone throwing flowers into the casket."

The second group is the elderly. When a person has led a full and productive life, the sentiment tends to be more of a celebration of their passing than a mournful state of depression. An African colleague gave me some historical background into this cultural practice. He stated that when the young are mourned in certain parts of West Africa, black clothes are worn, but when the elderly and those with a full head of gray hair are mourned, white clothes are worn.

The Nature of Grief and the Ritual of Mourning

In the old African-American communities, death was expected to be expressed openly and fully. When a family member died, especially a child, a death wail was not uncommonly heard throughout the com-

156

munity. As the mother or matriarch sounded the wail, other females in the community would pick it up. This death wail would marshal the community to the support of the bereaved person. Community support would be considered an important part of the ritual of the African-American community for its bereaved members. This support ranged from almost complete takeover of the home, with cooking, cleaning, and child care, to financial support and assistance with the formalities of funeral and burial arrangements.

The wake is an important ritual aspect of bereavement in the African-American community. In the old South, the body was often laid out on the "cooling board" for the wake. During the wake, the family and friends would gather for a part of the night and share remembrances, food, and drink. Various regions had various customs for the wake in the old South. Some of these customs would include such rituals as setting a place with a candle on the stomach of the deceased or setting a glass of water at the head of the deceased.

The wake remains as an important ritual aspect of bereavement. However, with acculturation into the Eurocentric model, many of the old rituals and open expressions of emotions have been suppressed and replaced with a more stoic approach to death, where one is expected to keep one's feelings inside. This stoic approach is definitely evident in the more Eurocentric Black churches, where it is often rumored that "you can't clap your hands, cry out, shout or pat your feet." This stoicism carries over frequently into the funeral and bereavement service and often does not allow the family the opportunity to express their emotions openly. After such funeral services, one frequently hears comments such as, "That was a very White funeral," or "There was no soul in the service." This is in contrast to the more traditional Black church, usually of Baptist denomination, where full expressions of emotions are encouraged through the music and preaching. The preaching usually is designed to review how the deceased's life served as some constructive lessons for the surviving family and community members.

Members feel free to cry, scream, clap their hands, pat their feet, and even shout if the Spirit so hits them. There are some hymns that have archetypal significance and evoke a deep empathy to the grief and mourning process for the family and the community. Often those approaching death, and others who want to assure that their funeral service will be conducted properly, will select their hymnal arrangements and sometimes designate the person they want to sing them. Such popular hymns that evoke deep sympathy and empathy are standard hymns such as "Swing Low, Sweet Chariot," "The Old Ship of Zion," "Just a Closer Walk with Thee," "You Will Never Walk Alone," "Precious Lord," "Will You Be Ready," "Let the Circle Be Unbroken," "Come on Up in Glory," "Amazing Grace," "When I Wake Up in Glory," "In My Home over There," "Nearer My God to Thee," "Abide with Me," "Guide Me Over," "There Is a Balm in Gilead," and many more.

Many African Americans include in their ritual of bereavement such actions as making regular visits to the grave site of the deceased, especially on birthdays and other special holiday occasions. Others employ rituals rooted in the African tradition of placing a glass of water and white flowers in a special location and burning a white candle in memory of the deceased.

Other rituals may be practiced in the funeral procession and burial, such as having the funeral procession pass the home of the deceased for the final time, with a brief stop of the hearse at the front door. At the burial site, usually the minister officiates with a traditional Christian closing prayer, but often family members may include some cultural elements, such as leaving certain articles in the casket and placing a glass of water at the head of the grave site.

Death: An American or an African Rite of Passage

Due to the immensity of the problems confronting us around the death issue, it is imperative that we devise new treatment strategies and paradigms of intervention. There are not enough trained psychotherapists in mental health to handle the immense problems, on a one-to-one basis, that we are facing. Adding to the problem is the Western-American cultural orientation toward dying and death, as well as the current treatment orientation of the mental health model. The Western-American cultural orientation stresses youth, joy, this-worldliness, and material development. This orientation discourages a view to the continuous existence of spirit and therefore frequently offers no ritual preparation for the dying and death stages of human development. The mental health model that is employed in the Western-American orientation is too frequently geared to treatment of failure of the psychosocial-spiritual functioning of the individual. The issue of dying-death rarely figures into the model of developmental issues for the training of mental health professionals.

African Americans are of mixed cultural backgrounds and enjoy a mixed world view. They have been both involuntarily and voluntarily

158

Amer: Joy - youth

acculturated to be in tune with mainstream American religious practices and philosophy surrounding the process of dying and death. Because of this acculturation process, African Americans often struggle in their ritual loyalties to American traditions while at the same time trying to express something of their African cultural traditions. Traditionally, Africentric culture provided for this crucial stage of death and transition into the spiritual world by institutionalized practices and rituals, which served as "marking-off experiences." These cultural practices and rituals were, and still are, referred to as *Rites-of-Passage* rituals. These rites-of-passage rituals serve to mark off one stage of maturation from another stage. These rituals are designed to guide the personality-character-soul through the passage from one stage of existence to another. The uniqueness and difference with which African Americans approach the dying-death process can be attributed to the retention of African spiritual beliefs that are rooted in this rite-of-passage process so indigenous to African culture.

As African Americans become more educated and exposed to their culture through media, travel, and research, there is a resurgence of efforts in assuring that dying and death practices contain some of the new as well as recapture some of the old. This blending of the old and new, the African and the American, in many ways may be viewed as a manifestation of the old gospel hymn, "Let the Circle Be Unbroken," which celebrates the unity of life and death as a continuous spiritual journey.

CHAPTER TWELVE

May the Circle Be Unbroken: The African-American Experience of Death, Dying, and Spirituality

Martha Adams Sullivan

Any discussion of the African American, or of Black people of African descent throughout the diaspora for that matter, must necessarily begin with some understanding and appreciation of African culture. Thus, an Africentric perspective will be employed here to examine death, dying, and spirituality; these phenomena will be viewed through the lens of African philosophy. While the African continent includes fifty-two countries and over one thousand ethnic groups, scholars have been able to describe an essential African philosophical thought. Imperialism, colonialism and neocolonialism, slavery, modernization, and urbanization, however, have magnified the diversity of people of African descent around the world. Within the United States, there are Black people of African descent who share Caribbean and South and Central American heritage, as well. The focus here will be largely upon those who hail from the "Southern" experience. Although we have much in common with the African-Caribbean, for example, based upon our common African heritage, history and geography have meant that we are also a very diverse people. While all of what is described will hold true much of the time, none of it will hold true all of the time. As with any other group of people, individual, gender, class, and religious differences, to name a few, mean that African Americans are quite a heterogeneous cultural group.

African Philosophy and Culture

Numerous volumes have been written on African philosophy. Some important principles of African philosophy and culture are particularly relevant in understanding how African Americans understand and experience death and dying.

A core concept is that of dual unity wherein polarities are opposites; for example, day and night, dead and living are viewed as having reciprocal and unifying functions rather than dichotomous ones, which dynamically unite them such that they create a whole, maintaining equilibrium by adjusting each to the other. Death, then, while it represents the soul leaving the body, is not simply the opposite of life but is inherently related to life; it is another dimension or phase of the same phenomenon.

A second concept derived from the first is that spirit and matter cannot be separated: "Both spiritual and material being arc necessary in order for there to be a meaningful reality" (Richards, 1985, p. 210). Mistakenly construed as animism by Eurocentric scholars, traditional African thought recognized that the material world is a manifestation of the spiritual world, both comprising a universe created by God. Life and death, the spiritual and material, never exist in the universe to the complete exclusion of the other.

Third, group orientation, including family centeredness, is key to understanding African culture. In fact, John Mbiti (Martin and Martin, 1985), noted African philosopher, states:

> The cardinal point of African philosophy could be summarized in the saying: "I am, because we are; and since we are, therefore I am," which means that traditional Africans did not see themselves as individuals with a concern for self over the group, but see that group as a corporate part of the individual personality.

Lastly, the traditional African concept of time has been influenced by what has been termed fatalism, "a world view in which it is believed that humans do not have the power to cause events and that their intellects are not such that they can understand or predict the future with any degree of confidence" (Pennington, 1985, p. 128). However, fatalism does not imply futility or promote inactivity; it does allow for action while simultaneously recognizing that life is unpredictable despite our attempts to affect it — that the Creator is ultimately in control. Therefore, one is able to maintain a sense of dignity in the

161

face of adversity, which may occur despite one's best attempts to avert it.

These principles and others will permeate the examination of the African-American experience of death and dying. Death and dying will be viewed from the perspective of the family and the community's experience and coping styles. The meaning of death and dying will be explored as part of the life/death duality. Spirituality will be attended to throughout, as the spirit is inherent in all aspects of life and death. A grasp of these principles is especially useful in understanding how older African Americans cope with death and dying, as they tend to hold more traditional beliefs and values than the younger generation.

Death and Dying

Like any challenge, hardship, or "cross to bear" — a euphemism from the Black Christian experience — death is experienced as a group event; family and community experience a transition as a member "passes over" to the other world. Members often avoid using the term "dying," perhaps because it is unidimensional and unidirectional. To "pass on," to "make a transition," connotes movement, a change in form more than a termination with no future. The future, despite one's best attempts, may not be entirely determinable, but there will surely be a future life as an ancestral member of the community. The family, in particular, is viewed as extending into the other world. The "passing" is experienced as a struggle, a central theme of African-American existence. The act of dying is an extension of the struggle, throughout this existence, to live. Discussions of how much the dying person suffers, or struggles through the pain of illness or the pains of life, are common. When the family "rationalizes" the death as an end to suffering, frequently they are referring not only to the final days but to life's suffering. For example, one elderly mother believed that the reason her son died at age thirty-nine was because "God took him away to stop people from using him." She fully understood the medical explanation that he died from complications resulting from an infection. Holding this medical explanation of his physical demise in the material world was not experienced as contradictory but perhaps complementary to the spiritual occurrence; through death to this world, God provided her son life in the next world, a resolution to his problems, and protection from harm in the form of exploitation.

As previously mentioned, the sense of family and community extends into the other world. Ancestors (i.e., those who have already died) are often thought of as playing a role in easing this passing over. For instance, a family member may be visited by an ancestor, often in a dream, notifying the family that the actual death is at hand and thus preparing the living family.

Mr. F.'s niece, Ms. B., awoke one morning and rushed her family to the hospital to see him. The family knew he was not expected to recover, but at first they questioned the urgency of visiting. When she explained that her mother, Mr. F.'s sister-in-law, had come to her in her dream to tell her that he was "coming up soon," they complied. He died while they were in transit.

The ancestors also prepare the dying and are thought to ease their transition. It is commonly recognized that dying family members sometimes begin to talk to people who have already died. This is experienced as both upsetting and comforting to the family, for while it signals that the transition is at hand, it also reassures them that their family is there awaiting them.

The dying person is often viewed as playing a role in determining the time of death. The notion that people "let go" of, or disengage from, this life is accepted. Behaviors such as the dying elder turning her back to a visitor or deliberately making a last contact with relatives are considered signs of "letting go" as much as a decision not to undergo further treatment.

Mr. W., age seventy, had spent nineteen years on hemodialysis. Everyone marveled at his perseverance and stamina; he pursued his hobbies of fishing, gardening, and some hunting throughout his illness. It was apparent, however, that his physical condition was becoming greatly deteriorated and that he could not survive much longer.

He had a very unhappy marriage of almost forty years. One month after his wife was diagnosed with cancer, he died. During that month, he telephoned all of his closest family members and told each that he loved them. Upon her visit, he shared with his niece that he wanted a real home—something he'd felt he never had in his life—and that he intended to get one—alone. The family was clear that he was letting go—and saying good-bye.

The collective experience of dying and death means that these events happen to the community, as the community is an organic whole which includes the living, the dead, and those yet to be born (Richards, 1985, p. 212). Babies are often experienced as "old souls" that have "been here before," the notion being that the spirits of the ancestors may regain physical form in the community in these babies, completing the circle through which a "timeless regeneration" occurs (Kamalu, 1990). Thus, the group has an important role to play in the dying process.

Care-taking activities become a priority as members of the family and community take care of the dying person and each other. The role flexibility commonly attributed to Black families is most notable at this time, especially among extended family members living in close proximity with each other. Clinicians should not overlook this, however, even when families are living far apart, as emotional support, advice giving, and decision making often continue to be extended family/community functions despite geographical distance. For instance, when Mr. W.'s daughter was ready to sign the "do not resuscitate" order, it was his niece, her cousin, whom she consulted, for the family had known that he was very close to his niece. With her cousin's approval, Mr. W.'s daughter, who was legally able to sign, could do so without guilt.

Taking care of the dying member means organizing medical care, home care, legal affairs, and so on. It also means continued hands-on care of the person's soma, that is, the physical self. Family members will oil their loved one's skin, groom his or her hair, and pay close attention to body temperature, becoming upset, for instance, if the person's skin feels cold or the room is drafty. Professionals at times become irritated by the family's attention to, or complaints about, these issues. However, these tasks involve the family in making the process more comfortable, not just for the dying member but for themselves, as well. This explains the seeming preoccupation prior to and after death with "How did she look?" The deceased member who looks "at peace," "resting," or "just like herself" is experienced as a comfort to the family. Since the physical self is not merely physical but manifests the spirit, attending to the body is a means of attending to the spirit. Having successfully assisted the spirit in its transition, the family can more easily reincorporate the deceased into the community as an ancestral member.

Care-taking also means "being with." In many families, a terminally ill member is never left alone. Neither are very close relatives left alone after the death. Comforting the dying and comforting each other means being together. Rules which restrict visiting are particularly baffling and sometimes infuriating to families, and families will often ignore them or seek ways of getting around them.

Families differ more in their involvement in organized religion, less in their need to come together as a group to comfort each other,

> for there is no closer bond that a group of Black people can feel
> than that which comes from the experience of feeling and express-
> ing our deepest emotions together. The group becomes a sacred
> community once again, and so its members gain strength from
> communal experience. (Richards, 1985, p. 220)

Community well-being during the dying process necessarily includes
some religious or spiritual ritual. The form varies from bedside prayer
groups including hand-holding, singing, and recitations from religious
scriptures, to congregational prayers, administration of sacraments and
blessings by ministers, and offers of prayers made by individuals. Black
religious congregations play a major role in care-taking. The congregation is a community and a spiritual family. "Brothers" and "sisters,"
as well as ministers, participate fully in caring for the dying and for
the family. The support which Black congregations offer is particularly limitless. As Boyd-Franklin (1989, p. 92) notes, the congregation's
support is highly accessible, as it "mobilizes quickly and without the
bureaucratic process of social agencies." Even for those families who
are not members of a religious congregation, clinicians should not lose
sight of this important potential source of support for African Americans coping with death.

Once the transition is complete (i.e., death occurs), the family
and community begin to respond emotionally and practically by making funeral arrangements. Clinicians are often baffled by the lack of
information families have about the medical cause of death, that is,
the diagnosis, the progression of the medical illness, and so on. Even
when medical care has been questionable or clearly substandard, some
families don't consider legal recourse. This reflects the family's understanding of the process as not merely a medical/physical one— as not
totally in the hands of humans. For example, upon her mother's death,
an elderly woman's adult daughter was confronted with the fact that
her mother's colon cancer had not been diagnosed even though she
had regular medical care and pursued treatment for specific symptoms.
The daughter acknowledged that this was so but stated, "I know doctors don't have all the answers." The African-American family's acceptance of the death-life duality, the physical-spiritual duality, means
that professionals and families may be out of sync. Families may rely
on and aggressively pursue the best medical care they can obtain, while
simultaneously placing their faith in God, not the professionals—
including medical professionals. In fact, heroic or unusual medical
efforts may be met with distrust and perceived as "experimentation."

This reflects not only a fatalist philosophy but also an understanding on the part of African Americans that in this physical world, the institutions one must sometimes rely upon are also racist and cannot be wholeheartedly trusted to not exploit or do harm.

Healing Grief and Bereavement

Once death has occurred, families are generally faced with the process of adapting and "reestablishing levels of well-being" (Lattanzi, 1984, p. 96). The African-American family has a specific task as part of that adaptation—the reintegration of the deceased member into the community so that the sense of wholeness of the community is regained; the circle is mended. The funeral rites provide an opportunity to begin this process:

> Our funerals have traditionally been rituals, not in any ordinary sense, but in the sense of African-American ritual drama. The group is called together from wherever its various members have migrated. The ritual is performed according to prescribed regulations, one enactment following another, until the family is transformed once more into a sacred community bound by a common experience, then cleansed, energized, and raised briefly to spiritual heights through their ability to experience and express the suffering within. The family renews its kinship ties, and the deceased is aided in his or her transition to another phase of existence. Crisis is understood communally. The order is restored. Things are put right. "We sent him off well." (Richards, 1985, p. 222)

Funeral rites, of course, vary according to many factors, including religious identification, income, and so on. However, there are some universals stemming from African culture. As Richards (1985) points out, the funeral is ideally a communal experience. Whether elders and children should attend the actual funeral service may vary according to health-related factors, but all generations and the community participate in some gathering during this period. Accessibility is therefore important in choosing a location.

Mrs. C. and her husband were both placed in different nursing facilities. The goal had been to move her to his facility as soon as a bed became available. However, very shortly after she was placed, he died. She insisted that her social worker help her to have a simple funeral service at a funeral parlor in their neighborhood, although it was far away. The social worker met considerable bureaucratic resistance but was supported by her supervisor and managed to do so. All their friends from the neighborhood, who were also elderly, were then able to come to "pay their respects" and to comfort her.

In contemporary Nigeria, funeral services often occur as much as two months after death so that disbursed members may travel to the service. Until then, media announcements spread the word. There, the funeral is referred to as an "outing service," as it is a ritual to aid the community in releasing the deceased's spirit. Increasingly, African Americans are referring to funeral rites using terms such as "home-going" services. The term reflects not only the strong belief in an after-life but also the reinclusion in the community, since the community's "home" extends beyond this physical world.

That funeral rites be conducted with dignity is extremely impor-tant for African Americans. Typically, funerals are formal, and the size of the gathering and the seeming extravagance, including the abun-dance of food, flowers, limousines, and so on reflect the dignity and respect one may achieve in death that may have been difficult to attain in an oppressed earthly existence. The movie *Imitation of Life,* wherein the maid has a very elaborate New Orleans–style funeral parade through the streets, makes this point. Younger generations are moving toward more simple funeral services and even memorial services; however, the emphasis that the service be special and dignified is unchanged.

The tone as well as the particulars of the services are evaluated by how much they reflect the character and spirit of the deceased. This gives the family an opportunity to talk about the deceased, making the person present by discussing what he or she would have wanted and how he or she would have felt about the service. The deceased may even be called upon to comfort the living. For example, a close friend of the deceased broke into tears after the interment. His sister tried comforting her at first, but this seemed ineffective. The sister, then remembering that her brother was known to be humorous and irreverent, reminded the friend that her brother would probably laugh at her if he were there. The friend then had to smile through the tears and acknowledge that this was true, and she, in turn, would have become annoyed and bickered with him.

The characteristics and wishes of the deceased, especially of an elder, are extremely important to the family. Sharing their knowledge of these and carrying out the deceased's wishes keeps that person "in" the community and also gives the family a sense of order and direc-tion. Any conflicts which arise around funeral arrangements, settling the estate, and so on can quickly be diffused with, "He wanted it this way," for the desires of the deceased take precedence over all others. Sometimes, however, the family goes too far as deathbed wishes become enforced narrowly and rigidly, resulting in dysfunction.

Wendy, a thirty-seven-year-old woman, entered therapy complaining that she was "stuck" in her life. It became apparent that she was underfunctioning at work and was able to organize people around her, especially her family, to infantilize her and expect very little of her.

The youngest of nine children, Wendy lost both of her elderly parents when she was young. Her mother died when she was fifteen and her father when she was eighteen. On his deathbed, her father made her older siblings promise to take care of her.

Wendy was coached in therapy to help her family to take care of her as a younger adult sister rather than as an eighteen-year-old child.

This sense that the deceased remains in the family as long as the family keeps them in by remembering them and talking about them can be very useful in therapy. The therapist can bring the deceased into the session via the family members' feelings, memories, and dreams. The ease with which the therapist incorporates discussion of the deceased can become a model for families who have been unable to do so. Challenging family members' interpretation of deathbed wishes can also be useful if it is framed as the family's misinterpretation of the deceased's true intent. For example, the therapist asked Wendy if she felt her parents wanted her to be treated like an eighteen-year-old forever. Wendy stated that they certainly did not want that for her, although she'd never thought about this before. She was encouraged to talk more about what her parents would have wanted for her at age thirty-seven; it became clear that they had very high aspirations for her as the youngest of an upwardly mobile Black family. The genogram was helpful in revealing the severity of her conflict; while the youngest siblings were expected to achieve the most, her two next-eldest siblings had failed to do so due to mental illness and substance-abuse problems. Wendy, then, had to be the family success, and yet she was being held back by a conflicting message not to grow up.

Wendy had been troubled by the fact she'd never dreamed of her parents since their deaths. After this session, Wendy did dream about them. She interpreted the dream as her parents coming to her to give her and the family their blessings for having taken care of her well and to tell her it was time for her to move ahead with her life.

The therapeutic goal once death has taken place is adaptation to the change that has occurred; the living must reorganize themselves

in order to recreate a functioning system. The role flexibility common
in Black families generally facilitates this process, which begins as part
of the care-taking function before death actually occurs. The therapist
can assess how the family works by first understanding what shifts
took place during the dying process. Sometimes, however, the death
actually exacerbates a long-term dysfunctional family pattern, making adjustments to the loss more difficult.

Nancy, thirty-nine, complained of feeling misunderstood by her
family and unsupported by her mother. A single parent, Nancy was
independent and a successful professional. Her mother catered to her
brother, who became increasingly dependent and dysfunctional.
Although he and his wife worked, he moved his family in to live with
his parents. Her sister, terminally ill, having been diagnosed with AIDS,
also lived with their mother. Throughout her sister's illness, Nancy
could not get her mother to talk about the impending loss. Mother
and sister had joined a fundamentalist religion which supported their
apparent denial; illness is the work of the devil, so they had to pray
harder. The more Nancy pushed, the more they seemed to deny and
the more emotionally distant Nancy felt from her family, who just
"didn't see things the way [she] did."

Once her sister died, Nancy was left with making all of the funeral
arrangements. Her mother lay in bed grieving, her father "watched
over" her mother, and her brother took to the streets hanging out.
Nancy was overwhelmed and resentful; her feelings of aloneness in
her family were exacerbated.

It is important to note that, despite what Nancy considered the
family's "denial," the family was actually preparing for her sister's
death. All the care-taking functions were carried out vigilantly.
Although her mother, age sixty, was still working, she made necessary adjustments by taking her daughter to live with her, managing
her daughter's medical care, escorting her when necessary, and caring
for her at home and during her frequent hospitalizations. Through
their church involvement, mother and daughter had become emotionally and spiritually closer, as well. Just before Nancy's sister died, her
mother had even initiated a review of her insurance. It is typical for
women to take primary responsibility for the care-taking functions,
and Black women are certainly no exception. The family coped with
the sister's death according to previously prescribed family roles which
were too narrowly defined. Mother, cast as the main care-taker in
general, and the emotional care-taker of the family, could now grieve.
Her husband, who was cast in the role of assisting his wife in caring

for their daughter, continued to assist her in grieving by watching over her. Nancy, cast as the capable one, was left to do it all with regard to tasks.

Another clinical situation which may present involves the death of a parent who has a dysfunctional cross-generational alliance with adult children. This presents great difficulty for the bereaved parent and the surviving adult children. A surviving elderly parent may be particularly vulnerable in this situation.

Mr. B., age seventy, and Mrs. B., age seventy-five, presented long-standing marital conflict. The eldest of their three adult children was very close to his father until he drowned when just over age twenty. The two younger children, now in their forties, were closer to Mrs. B. One son, who lived nearby, attended to his mother almost daily. Mr. B. was quiet and very independent, never asking for help or support from his sons. Mrs. B. constantly sought her sons' support for her differences with her husband, creating a triangle which stabilized their conflictual relationship.

When Mrs. B. died, Mr. B. expressed fear that he would not be able to rely on his sons, who "only cared about their mother."

The therapeutic task here is a significant one: to restructure the family system such that the family will be able to carry out the basic task of caring for the elderly member. Directing and clarifying the wishes of aged or dying members can become a potent therapeutic intervention which prevents or mitigates dysfunction related to death. The therapist had anticipated the impact of Mrs. B.'s death and was able to use this in treatment. Mrs. B. was then able to tell her sons that should she pass on, she wanted them to take good care of their father regardless of any differences she had with him. Initially, adult children can be encouraged to do so out of loyalty to the deceased parent with whom they were aligned. The performance of basic care-taking functions can then become a springboard around which a more positive relationship can be built. Even when the problem was not anticipated, the therapist can help the adult children to surmise the deceased parent's wishes, pointing out that the parent probably would have wanted them to care for their surviving parent since they themselves never abandoned their spouse, despite their differences.

Other clinical interventions working with African-American families who are coping with death have been discussed earlier but bear reiterating here. The family and community are both units of clinical attention and provide key resources for concrete, emotional, and spiritual support during the process of dying. Families undergoing this process may operate according to a dual reality (i.e., physical and spiritual), of which clinicians need to be mindful. Ascertaining family members' belief systems is important to entering the emotional level of the family. One can simply ask, for example, "What do you really think happened to her?" or "Why do you really think he died just then?" Asking, "Who else could help with this?" allows the clinician to assess key roles in the family and to identify functions which may be problematic. These functions can then become the target of the clinical work, again keeping in mind that utilizing resources which foster connectedness to the community, such as neighbors and religious congregations, will be most comfortable for the family.

Through an assessment which is based upon a recognition of cultural group differences, the therapist is also able to move to a more specific understanding of the unique "family culture" of a particular family. It is crucial that clinicians understand that reliance upon their own beliefs or knowledge about African-American culture, including that provided here, cannot suffice for learning about the unique culture of each of the families with whom they work.

Conclusion

The African-American experience of death and dying must be understood from an Africentric perspective. The death practices of African Americans mirror the same essential beliefs which guide African Americans through life-long struggle. In death, the struggle is to mend the circle; that is, to reestablish the sense of community and wholeness which a physical change has shaken. Psychotherapy can be particularly conducive and culturally syntonic with this goal, since it is based upon talking, and talking about the ancestors is the way to keep them spiritually alive in the family.

Understanding Death, Dying, and Religion: A Chinese Perspective

Peter Ching-Yung Lee

As human service professionals are increasingly engaging in practices with clients of diverse cultural backgrounds, little attention has been directed toward educating social work professionals to integrate multi-cultural perspectives into intervention with ethnic clients (Keys, 1991; Asamoah et al., 1991; Lum, 1992). Perhaps one of the most neglected areas about the issue of death is the extent that various aspects of death and dying are currently undergoing dramatic changes and being dealt with from cross-cultural perspectives. This chapter is intended to reflect these changes in relation to death, dying, and religion from a Chinese perspective—ranging from societal strategies for dealing with death as a cultural and religious concept to individual practices for dealing with death as an inevitable reality.

To understand the Chinese view of death and dying, we need to know something of the ways in which Chinese society and its people have attempted to come to grips with the fact of death throughout history, particularly their religious creeds, philosophical beliefs, and cultural practices. We begin by presenting some facts about China and its religions, then follow by touching upon historical religious views of death and some contemporary practices and reflections.

Chinese Societies and People

Since about 200 B.C., China has been one of the largest and most populous countries in the world. Today China has a population of well over 1 billion, about one-fifth of humanity. Situated on the eastern part of the continent of Asia, China has a total area of about 3.7 million square miles, accounting for some 7 percent of the world's landmass. Since the disintegration of the Soviet Union, China is the second largest country in area (after Canada), extending from the Pacific Ocean in the east to India and Central Asia in the west, and from Indochina in the south to Siberia in the north. Ethnic Chinese (the so-called *Han* people) constitute approximately 94 percent of China's population, while the remainder consists of over fifty ethnic groups (Blunden and Elvin, 1981; *Kaleidoscope*, 1990).

There are also other major Chinese societies besides China, including Taiwan, Hong Kong, and Singapore, which have an overwhelming majority of ethnic Chinese in their populations and have been heavily influenced by Confucianism (Tai, 1989; Lee, 1992).

Religion in Chinese Society

Among the three leading centers of civilization—Europe, India, and China—the place of religion in society is the least clearly recognized in the case of China (Yang, 1961; Kung and Ching, 1989; Fairbank, 1992). The word *religion* (*tsung-chiao*) did not exist in the Chinese vocabulary until the late nineteenth century, when it entered through Japanese translations of European works and terminology (Kung and Ching, 1989).

Are the Chinese a religious people, and is their civilization rooted in religious beliefs? But exactly what is Chinese religion? There is no generally accepted name for the religion of traditional China considered as a whole. For the most part, Chinese culture and religion developed on their own terms, the product of centuries of village agricultural life. At the dawn of Chinese society 4,000 years ago, we find a society where ancestral religion, sacrifice, and divination permeated daily Chinese life. A plurality of traditions have developed, including Confucianism and Taoism. Chinese religion includes a dimension of nature worship which was transformed by Confucianism, Taoism, and Buddhism and incorporated into each societal system in a different way (Wolf, 1974; Blunden and Elvin, 1983; Fairbank, 1992).

Ancestor Worship

As in many traditional societies, the family in China was the basic unit of ownership, economic activity, emotional support, and prestige.

Since the family was so central (and still is), it is not surprising that the single most important religious activity was ancestor worship, the veneration of predecessors in the father's line of descent, beginning with his parents. The importance of ancestral worship in Chinese family life was indicated by the ancestral altar in the main hall in every house. Each altar holds a number of wooden spirit tablets, each of them representing a deceased ancestor. Many Chinese have kept records of their families for generations, records that indicate what their ancestors did and stood for. This practice has taught each generation to be grateful and loyal to the family tradition and to work hard to keep it going.

It is the belief, in the Confucian tradition, that assumes the continued existence of the dead in the form of the soul, and mutual dependence between the soul and the living, which gave rise to much of the behavior in ancestor worship. The cult of ancestors in Chinese culture remains very much a family practice—an expression of a community of both the living and the beloved deceased. Even today, in many Chinese households in Hong Kong, Taiwan, and Southeast Asia, the ancestral shrine is maintained (Blunden and Elvin, 1983; Kung and Ching, 1989).

Confucianism

Providing structural principles and key instrumental values for the family and the state, Confucianism has been a major factor in Chinese culture. Confucius (552–479 B.C.) and the school named after him offered a moral or ethical answer to the question regarding life's meaning and order in society. Since it poses no god or supernatural dogma as the symbol of its teachings, Confucianism is not a full-fledged theistic religion. However, a close examination of the Confucian doctrine reveals that it contained a subsystem of religious ideas based on belief in Heaven, predeterminism, divination, and the theory of Yin-Yang (Yang, 1961; Kung and Ching, 1989; Fairbank, 1992). Confucianism became institutionalized around the first century BC in China, when it was first granted a status of a "state religion." The Confucian doctrine, as conceived by Confucius and Mencius and developed by most of the leading Confucians through the succeeding centuries, is well reflected through Four Books:

1. *The Analects of Confucius,* which contains the conversations between Confucius and his disciples; the issues related to life and death were often discussed.

2. *The Book of Mencius,* also a collection of conversations.

3. *The Great Learning,* short treatises focusing on moral and spiritual cultivation for good rulership.

4. *The Doctrine of the Mean,* also short treatises concentrating on the inner life of psychic equilibrium and harmony.

One major merit of Confucianism is its discovery of the ultimate in the relative—in the moral character of the well-known five human relationships, including the ruler-subject, father-son, husband-wife, elder and younger brother, and friend-friend. Within Confucianism, three of these are family relationships, while the other two are usually conceived in terms of the family models; for example, the ruler-subject relation resembles the father-son, while friendship resembles brotherliness. While five relationships emphasize the vertical sense of hierarchy, the responsibilities ensuing from these relationships are also mutual and reciprocal; for instance, a subject owes loyalty to the ruler, and a child owes filial respect to the parent. In return, the ruler must also care for his subjects, and the parents for their children.

Confucius's central doctrine is that of the virtue of *jen*—translated variously as goodness, benevolence, love, affection, and humanity. *Jen,* while rooted in human sentiment as well as in a fundamental orientation of life, is also concerned with human relationship. For Confucianism, parental love for children can be extended to cover other people's children, just as filial respect for the elderly can be extended to cover other people's parents and elders. Thus, the natural order serves as a starting point and an experiential guide in achieving universal love.

In addition to social behavior, Confucianism gives a definite importance to rituals, including religious rituals. Confucian belief in a supernatural Heaven and in fate has special significance for the Confucian doctrine as a moral cause. Thus, on the positive side, the belief in Heaven and fate inspires moral strength when one succeeds, and, on the negative side, it upholds people's faith in doctrine in the event of failure, or even in death.

Taoism

As China's earliest organized religion, Taoism is a priestly or theological religion that developed in China beginning in the second century A.D., with its own rituals, scriptures, and organizations (Wolf, 1974; Kung and Ching, 1989; Fairbank, 1992). Taoism emphasizes the revival of life power through contact with cosmic forces.

175

——————————— **Chapter Thirteen** ———————————

Unlike Confucianism, Taoism is a salvation religion. It seeks to guide its believers beyond this transitory life to a happy eternity. But Taoists do not conceive of eternal life in terms of spiritual immortality alone. Since there is no strict separation of spirit and matter in Chinese thought, Taoists look forward to the survival of the whole person, including the body. To live according to nature is to respect its laws, including that of dying. Such acceptance of the natural indicates an attitude of equanimity regarding life and death, rather than a sole desire to prolong one's life.

The Taoist religion has developed the doctrine of the Three Life Principles of breath (*ch'i*), vital essence or semen (*ching*), and spirit (*shen*), each of which has two dimensions being present at the same time—in the human being as microcosm and in the cosmos as macrocosm. It also gives much attention to ritual expressions; for example, exorcism rituals are often carried out in case of sickness, with the exorcist struggling for a victory over the evil spirits. Many other rituals are regularly performed around the lunar year and its festivals. The best-known ones center around the Chinese New Year, with dragon dances and firecrackers to chase away the demons. Some of the Taoist priests who lead the rituals are also *shamans,* or spirit-mediums, who can assist the faithful with their counsels and assist communication with the spirits of the beloved dead.

Buddhism

The introduction of Buddhism to China during the first century A.D. was an event with important consequences, both for the development of Chinese thought and culture and for the evolution of Buddhism itself. The essence of Buddha's teachings appears to be contained in the so-called Four Noble Truths: that life is painful, that the origin of pain is desire, that the cessation of pain depends upon the ending of the desire, and that the way to this end is through the rules for right living (Reischauer and Fairbank, 1960; Kung and Ching, 1989). In Buddhism, life is both painful and unending, since one existence is tied to another by *Karma,* a term which literally means "act" but also implies causality. Therefore, each act produces the next—birth leading to old age, death, and further births—in the endless chain of causality. In this context, death and dying are considered as essential elements of the never-ending life cycle.

The meeting of the Buddhist religion and Chinese culture became the occasion for conflicts and controversies, which were resolved only when Buddhism adjusted itself to the Chinese environment—taking account of Confucian moral values such as filial piety, while making use of Taoist ideas and terminology for its own survival and advancement. But Chinese realism and pragmatism have profound influence upon Buddhism—affirming this life and this world, including the values of family, longevity, and posterity.

Cultural and Religious Dimensions of Death and Dying

We have briefly discussed three Chinese religions—Confucianism, Taoism, and Buddhism—which were able to coexist and complement one another within the Chinese cultural context. While each religion serves a socially useful function, it is a spirit of harmony and reconciliation which is perhaps most characteristic of traditional Chinese culture.

To the living in the Chinese society, death is not an individual matter but a social concern involving the permanent removal of a member from the group. Death lingers on among the living, who emotionally refuse to accept it and who face the task of carrying on life in spite of it. In the context of harmony and reconciliation, one alternative to the tragic situation is to assume the continued existence of the deceased and use this assumption to mitigate emotional grief and demoralization, and for the family members to rally their efforts and carry on the business of the living (Yang, 1961; Hsu, 1981; Lin, 1992). This traditional belief is based on the existence of the soul of the deceased and on the perpetuation of the memory of the departed as perceived by the family members.

General Nature of Death and Dying

Basically, there are serious and complicated issues relating to death and dying in each culture. In the Chinese culture, death was considered evil, and the "spirit" of a deceased family member could become unpredictable and might do evil even to his or her own intimate kin.

The dying process, like stages in human development, is constantly affected by cultural traditions. In spite of current arguments over the patient's "right to know," which favor frankness with the dying persons, many families, and even the medical providers, are reluctant to speak with them of death (Hinton, 1984). They feel that most patients do not wish to raise the subject of dying except to get reassurance, and that the painful truth is likely to be hurtful. When the patient, medical staff, and family members know that the patient is dying but pretend otherwise—when all agree to act as if he or she were going to live—then a context of so-called "mutual pretense" exists (Glaser and Strauss, 1984). In the Chinese culture, this is a common attitude and on some hospital services it is the predominant context (Lin, 1992).

Dying is fundamentally shaped by the sociocultural milieu in which it occurs. Generally speaking, dying at home has been the traditional arrangement for most Chinese families, since it allows more latitude for them to handle it in culturally appropriate ways. There is also the traditional Chinese belief that people who die away from home will become lonely spirits, ghosts in the wild. Further, the dying person at home is often integrated into the round of daily life and therefore is involved in living as he or she prepares to die. From the Chinese perspective, one of the most important implications of dying at home is that the dying person, family members, and relatives may come to feel that they have realized a symbolic completion of their shared relationship and solidarity.

The entire set of mortuary rites was once regarded as unclean and unlucky, contaminated by evil. Mortuary rites, therefore, made it necessary to choose a propitious date by consulting the Chinese almanac or by divination for practically every ritual act so that evil spirits might not be aroused into action, good spirits might not be offended, and favorable influences might be called into play. Ancestor worship was basically a means to cope with the emotionally shattering and socially disintegrating event of death of an intimate family member. The living developed a deep emotional, social, and even economic dependence on the dead, particularly if the deceased were an adult person who had raised a family. To whom could the living now turn for comfort, companionship, and economic support? And how could the living face the feeling of emptiness and futility that suddenly descended upon family activities, as characterized by the familiar Chinese poetic line, "Grief is futile as the person is gone, leaving but an empty chamber"?

The Expression of Grief

The rituals to fulfill the function of grief begin with the sending of obituaries to relatives and friends, not only to inform them of the tragic event but also to invite them to participate in the funeral procession and mourning feast. This is an attempt to assemble the social group of relatives and friends, and the size of the group often symbolizes the socioeconomic status of the family. Relatives and friends are expected to come with condolence gifts which might be in the form of condolence scrolls with words of comfort for the living or glorification of the dead, or in the form of money to help defray the costs. Condolence gifts, scrolls, or money represent collective emotional and material assistance from the wider social group to the bereaved family and symbolize the extent of social ties the family has with relatives and friends.

During the mourning period, another means of mitigating the emotional shock of death include such matters as the ritualistic weeping, eating lightly, and the wearing of the mourning garments made of the cheapest rough materials as a genuine expression of grief; for example, when Confucius was eating by the side of a mourner, he never ate to the full (*Four Books*, 1977). There is also the suppression of events of happiness such as weddings or the celebration of birthdays. Aside from the function of treating the emotional shock of the death, it should be noted that these expressions of grief also have the significance of reaffirming the cohesion and solidarity of the family.

Another significant dimension is the gradation of the expression of grief for various types of relations. In general, the closer the family members and friends with the dead, the greater the degree of grief required by convention; for example, the children of the deceased are expected to weep most sadly and observe mourning rules and rituals most faithfully and for the longest period. Confucius once commented on the expression of grief that it was better there be deep sorrow than a minute attention to observances (*Four Books*, 1977; *Discourses and Sayings of Confucius*, 1982).

The Significance of Death for the Living

The Chinese believe that the body should remain in contact with the earth following death and, therefore, prefer interment to cremation. Preparations often entail consulting a fortune teller or geomantic master for an auspicious burial site and date. The belief behind this behavior is that the spirit of the deceased will be happy only if the final resting place has good soil and luxuriant trees and grass. It is also believed that the ultimate burial site of the deceased is going to influence the fortunes of his or her descendants, even for generations to come.

After having done the impressive and elaborative burial and grieving processes, the next step is to stabilize the relationship between

179

the dead and the living by periodic offerings so that this memory and relationship will not be affected over time. As an act of making an offering to the spirits of the deceased, the family members offer daily morning and night burning of incense and bowing to a symbol of the spirit, usually a wooden tablet or a portrait of the dead one. The offerings of food and drink are more elaborate on such family occasions as the anniversary death date of each deceased member, festival days, the first and fifteenth days of each Chinese lunar month, and special events such as births or weddings. In Taiwan, for example, a special event such as "Tomb Sweeping Day" (April 5 of each year) is a national holiday on which respect is shown for one's ancestors by tending their graves.

The offerings to the dead, and later, the sharing of them by the entire family on various occasions, has a significant social implication. First, serving for the continuity of the relationship, this mode of communication with the deceased symbolizes a reminder of the existence of the role of the dead among the living in the family. Second, in sharing the food in the presence of the ancestral spirits, who have presumably returned for the occasion, the family also reinforces the ties of loyalty and solidarity among its members. Third, in the sacred name of the deceased, the sharing of good food represents the symbol of the family's good fortune and abundance, and all family members are expected to be present at this family reunion. Should some members be unable to attend, they remember such sacrificial occasions as a time of family reunion. This is especially true of such occasions as death anniversaries of parents and annual sacrifices at the graves, which take place in the spring and autumn.

Social Implications of Death

For the individual, the satisfying feeling that one has done his or her best for the parents from the beginning to the end serves to mitigate the psychological shock of the death of the parents. For the society as a whole, the inspiring of filial sentiments through funeral and sacrificial rites is a means of maintaining filial piety as a favored basic value within the context of the kinship system. Tsang, a disciple of Confucius, once remarked, "By cultivating the respect for the dead, and carrying the memory back to the distant past, the virtue of the people will grow in depth" (*Four Books,* 1977; *Discourses and Sayings of Confucius,* 1982).

It is interesting to note that the group integrational function is further seen in other aspects of a death within the family. For instance, those who die at an advanced age receive more elaborate mortuary and sacrificial rites than those who die younger; a deceased male member of the family is mourned with more elaborate rites than a female, and the rites for the head of the family are the most significant in the family. This differential treatment appears to lend religious support to the stratification of the family organization based on the factors of age and gender role. Thus, the basic function of ancestor worship is still the integration and perpetuation of the kinship group (Yang, 1961; Wolf, 1974; Hsu, 1981; Fairbank, 1992). Even the cultivation of social values such as affection and filial piety contribute directly to this end. When asked about the meaning of filial piety, Confucius replied, "That parents, when alive, should be served according to propriety; that, when dead, they should be buried according to propriety; and that they should be sacrificed to according to propriety" (*Four Books,* 1977).

Chinese people take neither death nor the treatment of the deceased lightly, for they also regard death with awe and fear. It is a taboo subject around which revolve numerous superstitions and customs. People try, for instance, to avoid the number "four" which, in Chinese language, is a homophone for the word "death." Many buildings, including hospitals and hotels, have no fourth floor. Further, children are often scolded for wearing white, the color of mourning, in their hair.

Conclusions and Implications

In the context of a Chinese cultural perspective, death is treated with great respect and ritual, the purpose of which is to express the deceased individual's solidarity with his or her family and community. In the past, so long as death was concrete, personally experienced over and over in life, familiar ritually in the family and kinship community, it was comprehensible and acceptable, at least to a greater degree than it is now in the Chinese society. In referring to death, one thinks of the linguistic abominations "passed on," "pass away heavenward," "going to the happiest land of the West"—words as noble as any to be found in the Chinese language.

From the acceptance of the finality of death, Chinese culture developed a group of religious acts which also aimed at the comfort and happiness of the dead in the other, yet unknown, world. The very elaborateness of such behaviors and their symbolic meaning served to confirm to the remaining family members the reality of the continued existence of the soul. The belief of life after death as a state of repose or peaceful existence of soul lasted much longer than one might expect and is surely one of the most tenacious forms of Chinese attitude toward death. But more important than the physical onset of death in the individual is the place of death in Chinese society. Unlike anonymous, impersonal Western society, death in the Chinese sense is, first and last, communal, not individual.

What will be the dimension of death in the future? Given the changing nature of the multicultural diversity of American society, how might our conceptions of the nature of death and dying change in the future? Does the cross-cultural issue of death and dying challenge ongoing practices of care of the dying? To answer these questions, we need to put into perspective some major issues discussed in this chapter. In that way, we can examine current cross-cultural trends in relation to their implications for the future.

Arguments have already been made that the character and meaning of death and dying are changing as they are increasingly brought into empirical assessment and discussion (Hinton, 1984; Stephenson, 1985; Kotre and Hall, 1990; Bloom, 1992). Ultimately, the issues surrounding death and dying may encompass a recognition of quality human living, human rights, and humane care. When his disciple asked about serving the spirit of the dead, Confucius said, "While you do not know life, how can you know about death?" (*Four Books,* 1977).

In conclusion, the beliefs, value systems, norms, and cultural practices constituting the reality of death and dying are constructions of interacting persons who shape both the culture and society, and above all, our professional practices.

Chinese attitude toward d.

CHAPTER FOURTEEN

Death, Dying, and Grief in the Chinese-American Culture

Jane G. Tanner

In 1980, the United States statistics on minority groups estimated that there were 800,000 Chinese Americans in the United States. Between 1960 and 1980, the Chinese-American population grew by 89 percent, with approximately 30,000 Chinese immigrating to the United States each year (Tsai et al., 1981). Many of these immigrants left their homeland with the hope that they would return to China. Currently, as many Chinese leave for political, economic, and social reasons, they dream of one day returning to their country. Chinese Americans, therefore, continue to maintain a strong allegiance to their homeland, retaining their culture, customs, and rituals. This is most noticeable in their beliefs and rituals surrounding death, which differ greatly from those of mainstream America.

Lack of understanding of a minority's culture can lead to conflict, discrimination, prejudice, and racial self-hatred; however, cultural awareness generates solutions, acceptance, and admiration. The purpose of this chapter is to describe the death rituals and the care of the terminally ill practiced by Chinese Americans in order to increase our awareness and understanding of this ethnic group as social worker practitioners working in the area of death and dying.

Care of Terminally Ill

The traditional Chinese beliefs about illness, health, and disease are based on the ancient principle of the body's Yin-Yang forces (Parry,

183

1990). The balance of these hot (yin) and cold (yang) forces is believed to be essential for good health. Illness and disease are "due to disharmony or lack of ebb and flow between yin and yang forces" (Foster, 1978, p. 39). Therefore, traditional Chinese healers treat illness and disease with foods or herbs that are either hot or cold to correct the body's imbalance; for example, if the body is hot with a fever, the healers would administer cold food and herbs that had a cold value.

To maintain health, the Chinese eat a diet that is balanced with hot and cold foods. This dialectic represents the basis of Chinese medicine, which continues to exist simultaneously with modern Western medicine among Chinese and Chinese Americans (Parry, 1990). In a study examining the health practices of Chinese Americans, Hessler, Nolan, Ogbru, and Kong-Ming-New (1975) found that they utilize Chinese and Western medical care in an interconnected fashion reflecting their intraethnic diversity. Hessler et al. (1975) also state that traditional Chinese medical practices should not be characterized as nonscientific folk medicine that is based in magic, because Chinese medicine actually has a scientific foundation. It is not founded on primitive concepts of magic and has survived for thousands of years. In concluding, Hessler et al. recommend that we offer medical care complete "with the compelling authority and power of cultural traditions and turned to the complex and diverse social order of ethnic survival" (p. 202).

It was the aim of this study to provide knowledge of the medical practices of Chinese Americans in order to reduce confusion and discrimination and promote acceptance and admiration. Modern Chinese-style practitioners understand the patient's desire to be treated with herbs as well as Western medicinal techniques, especially when the patient is terminally ill. The healers serve a purpose in modern China, as they provide the patient and his or her family with support and hope when the patient's condition continues to deteriorate despite the use of modern medicine. The healers also deal with the social and psychological problems associated with a terminal illness within the family. This role is abdicated by occidental physicians, especially when treating the terminally ill (Kleinman, 1980). It is, therefore, understandable that the terminally ill patient and his or her family avail themselves of modern medicine while simultaneously using traditional Chinese healers. Although the practice of medicine in China is modern and westernized, Chinese physicians understand the role of the healer, whereas Western physicians are generally not aware of the support the healer may offer a patient and his or her family.

When a member of a family is terminally ill, Chinese Americans prefer that the physician address the family rather than the patient when explaining the illness or treatment. The family members actually make the decisions regarding the treatment of the illness. When the physician addresses the Chinese-American patient, it is not uncommon for the patient to direct the physician to a family member. This supplants the fundamental communication pattern of patient-practitioner (which is typical in the United States) with "practitioner-family" and "patient-family" (Kleinman, 1980).

Chinese Americans believe that it is their duty to support the dying patient by being involved in the management of his or her care. The dying patient is never isolated, as the family is the main vehicle of communication in the hospital (Kleinman, 1980). Therefore, the Chinese cultural approach of managing the terminal illness of a family member encourages the support and involvement of the family when a member is dying. This is therapeutic for the patient as well as the family. However, this continues to be misunderstood by American physicians, who feel an ethical responsibility to directly address and consult with the patient about his or her care. This might also explain why terminally ill Chinese Americans do not complain about pain to their physician; however, they will tell family members that they are in pain. At San Jose Medical Center, on the oncology floor, rarely does a Chinese American ask for pain medication. However, family members will often request medication for the patient. The patient is seen as having a high tolerance for pain. Another explanation is that patients do not want to be "seen as a chronic complainer, lest they not get any attention and may even be ignored" (Parry, 1990, pp. 155–56). Hospitalization is feared by many elderly Chinese Americans as many in this age group are not bilingual and strictly adhere to their culture. "Chinese patients feel utterly helpless and isolated in a strange environment which may be insensitive to their anxieties" (Fujii, 1976, p. 206). Some of their anxiety is reduced as the family remains with the patient as much as possible. However, unlike hospitals in China, U.S. hospitals have strict rules regarding visiting hours and the number of visitors allowed to see a patient at one time. This creates anxiety and conflict between the patient's family and the hospital staff, as the family feels responsible for the patient's care. This is consistent with Chinese physicians' belief that the family is responsible for the care of the patient (Kleinman, 1980), but in sharp contrast to the United States, where the physician is viewed as solely responsible for the care of the terminally ill patient.

——————————————— Chapter Fourteen ———————————————

Death and Grief Rituals

According to an old Chinese saying, "The most important thing in life is to get buried well" (Hom, 1971, p. 62). The Chinese religion is a mixture of Taoism, Buddhism, and Confucianism (Hom, 1971). The colorful and lavish funerals of Chinese Americans are grounded in their religious beliefs and ancient customs. They believe that the soul has two forces, Shen and Kwei. Consistent with the principle of Yin-Yang, Shen and Kwei represent hot and cold forces. Shen represents the good characteristics of the deceased: warmth, productivity, light, and personality. Kwei represents the negative attributes, such as the animal nature of man, darkness, and cold (Hom, 1971). When the individual dies, the souls separate and leave the body. However, if the funeral rites are not lavishly performed or if the ceremony is carried out incorrectly, the Kwei soul will reenter the body and haunt the friends and relatives of the deceased (Watson and Rawski, 1988). The degree to which these beliefs pervade Chinese-American culture is not clear. However, Chinese burial rites continue to be performed in modern America.

When an individual dies, the family gathers in the room where the death occurred and weeps. This is the only time men can openly express their grief. The funeral rituals in China take place in a Buddhist temple and the family house. However, in the United States, Chinese Americans use mortuaries that accommodate their practices. At the funeral home, blue and white flowers are arranged around the coffin. David Stern, director of Oak Hill Cemetery, stated that the mourners wear white robes and burn incense during the funeral. These practices date back to late Imperial China. The women in the family wail loudly during the funeral and the men remain silent (Watson and Rawski, 1988). The closer the relationship to the deceased, the louder the women should wail. For sixty days after the death, the men do not shave and the women do not wash their hair (Hom, 1971).

After the rites are performed by the Taoist and Buddhist priests, the funeral procession begins. The procession is loud and elaborate, with drums, music, wailing, and firecrackers. The coffin is placed on a coach which travels from the chapel at the mortuary to the grave site. In the early 1900s in San Jose, the elaborate procession took place in the streets of the neighborhood. The length of the procession was equated with the family wealth and esteem. In fact, the death is "a time of community reckoning in which people who attend are only those who admire the deceased" (Hom, 1971, p. 65). When the procession ends at the grave site, each family member throws a handful of dirt on the coffin. The procession is actually symbolic, as it moves the deceased to his or her final place, acknowledging that the person is no longer with the living. The procession away from this final place represents a movement back to life without the deceased.

Three days after the funeral, the family has a picnic on the grave; they burn fake money and food for the deceased to have in the after-life. Ceremonies continue on the grave site on the twenty-first, thirty-fifth, and forty-ninth day after the death (Hom, 1971). David Stern states that these practices currently take place at Oak Hill Cemetery at least two or three times a week.

Chinese Americans have a strong belief in an afterlife, which is obvious in their practice of burning money and food for the deceased to have in the spirit world. This aids them in their acceptance of death among their elderly relatives. However, the premature death of a child or adult is not accepted. The funeral service is not elaborate, and public display of grief is not considered appropriate, even though there is significant grief. This practice is grounded on the religious belief that a child who died was, in fact, an evil spirit and not the real offspring of the parents (Fried and Fried, 1980). Currently, the reasoning behind the less-than-elaborate funeral service for a child might stem from the avoidance of a celebration for a premature death. However, even when an elderly individual dies, it is not uncommon for family members to exaggerate his or her age (Hom, 1971).

Comparison to Mainstream America

When comparing American white culture to that of the Chinese American, Tsai, Teng, and Sue (1981) make the following observation:

> The American way of life emphasizes individual centeredness—autonomy, assertiveness, and independence within a youth-oriented perspective. These values are in direct contrast to the Chinese values of generational continuity, family solidarity, respect for elders, and situation-centeredness whereby individual impulses are subordinate to the will of the family as a group. (P. 297)

This dichotomy is readily observed in each group's care of their terminally ill. Most Americans believe that the sole responsibility for their terminally ill family member lies with the physician, as opposed to Chinese Americans, who believe that the family *and* the physician are responsible for the patient's treatment. This is based on family solidarity and their belief in the causes of illness and self-treatment with herbs and foods. Most Americans rely on modern medical care for the treatment of terminal illness, as the cause is believed to be of a biochemical nature. Chinese Americans also utilize modern medical techniques, but in combination with ancient remedies such as herbs, hot/cold foods, and incense-burning rituals, as they believe the cause of illness to be a combination of a biological and a spiritual nature. Chinese Americans do not separate the mind and body as most Americans do. This is noticeable in the high incidence of psychosomatic illnesses among the Chinese Americans (Lefley and Pedersen, 1986). Therefore, the terminally ill Chinese American relies on both family and the physician to provide treatment.

The individual nature of most Americans demands that decisions about health care are ultimately up to them. The physician consults the patient's family as well; however, the physician is more comfortable with following the wishes of the patient. As was mentioned, the family of the Chinese-American patient decides the course of treatment. This includes the dispensing of pain medication as well as medication in general. Since the Chinese American believes in the assistance of herbs and foods to counter illness and relies on his or her family for decision making, he or she rarely requests medication for pain. Most Americans rarely hesitate to ask for medication to control pain. This is emulated in their daily lives as they rely on aspirin, sleeping aids, vitamins, and digestive aids, and the Chinese American relies on the balance of foods, herbs, and incense.

Whereas the Chinese culture encourages the family context of dying, the traditional American white culture does not. However, the hospice movement has been successful, to some degree, in combating isolation felt by the terminally ill by shifting care from the patient to the patient and his or her family. Before hospice, the management of dying in the health care system was labeled as maladaptive and handled poorly. There is increased isolation felt by many dying persons as compared to the dying Chinese-American patient for two reasons: (a) attitudes surrounding death and (b) hospital visiting regulations. Chinese Americans more readily accept the death of the elderly family member. In fact, elderly parents are honored when their eldest son purchases their coffin and grave site before they die (Hom, 1971). However, most Americans are raised in a death-denying culture which is youth oriented. As a result, the dying patient, as well as the family, experiences loneliness and abandonment. By limiting their contact with the dying person, most Americans decrease their contact with death and reduce their emotional involvement with the patient. This has been observed at San Jose Medical Center especially in a prolonged death. Most American families also believe that the hospital staff are the best caretakers of the dying patient. They rationalize that the patient is getting the best possible care at the hospital, leaving them little to do for the patient. The Chinese-American family, although they seek modern medical care, believe that they can offer the dying patient the care he or she needs.

There are many similarities, as well as differences, between the funeral and grief rituals of the Chinese Americans and other Americans, particularly those of Irish Catholic descent. Virtually all cultures have some type of funeral rituals which satisfy important needs for the grievers. Both the Chinese-American and Irish Catholic funeral provide affirmation that a loved one has died. Sympathy is extended to the families through social support and attendance at the funeral in both cultures. The ceremonies in each culture are religious in nature. Chinese Americans utilize Buddhist and Taoist priests, while the Irish Catholics have a mass in the Catholic church after a three-day viewing of the body. The three-day viewing in the Irish-Catholic culture is similar to that of the Chinese, who believe the deceased should not be buried for at least seventy-two hours. However, the body is sometimes viewed for up to two weeks awaiting the arrival of relatives from China. Both cultures have open-casket viewings. The last similarity is that alcohol is part of both rituals. An Irish Catholic wake is notorious for the consumption of alcohol. However, at the Chinese-American ritual, wine is poured into a brass container by each visitor (Hom, 1971). The brass container is placed in front of the coffin as an offering to the spirit of the deceased. Chinese Americans drink the wine in moderation.

Social changes in America have impacted funeral practices in many ways. There has been a decrease in participation in the funeral among Anglo-Americans (Rando, 1984). The details are left to the funeral director, and attendance has declined due to the replacement of the large extended family with the mobile nuclear family. Rando (1984), in her book entitled *Grief, Dying and Death,* states, "It is a uniquely American custom for the family to participate so minimally, other than by attendance, in funerary rituals" (p. 176). Rando explains this phenomenon by suggesting that "advances in medical science, changes in mortality rates, and segregation of the ill and elderly have made death seem remote in America" (p. 176). She adds that it is now easier to deny death and funerary rites. In the Chinese culture, it is unheard of to not attend the funeral of a friend or family member.

When President Kennedy was killed, Jackie Kennedy became our role model, defining how America should grieve. She was strong, stoic, and quiet during the funeral and the procession. Display of public grief became taboo. Today, the typical American is reluctant to grieve in public, whereas to the Chinese American, the wailing and crying of the deceased's daughters are required to open the gates of heaven. In fact, a parent without daughters is considered to be unlucky for this reason (Hom, 1971).

The void left when a family member dies is felt in all cultures; however, adjusting the family's equilibrium is less harsh in Chinese-American families for two reasons: (a) the deceased is considered to still be with the family, and (b) the extended family members fill the functional roles once occupied by the deceased. "The idea that the dead are at least as important as the living, if not much more, is so basic to much of Chinese belief, behavior, and social organizations" (Fried and Fried, 1980, pp. 169–70). Members of a non–Chinese-American family may, in this respect, have a more difficult adjustment period, but their adjustment to the loss can be aided through professional mental health intervention or by participation in support groups. Chinese Americans may benefit less from this kind of intervention, as many become uncomfortable when asked personal questions or when expressing feelings in front of those who are not family members. In addition, language and cultural barriers interfere with appropriate assessment of problems displayed by Chinese Americans. Without a reasonable understanding of this ethnic group's behavior and beliefs, the odds of a professional providing effective intervention are drastically reduced. The differences among cultures are summarized in a statement by McGoldrick and Carter (1989) in their book, *The Changing Family Life Cycle*:

> Ethnicity patterns our thinking, feeling, and behavior in both obvious and subtle ways, although generally operating outside of our awareness. It plays a major role in determining what we eat, how we work, how we relate, how we celebrate holidays and rituals, and how we feel about life, death, and illness. (P. 69)

The Role of the Health Professional

When working with the family of a Chinese-American patient who is terminally ill, the worker's roles consist of educator, mediator, and helper. First and foremost, the worker must educate the hospital staff and the physician on the cultural differences between the staff and the client; these differences may include beliefs, attitudes, and behaviors. For example, a social worker might educate the physician on Chinese-American patterns of communication, described above as "practitioner-family" and "patient-family." Second, the social worker may mediate between the family and the hospital staff regarding cultural practices and hospital rules. The worker might negotiate a special diet consisting of a balance of hot and cold foods to please the family and the patient, thereby respecting their cultural beliefs and practices. The worker in every situation is a helper. The worker must help the dying patient and his or her family by facilitating the expression of feelings and encouraging resolution of "unfinished business," while simultaneously respecting their cultural beliefs and practices. This is illustrated by the following case example.

A fifty-one-year-old Chinese-American man died of cancer at San Jose Medical Center. He had one adult son, a wife, and an extended family who carried out a bedside vigil. Upon his death, the family gathered and cried. The son requested some time alone with his father, and the request was honored by the family and the worker. After a while, the worker decided to take the son a glass of water, as he was extremely upset. When the worker entered the room, the son was expressing his deep regret and sadness that he had never revealed to his now dead father his awareness that he was an adopted child. He was explaining that his aunt revealed the truth to him years ago. The aunt had told the adopted son that his father feared that he would lose his son's love if the truth were known. The son told his dead father that his love for him was never diluted by the true circumstances of his birth. Afterwards, the son expressed his regret to the worker, who inquired why the son had not resolved this while his father was dying. The son informed the worker that he did not want to show disrespect to his parents by confronting them with the truth, but that he now intended to tell his mother.

The above case demonstrates the unfinished business between a dying father and his son which could have been resolved by just giving the family permission to express feelings previously left unsaid.

The above example also demonstrates a central role of the worker when working with any dying patient and his or her family. Encouraging both the patient and family members to resolve unfinished business can prevent a prolonged and severe grief reaction and, subsequently, can enhance the psychosocial functioning of the family after the death. This might be difficult in the face of denial, which tends to be more pervasive among those groups who are less accepting of death. Although denial is a normal coping mechanism, it can become abnormal when it is prolonged and can interfere with the grieving process. With prolonged denial, the worker intervenes with the patient and the family by gently reinforcing the reality of the patient's illness.

Last of all, when working with patients and their families that are not Chinese American, the worker may need to encourage continued family involvement with the dying patient, consequently preventing feelings of isolation. When discussing the dying patient and his or her family, Rando (1984) states that "the treatment goal is to maintain the patient and family relationship by facilitating open communication and interaction patterns to the extent the family style allows" (p. 340).

The most important area of concern for the Chinese-American patient and his or her family is continuous family involvement in the management of the dying patient's care. This is expanded to the funeral rituals when the patient has died. The Chinese-American patient does not want to lose his or her dignity and sense of self-worth, which are derived from the family, as they value "family solidarity" and "situation-centeredness" (Tsai et al., 1981, p. 297). Family members, in turn, need to carry out their job of supporting and taking care of the patient. The social worker is concerned with properly identifying the needs of the patient and his or her family and meeting those needs within the constraints of their culture and the dominant culture. The social worker must assist the patient and family with the life transition within a cultural framework.

Most non-Chinese patients are concerned with continued family interaction, loss of independence, loss of identity, loss of relationships, and control of pain. The family is concerned with coping with the terminal illness and adapting to the impending death. The worker must be concerned with assisting the patient and his or her family to increase their adaptive capacities and maintain family equilibrium. The worker should identify the family's needs, strengths, and weaknesses in an attempt to assist the family in their coping, functioning, and grieving. Self-awareness is crucial when working with the bereaved. This position is supported by Cassidy (1977) as summarized in her chapter on "Helping the Social Work Student":

> To engage in a productive helping process with patients and their families amid the grief, sorrow, and crisis aspect attendant on the death, the student must become aware of his own reactions, know his own feelings, and be willing to plunge into self-scrutiny as a preface to development of insight. (P. 321)

The Korean Perspective on Death and Dying

Daniel B. Lee

Life is an empty carriage, an empty hand
If you go now, when do you come back?
Eh hey, eh hey . . .
Life is a day-length, a dream of Spring time
If you go now, when do you come back?
Eh hey, eh hey . . .

—Korean village funeral chant

This chapter is organized around cross-cultural perspectives on death and dying relevant to Koreans in their traditional practices and Korean Americans in their adaptive modes in dealing with bereavement, loss, and grief. Supportive data consist of literature review, participatory observations, and survey results. Special attention is given to clinical implications in working with Korean clients and families in mourning. Thematic topics include: (a) an overview of Korean belief systems; (b) traditional funeral rituals; (c) contemporary practices of burial and ancestral worship; (d) research findings on Korean immigrants' attitudes toward death and dying; and (e) clinical implications on bereavement, grief, and mourning.

Korean Belief Systems

Korean culture is permeated with spiritual concepts and practices from diverse religious traditions. Many Koreans may not be affiliated with any particular religious institution although their values are still significantly shaped by spiritual systems. Korean religiosity is highly syncretistic; traditional religious systems influence and absorb elements from each other. Shamanism, as the oldest faith in Korea, has combined not only various primitive forms of worship but also Buddhism, Taoism, Confucianism, and even Christianity (Han, 1982). A Korean may profess Buddhism while practicing Confucian rituals and Taoist-inspired magic. However, the indigenous shamanistic tradition underlies all the Korean forms of religious practices.

Shamanism emphasizes the necessity of harmonious and personal relationships among all beings, humans, animals, plants, geographical features, ancestor spirits, and other spiritual powers. The most prevalent shamans now are women (*mudang*), who use ecstatic states of consciousness and impressive rituals to heal, divine the future, and mend relations between humans, heaven, earth, and underworld. Shamanistic rituals often enable emotional cathartic release of stress and repressed emotions, especially for psychologically oppressed lower classes and women. The shamanistic tendency to view human and non-human relations in personal and supernatural terms is prevalent in Korean culture, although it is often ostracized by upper-class and Westernized Koreans.

Korean Buddhism, which entered the country in the fourth century B.C., belongs to the *Mhayana* (Greater Vehicle) branch. It emphasizes the integration of meditation, doctrinal learning, and ritual practice. It stresses cultivation of virtues of expression such as care, loving language, sacrifice, and helping. It also teaches seven virtues of attitude: interest in others, obeying the law, compassion, perseverance, progressiveness, concentration, and wisdom (Yoon, 1987). Although Buddhism is essentially nondualistic, common practice involves the veneration of deities that represent aspects of the ultimate reality, Buddha-nature, which is identical with the true self. The attainment of enlightenment (*haet'al*), which pierces through egocentrism, duality, and illusions, is the goal. Buddhism is strongly metaphysical and cultivates emotional, intellectual, and transcendental aspects of spirituality.

Confucianism has been an important component of Korean political and ethical development since A.D. 300–400. Most Koreans would not consider themselves to be Confucianists in an institutional sense, but Confucianism permeates world views and ethics. The ideal of compassionate mutual responsibility in the context of hierarchical social relations is Confucian. Social ethics, including filial piety and propriety, are addressed in every aspect of social and political intercourse, from a family ancestral worship to the governmental entrance examination. Everything in the universe is the result of the interaction between two primary poles, *yang* (light, creature, masculine) and *um* (dark, receptive, feminine), which are one in the Great Ultimate (*tae kuk*). Achieving harmony between the two poles in all aspects of life, especially social relations, is the prime ideal of Confucianism. Confucianism considers that humanity in harmony with the *Tao* ("the Way") can serve to fulfill the creative potential of heaven and earth in interaction.

Although Taoism is not practiced as a formal institutional system in Korea, certain Taoistic elements remain prevalent in the Korean world view. Its mystical transcendentalism and nondualism are known to philosophers. On the common practice level, the magical attempts to gain long life (*su*) and blessings (*bok*), as well as the use of geomancy (*pungsu*) for location of auspicious grave, home, and temple sites, are most widely known.

Christianity, a Western religion, grew strongest in modernizing Korea, despite many repeated persecutions by the Confucian rulers in the eighteenth century, as well as the colonial Japanese and North Korea's Communist rules in the early and mid-twentieth century. The similarities between historical backgrounds of Koreans and ethnic Jews, and the strong desire of Koreans toward modernization and Westernization, are thought to have influenced the rapid development of churches and Christian congregations in Korea. The introduction of modern education, technology, and democratic ideals initiated by Christian missionaries in Korea during the era of international expansion became not only an impetus toward integration of Christian world views, spiritual significance of hope, and social renewal, but also their applications to national independence and modern ideas of democracy in Korea (Yoon, 1987). Christianity proclaims personal salvation in the personification of Christ through the works of Divine grace.

Traditional Funeral Rituals

Although Korea has modernized many of its traditional rites, including funeral rituals, it is important to revisit village conventions that underline the ethos of Korean cultural tradition, since many Koreans in rural communities adhere to traditional folklore and customs. Han (1982) views the village as an important framework from which the

Korean traditional mode of behavior can best be observed and understood. Roh (1987) notes the importance of the mourning process in conjunction with funeral rites from cross-cultural perspectives. He outlines eight progression components of funeral rituals commonly practiced in rural Korean communities: (a) preparations for the funeral; (b) announcement of death; (c) preparations of funeral uniform and foods; (d) stages of the funeral process; (e) burial site; (f) preparation of the "death carriage"; (g) funeral processions; and (h) ending the funeral ritual.

Funeral Preparations and Announcement

Ch'ohon or *Bok* is the first ceremony upon the death of a person—an initial gesture that is intended to call the deceased person's soul or spirit back with a hope for its restoration. It is done in the belief that one's soul does not depart immediately and that it wanders around for some period of time before it departs for a journey to the world beyond, so immediate family survivors sustain hope for a return of the soul within three to five days before funeral processions take place (Han, 1982; Roh, 1987). During this waiting period, *Sangjoo*, the chief mourner announces the death to other relatives, neighbors, and friends, and prepares for funeral arrangements to proceed. Special mourning garbs (*Sangbok*) and foods are prepared; signs are posted at the gate of the chief mourner's house. Wailing takes place, and visitors, *Moonsang*, are received for their condolences. Much of the funeral expense is met with the funeral contributions offered at the time of their visits. The preparation of food varies considerably and depends on the socioeconomic status of the mourners and their family backgrounds. The family reputation is often measured by the expectations of visitors around how well they are treated with food during this period of funeral visitation. This occasion also lays a testing ground for solidarity among the mourners' kin, as well as mutual help among the neighbors.

Funeral Process and Burial

While the chief mourners engage in much of the early phase of funeral preparations, including periodic wailing, the supervision of the funeral process is often conducted by a funeral director who is more experienced with funeral rites. There are four stages of handling the dead body: (a) *cho'jang,* which is the first-day preparations; (b) *soryom,* the process of clothing the deceased and covering the corpse with cloth, at which time the dead body is cleaned with honeyed water; (c) *taeryom,* the process of wrapping the body with a blanket and binding it with ropes on the second and third days; and (d) *ipkwan,* the process of placing the body in a coffin. No conversation is allowed during this period, and, as a way of respecting the departed person, callers are expected to show and reflect deep sorrow and somber feelings (Han, 1982; Roh, 1987).

The funeral procession begins at the chief mourner's house. *Sangyo,* or the death carriage, is carried by men, ranging in number from eight to forty, depending upon the family's prestige, and is accompanied by the chief mourners and other members of the bereaved family. Along either side of the carriage are displayed colorful banners inscribed with the name, family origin, and honors of the deceased. On its way to the graveyard, it stops at houses of relatives and friends where *noja,* or a ritual of treating the deceased with food and wine, is observed. This is the period in which many people in the village and community can bid farewell to the dead person (Roh, 1987).

Interment or burial in the ground is the most commonly practiced burial system in Korea — cremation being rare. The burial site is carefully chosen according to divination by configurations of the ground by the geomancer, who performs "a ritual in honor of the earth deity to inform him of the opening of the ground" (Han, 1982, p. 120). The grave diggers are employed to dig a burial hole, and the dead person is buried. The funeral rituals come to an end formally when a final rite to call the soul of the deceased back is completed after the burial. When the burial is finished, in memory of the deceased, a tablet made of a chestnut wood is enshrined in the family shrine. The post-funeral rituals include: (a) *Cho'ouje,* or the first rite, is performed by the mourners to console the soul of the dead upon returning home from the funeral; (b) the second rite is performed on the next morning to console the dead; (c) the third rite is held at the graveyard on the third day; (d) afterward, on the first and fifteenth days of each month, the mourners are required to offer a meal to the dead; this continues throughout the first year following the funeral. The first (*sosang*) and second (*taesang*) anniversary rituals are commemorated on a large scale with food and wine shared by relatives and other attendants. The mourning period ranges from three months to three years, depending on the degree of relationship (Yoon, 1987).

Contemporary Practices of Funeral and Burial

Trends and Variations

A trend toward simplicity of funeral rituals is becoming obvious in Korea today, in both rural and urban communities. Under governmental pressure to alter their conventional funeral practices (*Family Ritual Standards*), Koreans find themselves in a dilemma as to whether to adhere to their traditional rituals or to break away from them (Roh, 1987). However, a great variation of funeral rituals exists across geographical, religious, socioeconomic, and family backgrounds. Modern medicine and health care systems, as well as Christian influences, have significantly altered the role of the bereaved and cultural practices in funeral and mourning processes.

Case Illustrations

The author's recent encounter with two deaths in Korea illustrates such divergent examples of funeral rituals and dilemma.

Mrs. K., seventy-five years old, died of high blood pressure at home in Pusan, a southern harbor city, in the fall of 1987. She was a devoted, life-long Buddhist, but the chief mourners — her daughter and son-in-law, who are converted to Christianity — were faced with a dilemma, being caught between the conflicting pressures of their cultural and religious expectations. Many relatives of the deceased were gathered to observe traditional funeral rituals, and prepared the dead body according to traditional Korean funeral customs. But the chief mourners insisted on altering conventional rituals by bringing the pastor of their church to perform a memorial service at home. In the midst of the early funeral stage, an hour-long Christian memorial worship was conducted by the visiting minister for the dead and the family of the deceased. The prayer, hymnal, meditation, and condolence were parts of the service. It was soon followed by the Buddhist ritual performed by a group of monks from the Buddhist temple where the deceased maintained her membership. A long group chanting of funeral orations reflective of her faith journey in this world and beyond was accompanied with sounds of wooden instruments. Incense burning and bowing were made in tribute to the dead. Both religious rituals were ceremonial and did not allow mourning processes for the bereaved family members. At the third day of funeral, the body was cremated at one of the public funeral places after the dead received the last prayer offered by the chanting Buddhist monks; this was done according to the wishes of the deceased person.

Mrs. C., sixty-eight years old, died of kidney failure at a metropolitan hospital in Seoul in the winter of 1987. The pastor of her church paid a visit upon her death, and attending hospital staff provided the bereaved family members their condolences. The body was cleaned and clothed by the specialist at the hospital and placed in the casket in the calling room where callers were received. The announcement was made to the relatives, friends, and church members through multiple methods including telephone contacts, telegrams, newspapers, and word of mouth. The female mourners were in formal traditional Korean dress, while the male mourners dressed in Western-style black suits. Visitors were received for their condolences and provided with food. On the third day, the funeral procession took place; the casket was carried on the funeral van from the hospital calling area to the church graveyard. The first stop was the church where the farewell memorial worship was given, then a short stop was made at the house of the deceased. The burial memorial service was given at the graveyard sanctuary in the countryside. The body was buried in the designated burial site, which had been prearranged. Later, the tombstone was installed containing inscriptions of the name, birthday, date of death, church stewardship status, and the remaining family members of the deceased. The mourners visited the graveyard on the third day after the burial and periodically during the first year. At minimum, the bereaved family members visited there on the anniversary date of the death, the Korean harvest festival day, and/or memorial day.

The above case examples depict not only variations of funeral practices in modern time, but also some conflicting aspects of religious and cultural forces shaping the mode of mourning behaviors and burial practices. In the former case, kin played a significant role in bringing traditional rituals to the funeral, although cross-religious rituals broke the rhythms of traditional folklores. The latter case reflects a changing pattern of funeral rites under the influence of the Christian community, professional health practitioners, and modern technology. These combinations of traditional and contemporary practices of funeral rites and customs present clinical implications for helping professionals in working with the bereaved Korean immigrants residing in the United States. These concerns will be discussed in more detail later in this chapter.

Ancestral Worship

Ancestral worship, a traditional Korean memorial rite, is an expression of filial piety of children toward parents. It is an important ethical norm for Korean families to observe. As a guiding principle in the life of Koreans, filial piety is expressed in the conduct of serving one's own parents with deference and devotion. Such devotion is expected to continue even after the deaths of the parents. Choi (1982, p. 21) notes: "For three years after the death of one's parents, one should be circumspect in all conduct, behave oneself, and perform rituals on a large scale to honor one's ancestors."

Another aspect of ancestral worship is the inheritance system of the patriarchal lineage, which stresses the ancestral rites. Choi (1982, p. 21) argues from a socio-historic perspective: "The emphasis of rituals to honor paternal ancestors naturally resulted in the strengthening of unity among clansmen. The central figure in the society composed of paternal male relatives was the eldest son of the eldest grandson who succeeded to ancestral rites." The discriminatory treatment by gender and seniority in ancestral rites, and thus in inheritance, has prevailed in the ruling social class, *Yangban* for the Yi-Dynasty, between sixteenth and twentieth century Korea. Although serious practices of filial piety and the dominant role of patriarchal lineage in inheritance of properties and ancestral rituals might have been substantially altered by changes brought upon by current family laws, urbanization, Western influences including Christianity and equality movements, and migrations, ancestral worship is still practiced today not only in Korea but also in many parts of Korean immigrant communities in the United States, including Chicago.

Ch'usuk (Korean harvest festivity in autumn) and *Tano* (holiday in spring) are annually observed as occasions to perform ancestral rituals. Family members gather to pay tribute to their ancestors by visiting the burial sites of their ancestors, *s'ukmyo*. It is estimated by the Korean Red Cross that 10 million Korean families remain divided as a result of the Korean War in 1950. Many of these families have been unable to carry out their filial piety, including ancestral rites and clansmen and kin gatherings, and thus suffer from deep-seated emotional turmoil, guilt, and the painful social consequences of alienation, uprootedness, and intergenerational discontinuity (Lee, 1992). Until this tragic situation is improved, many Koreans, including approximately one-third of Korean immigrant families in North America, will continue to be extremely frustrated, some to a degree detrimental to their mental health.

Attitudes on Death and Dying: Research Findings

Sample and Data Collection Method

An exploratory study was conducted on the Korean immigrants' perspective on death and dying in the Chicago area during the month of April 1992. The sample was drawn voluntarily from adult members of a Korean Presbyterian church located in a Chicago suburb (N=46) and participants at the Korean-American Senior Center ESL classes in Chicago (N=28). A total of 74 returns out of 150 questionnaire distributions were used for this analysis. The survey questionnaires contained fifteen items and demographic information written in both English and Korean. They were distributed at each location by a graduate Korean-American student of Loyola University of Chicago, who is bilingual and familiar with both organizations. She assisted in collecting data and tabulating survey results.

Demographic Data

Although there were seventy-four participants, the survey respondents to demographic information consisted of thirty-one males and thirty-seven females. As shown in table 15.1, the ages of the respondents ranged from the forties (13%) to the eighties (3%), the mode being the sixties (34%). The majority were married (75%) and members of the Protestant religion (79%), as 62 percent of the sample were drawn from the church sample. More than half of the respondents (53%) had resided in the United States for more than ten years, and the remaining 47 percent had resided in the United States less than ten years, which reflects recency of their immigration history. Although more than one-third of the respondents had college educations, due to age factors, more than thirty percent did not have more than a ninth-grade education. Many of the respondents (44%) were presently retired or, if not, were unemployed. Others had professional (15%), clerical (14%), service (15%), technical (6%), and business (6%) occupations. A large proportion of the respondents (41%) perceived their health as fair, and others as excellent (17%), good (29%), or poor (14%). Although the majority (56%) had had no deaths in their immediate family over the past five years, the remaining 44 percent of the respondents had family deaths ranging from one (18%) to four (1.5%), mode being two (21%). More than one-third of the respondents (36%) had attended funeral services ten or more times over the previous ten years. Only 11 percent had no funeral experiences during the same period. Others ranged from one to three (23%); four to six (26%); and seven to nine (4.5%).

Table 15.1 • Demographic Characteristics by Gender

	Male		Female		Total	
	No.	%	No.	%	No.	%
Age						
40s	2	6.4	7	18.9	9	13.2
50s	8	25.8	10	27.0	18	26.5
60s	14	45.2	9	24.3	23	33.8
70s	6	19.3	10	27.0	16	23.2
80s	1	3.2	1	2.7	2	2.9
Total	31	99.9	37	99.9	68	99.6
Marital Status						
Married	29	93.5	22	59.4	51	75.0
Widowed	0	0.0	10	27.0	10	14.7
Divorced	0	0.0	4	10.8	4	5.9
Separated	1	3.2	1	2.7	2	2.9
Single	1	3.2	0	0.0	1	1.5
Total	31	99.9	37	99.9	68	100.0
Years since Immigration						
Less than 5	10	32.3	7	18.9	17	25.0
5–9	8	25.8	7	18.9	15	22.1
10–14	9	29.0	9	24.3	18	26.5
15–19	3	9.7	6	16.2	9	13.2
20 or more	1	3.2	8	21.6	9	13.2
Total	31	100.0	37	99.9	68	99.9
Religion						
Protestant	20	64.5	34	91.9	54	79.4
Catholic	7	22.6	1	2.7	8	11.8
Buddhist	1	3.2	1	2.7	2	2.9
Other	1	3.2	0	0.0	1	1.5
None	2	6.4	1	2.7	3	4.4
Total	31	99.9	37	100.0	68	100.0
Education						
6th grade or less	2	6.7	8	22.2	10	15.1
Middle school	8	26.7	3	8.3	11	16.7
High school	8	26.7	8	22.2	16	24.2
Some college	2	6.7	3	8.3	5	7.6
College graduate	6	20.0	14	38.9	20	30.3
Postgraduate	4	13.3	0	0.0	4	6.1
Total	30	100.1	36	99.9	66	100.0

Table 15.1 • (Continued)

	Male		Female		Total	
	No.	%	No.	%	No.	%
Occupation (present)						
Professional	6	20.0	4	11.1	10	15.1
Clerical	5	16.7	4	11.1	9	13.6
Technical	2	6.7	2	5.6	4	6.1
Service	4	13.3	6	16.7	10	15.1
Business	2	6.7	2	5.6	4	6.1
None/Retired	11	36.7	18	50.0	29	43.9
Total	30	100.1	36	100.1	66	99.9
Perceived Health						
Excellent	6	20.0	5	13.9	11	16.7
Good	9	30.0	10	27.8	19	28.8
Fair	11	36.7	16	44.4	27	40.9
Poor	4	13.3	5	13.9	9	
Total	30	100.0	36	100.0	66	100.0
Number of Deaths in Last Five Years						
0	16	53.3	21	58.3	37	56.1
1	7	23.3	5	13.9	12	18.2
2	7	23.3	7	19.4	14	21.2
3	0	0.0	2	5.6	2	3.0
4	0	0.0	1	2.8	1	1.5
Total	30	99.9	36	100.0	66	100.0
Number of Funeral Services in Last Ten Years						
0	3	10.0	4	11.1	7	10.6
1–3	7	23.3	8	22.2	15	22.7
4–6	7	23.3	10	27.8	17	25.8
7–9	1	3.3	2	5.6	3	4.5
10 or more	12	40.0	12	33.3	24	36.4
Total	30	99.9	36	100.0	66	100.0

Findings

Meaning of Death. Survey items 1, 2, and 3 contained questions pertaining to the meaning of death in terms of personal thought, meaning, and religious teachings. As reflected in table 15.2, the majority of Korean respondents viewed death and dying from a religious (predominantly Christian) perspective of eternal life, salvation, or peace. Other views included the inevitability of life to end, fear of death, or vagueness of the afterlife.

Table 15.2 • The Meaning of Death

Question 1: What comes to your mind first, when you think of death?

Responses	Number	Percent
I am afraid.	12	14.8
I haven't given it much thought.	15	18.5
Christian point of view	26	32.1
It's an inevitable happening	28	34.6
Total	81	100.0

Question 2: What does death mean to you personally?

Responses	Number	Percent
It means that I become peaceful.	17	21.2
It means that I go to heaven.	40	50.0
I have no clear idea what it means.	7	8.7
It means that one has to go eventually.	7	20.0
Total	80	99.9

Question 3: What does the religion you adhere to teach about death or dying?

Responses	Number	Percent
It teaches about faith in salvation.	41	51.2
It teaches about eternal life.	19	23.7
It teaches about peace.	18	22.5
Others	2	2.5
Total	80	99.9

Readiness for Death. Questions 4, 5, 6, related to preparation for death, the most important things to be done prior to death, and types of will to make before or at time of death as shown in table 15.3. Although the majority of Korean respondents mentioned their preparations for death in terms of spiritual salvation and conscientious efforts toward maximization of their life accomplishments, it seems clear that specific articulations were not made. Over 10 percent of the respondents were not dealing with death seriously, as they had not given enough thought to wills and any important matters they had to attend to prior to death.

Table 15.3 • Preparation for Death

Question 4: How do you prepare for your own death?

Responses	Number	Percent
I prepare myself for death diligently.	73	98.6
I do not give death much thought.	1	1.3
Total	74	99.9

Question 5: What kind of will do you wish to make before or at the time of your death?

Responses	Number	Percent
Wish for salvation	43	55.8
Best out of life	24	31.2
Not given it enough thought	9	11.7
Other	1	1.3
Total	77	100.0

Question 6: What are the important things you think you should do before you die?

Responses	Number	Percent
Physical and psychological preparations	57	79.2
Not given enough thought yet	8	11.1
Earthly arrangements, including wills	6	8.3
Others	1	1.4
Total	72	100.0

Ideal Way of Meeting Death and Conception of an After-Death Life. Question 7 was directed at assessing the views of ideal ways to meet death, and question 15 sought responses to the conception of an after-death life. Table 15.4 shows that the majority who believed in *heaven* and *another life after death* also expressed their ideal way of dying in a Christian context, although the contents of a *Christian way* of dying were not specified. *Dying peacefully* was also considered as an ideal way of dying for over 27 percent of the respondents. *Dying while working productively* was considered to be ideal for more than 10 percent of the Korean respondents. It is also noteworthy that to over 14 percent of the respondents it did not matter whether or not life after death exists; at least, over 10 percent who believed in a state of happiness after death held their optimism.

Regrets, Concerns, and Wishes. Emotional dimensions of death and dying were assessed in the areas of: the most regretful or painful things upon departure of this life (question 8); concerns over dying on foreign soil as immigrants (question 9); and the object most missed (question 11). The results are found in table 15.5.

Table 15.4 • Ideal Ways of Dying and Belief in Life after Death

Question 7: What is the most ideal way of dying?

Responses	Number	Percent
Christian way of dying	46	59.7
Dying peacefully	21	27.3
Dying while working productively	9	11.7
Beyond my will	1	1.3
Total	77	100.0

Question 15: What is your belief or thought about after-death matters?

Responses	Number	Percent
Believe in heaven	43	55.1
Believe in another life	16	20.5
Doesn't matter	11	14.1
There will be happiness	8	10.3
Total	78	100.0

Table 15.5 • Regrets, Concerns, and Missing Objects upon Death

Question 8: What would be the most regretful things or painful things to you when you die?

Responses	Number	Percent
Leaving others with pain or burdens	23	33.8
Being unfree from many attachments	21	30.9
Dying in miserable and disturbing conditions	15	22.1
Others	9	13
Total	68	100.0

Question 9: What is your thought about dying in this country as an immigrant?

Responses	Number	Percent
It's only a natural course.	50	69.4
It's a sad affair.	12	16.7
Have not given it much thought	10	13.9
Total	72	100.0

Question 11: Whom should you miss the most if you die now?

Responses	Number	Percent
Family	56	75.7
None	11	14.9
Friends	7	9.4
Total	74	100.0

Funeral Service and Burial Site. Questions 10 and 12 were designed to assess the respondents' attitudes on death management of funeral and burial considerations. The majority of Koreans residing in the United States (69%) wished to be buried where they reside by accepting the realities of life as reflected in table 15.8. However, 21 percent of the respondents still wished to be buried in Korea, their motherland, while 9.3 percent left that decision to whomever is responsible for their burial arrangements. Several kinds of funeral service were identified, as shown in the same table. More than half (51.4%) of the respondents wished to have their funeral services done on a small scale. Another 37.5 percent left that decision to those who would manage their funerals. Only two persons (2.7%) wished to have a grand-scale funeral service.

Recent Experiences with Death of Close Relatives and Friends. Question 13 was designed to assess the respondents' recent experiences with death of a close relative, including spouse, children, and parent, close friends, relatives, or church members. More than half (52.7%) of the respondents who had recent experiences of death of someone very close to them felt a sense of lamentation and void. Nearly one-third (29.7%) had a Christian perspective of death in terms of God's calling of one from this earthly life. Painful and sad experiences were common to 13.5 percent of the respondents.

Familiar Customs. Question 14 was on cultural aspects of death and dying with which the respondents were familiar. Table 15.8 shows several responses. More than one-third (37.8%) of the respondents stated that they were familiarized with a solemn climate, and almost the same proportion (36.5%) recalled the echoes of life's brevity. Others (20.3%) associated with the gathering of relatives at the event of death.

Table 15.6 • Funeral and Burial Considerations

Question 10: Where do you wish to be buried?

Responses	Number	Percent
Wherever I reside	31	41.3
In the United States	21	28.0
In Korea	16	21.3
It doesn't depend upon my wish	7	9.3
Total	75	99.9

Question 12: What kind of funeral service do you wish to be performed for you upon death?

Responses	Number	Percent
A small-scale funeral	37	51.4
At the wishes of the funeral master	27	37.5
Instruction already given	6	8.3
A grand-scale funeral	2	2.8
Total	72	100.0

Table 15.7 • Recent Experiences with Death of Relatives

Question 13: What were some of the most difficult experiences you had to deal with when one of your most significant persons (i.e., spouse, parent, children, close friends, relatives, or church member) died in the recent past (within the last five years)?

Responses	Number	Percent
A sense of lamentation	38	46.9
Pain and sadness	13	16.0
No particular feeling	2	2.5
Christian perspective	26	32.1
Other	2	2.5
Total	81	100.0

Table 15.8 • Familiar Cultural Aspects of Death and Dying

Question 14: What kind of cultural custom on death have you been most familiarized with?

Responses	Number	Percent
Solemn climate	28	37.3
Echoing the brevity of life	28	37.3
Gathering of relatives	15	20.0
Mourning sounds (eulogy)	2	2.7
Others	2	2.7
Total	75	100.0

Only a few (2.7%) recalled mourning sounds and funeral eulogy as linked to their cultural customs on death.

Selected Case Descriptions of Respondents

Respondent A: A Korean male in his sixties, married, a former accountant prior to his recent immigration to the United States, had some years of college education and is currently working as a bookkeeper. He attends a Korean Protestant church and has a few close relatives in the United States and in Korea. His perceived health condition is fair. He had one death in his family in the recent past and has attended at least fifteen other funeral services over the period of ten years from 1982 to 1992. His views on death and dying are summarized as follows:

"I begin to think that death is nearing. Death means that everything disappears from you on this earth, but I believe in the 'spiritual' world where no earthly pain exists. . . . Although I have not seriously prepared for my own death, I merely think I ought to get ready for it. I fear death, but one thing I should try is to hold no lingering attachment to life when my time comes. It is best to leave with the confirmation of love, forgiveness, and reconciliation which attest to humanness. It is ideal to die painless and as comfortably as you can. When possible, I'd like to prolong my life in healthy and productive ways, with no one condemning me for anything. Can you have any choice in the location of your death? I should only accept where it occurs. So it goes with my burial site, wherever it may be. I have no one whom I would miss. If there is one wish for my funeral service, I wish there are people who truly mourn for my passage. I feel an American funeral service arrangement is better. As death has visited others, it will, likewise, come to me soon. As my earthly passage has been full of difficulties, I only hope the passage beyond this life lies in a paradise if a spiritual world exists."

Respondent B: A Korean male in his forties, married but separated, immigrated to the United States within five to nine years, is doing clerical work. He has a college education and worked in a company clerical position before he came to the United States. He is Buddhist, and his parents and siblings are still in Korea. He has no relatives living here. His perceived health is good. None of his family members has died within the past five years, but he has attended seven funeral services over the past ten years, from 1983 to 1992. He has the following views on death and dying:

"When I think of death, I become fearful of it. Death's meaning is ambiguous to me, although the religious teaching on death suggests peace. I have been living without giving much thought to the preparation of my own death, nor to the making of my will. The ideal way of dying for me is dying peacefully. I have many attachments in my life, and it may become painful to let them go when I die. I would like to be buried in my home country, Korea. I have no one whom I would miss very much if I died right now. The difficulty I frequently encounter in the deaths of other people is my realization of the brevity of life. Although I have not adhered to any cultural tradition on death, I believe there is another life beyond this one."

Respondent C: A forty-year-old, married Korean woman, who has been living in the United States about fourteen years, is working in a clerical position. She has some years of college education and attends a Korean Presbyterian church in a suburban Chicago area. She has relatives, including parents-in-law, sister-in-law, parents, brothers, sister, nieces, and nephews, in Korea. Her perceived health is good. None of her family members have died within the past five years, although she has attended five funeral services over the past ten years. She has the following perspective on death and dying:

"Death is something that is inevitable to all. Heaven is meant to follow after death. Religion teaches about everlasting life, and I want to be saved when I die. The most important thing to do before your destination is to cleanse your mind and body. A Christian way of dying is ideal to me. There are so many things I will miss when I have to face death. It is only a natural thing that I die in this country where I have settled. I would like to be buried here. I will miss my family the most when I die, and my funeral service is up to whoever is handling it. When I attended other funeral services in the recent past, it was painful to find [someone] void of life. I believe that there is heaven after death."

Clinical Implications

To work effectively with Koreans who are going through bereavement, loss, and grief processes in clinical settings, it is important to understand their belief systems, cultural backgrounds, and contemporary practices of funeral rituals, attitudinal aspects in handling their loss, and bereavement processes. As noted earlier, individual and family variations also need to be taken into consideration when assessing both cognitive and affective domains associated with death and dying. Although Korean Americans have developed adaptational behavioral patterns of coping with life stress over the years, many recent-immigrant Koreans still hold onto their natal customs. At the same time, however, they struggle with letting go of their past attachments. Several approaches—cognitive, cultural, existential, and spiritual—briefly mentioned here may be applied to various settings, including hospital, clinic, church, or funeral places. Added to this are unresolved issues of grief work with their lost culture. It may be necessary for those close to the dying person that the mourning process be completed by effectively recalling various aspects of the lost culture and engaging more fully in the culture in which they now live (Levy-Warren, 1987).

Cognitive Approach

This approach stresses affirming clients' belief systems in defining the meaning of death from their cognitive reference points. Depending upon an understanding of their religious or spiritual interpretations of death and value systems, metaphoric messages are communicated to the bereaved in reaffirming their importance in framing the event of death.

The shamanistic interpretation of death, for instance, underscores a circular thinking by connecting all significant elements of life, death, incarnation, and ancestral spirit to achieve an ultimate harmony. Thus, death is not to be eradicated or buried unconsciously, but rather it becomes an integral part of the whole life that carries potential resources to be used in resolving current conflicts or afflictions. Shamanistic Korean clients who mourn need to be assisted in incorporating such a holistic perspective of death and to seek harmony within and without the self throughout bereavement processes and beyond.

Buddhist Koreans may become extremely sensitive to both reflective and affirmative assessments of the extent to which the dying or the deceased has maintained a virtuous life, as they believe in incarnation and causality in reward and punishment after death. Devotional prayers and benevolent deeds are viewed as prerequisites to leading one's destiny to a rewarding incarnation.

Christian faith also takes a cognitive approach, but from a different perspective or different metaphors. It stresses hope for resurrection and heavenly peace. Death replaces the afflicting journey of life and yields to a victorious entrance into the heavenly place where one joins one's predecessors. The degree to which the dying or the deceased has exhibited peace and hope during the terminal period often measures the depth of his or her faith. Thus, such belief serves an important cognitive energy to release tensions associated with the bereaved over loss. The following excerpt of the last words uttered by a Christian patient* to her attending family members carried an ongoing impact on their grief-resolving processes:

"Owing to your dedication in caring for me, I have come to a place of comfort. No words are found to appreciate you. Do not feel sorry, nor cry, my family. Rather, tell others that there's no one who passed away in glory like me though I am dying. I am so thankful to those people who have been involved in caring for me. Tell Reverends Lee and Kim whose words of prayer make me extremely comforting. Reverand Shin knows how our faith has been. Fear has long gone, and

---

*The author's mother-in-law, who passed away on December 14, 1985. The excerpt was from the last words spoken between the night of December 2 and dawn of December 3 prior to her death.

other than heaviness of my body, I am peaceful. 'Your time of freedom has come near,' said Jesus. What makes me anxious is your father. Although I miss my grandchildren, now I can see them from everywhere. Now, I'd like to rest my heavy body which did not take rest there. Your father did not take rest even though I told him so. Our marital life was faultless. Dr. Lee [attending chief physician] is a person worthy of receiving a grand award, and his wife must have given him her dedicated support! Heavenly father is one who provides us with comfort. What a wonderful place here I have come, away from the painful earthly life! Here I meet your maternal grandmother and Il-Chung [deceased son]. Good night is my last words. Children must be tired. Thanks for your loyalty."

Cultural Approach

Funeral rites provide the bereaved with opportunities for mourning in the contexts of kin-supportive milieu, emotional catharsis, life review, ancestral worship, progressive detachment, celebrating festivities, and spiritual reintegration of death and life. The rituals allow participants to mourn the losses of their close relatives, to offer prayers to comfort the spirits of the deceased, and to share their agony and guilt with those who console their spirits. Absence or circumvention of such rich cultural funeral rites for Korean immigrant families who do not observe traditional rituals may lead to a deprived sense of wholeness in connecting death to various dimensions inherent in the rites of passage. Periodic visits to graveyards on cultural holidays serve not only as commemorative occasions to renew their ancestral linkage, but also to allow any unfinished mourning to be carried out. A case example of delayed mourning from a cultural perspective is illustrated as follows:

> Dr. C. was a young refugee during the Korean War who was unable to fulfill his filial piety over thirty-three years due to the division of his motherland. When he recently visited his native land, he found that his mother had already passed away. His sorrow reached its peak when he kneeled down in front of his mother's burial site. He uttered in deep sorrow: "Oh mother! It was impossible to keep my three-day promise of return, but I came back to you even this late. And I am now in your bosom, don't you see? Why won't you respond to me? Mother, please answer me, please. . . ." (Chung, 1990, pp. 316–17)

Conclusion

Sands and Lee (1985) stress the importance of inclusion of children in attending to the issue of death and dying from their cultural perspective throughout the life cycle. It is important, however, to assess the family cultural milieu in terms of its contextual practice and the level of integrating family belief systems into mourning processes. Many first-generation Koreans, including the author, vividly retain their childhood memories of traditional rites of passage — funeral processions, foods, festivities, kin gatherings, wailing, and chanting. Although most of the emerging generations of Korean ancestry may never have experienced traditional funeral services, intergenerational accommodation of grief work is needed.

As noted in the findings of Korean immigrants' attitudes on death and dying, the majority of respondents held their religious beliefs, and they tended to become adaptive to their newly adopted sociocultural environments. While the majority think it is natural to die and be buried in the country of immigration, several concerns, such as being unfree from many attachments, leaving others with pain or burden, or dying in miserable conditions, are perceived to be sources of stress. While many significant cross-cultural considerations need to be articulated, death transcends various cultural rites in its existential contexts: it produces loss and grief; it creates existential crisis; it invites a new search for meaning; and it offers opportunities to regenerate and reconnect humanity.

CHAPTER SIXTEEN

The Filipino Perspective on Death and Dying

Ihande Weber

As Filipinos have been in the United States only since the beginning of the twentieth century, many people are unaware of Philippine history and traditions. The U.S. Census Bureau reported only 160 Filipinos in the United States in the 1910 Census; 5,603 in 1920; and 45,208 in 1930 (Wagner, 1973).

The Philippines are located some 600 miles southeast of the coast of mainland Asia and 7,000 miles west of San Francisco. Geographically, culturally, and economically, the Philippines have more in common with Indonesia and Malaysia than with the northern Asian countries of Japan and China. The Philippine people are predominantly of Malay stock, and Tagalog is the most common native language. English, however, is widely used and is taught in all schools. The majority of the people are Roman Catholics, and a small number of them are members of other Christian faiths, Muslims, or Buddhists.

Precolonial Filipino history was influenced by Indonesians and Malayans mixed with the early Negrito inhabitants. Hindu and Buddhist influences from India, Chinese traders, and Muslims from Arabia marked the time from the eighth century to the fifteenth century (Wagner, 1973). In 1565, the country became a colony of Spain. Although at different times the Portuguese, Dutch, and English claimed parts of the Philippines, Spanish rule was maintained until 1898. America, as a consequence of the Spanish-American War, purchased the Philippines by a treaty signed in Paris in December 1898. Under

215

the American colonial rule, Filipinos became subjects (not citizens) of the United States, and some limited immigration of agricultural workers to the States was encouraged. In 1934, the United States passed the Philippine Independence Act, and consequently, the Philippines were granted their independence on July 4, 1946, after a period of occupation by Japan during World War II.

Filipinos express their beliefs and attitudes about death by means of stories, images, and teachings rooted in both Western and Eastern spiritual traditions. Death in the Philippines is viewed as a destiny or fate, and part of the cycle of beginning and end. It is a natural occurrence, accepted with little hesitation if it happens expectedly, such as people dying of old age. Dying of old age is seen as a positive occurrence. Relatives are even thankful, for the deceased has already fulfilled his or her duties on earth, so deserves to be in heaven resting in peace. Death provides an opportunity to examine the deceased one's life, whether it was good and productive, or if it was full of challenges and shortcomings. For some people, this is the only opportunity they have to express their honest opinion about the dead person. Death of a family member also heals misunderstandings and conflicts among family members. This is an event that draws people together.

Death is also seen as part of the normal stages of life development. However, death that occurs before the expected time—death caused by a fatal accident and other tragedies—is very difficult to accept. People automatically put blame on that person for not taking charge and being responsible for their lives. They see that person as greedy, irresponsible, cowardly, and selfish for not being able to carry out expected responsibilities for self and for others. This initial anger and blaming is understood by all as the beginning of coping and dealing with the situation. Eventually, the dead person is forgiven, and sympathy and support are extended to the bereaved family. More prayers are offered to assure that the dead is forgiven for his or her sins to guarantee peace in heaven.

Death is also perceived with fear and apprehension, for it is the termination of biological life. Young generations of Filipinos, particularly, view death with fear. They are afraid to die and afraid of the dead as well. They believe the dead will come back as ghosts to haunt them. What makes it more vividly realistic to the younger generations is the supernatural power or "God-like image" that the older generations give to the dead. This supernatural power sends messages to the young ones that the dead will come back, invisible to the naked eye, and watch what they do with their lives on earth. This belief serves as a creative form of disciplining the young ones, instilling fear in them. It is believed to be an effective measure of curbing unacceptable or undesirable behavior.

Filipinos look at death as more than sorrow and loss. Happiness is also a part of how we view death. Generally, when people die at an expected time, people are happy and thankful because the dead have fulfilled their roles on earth and deserve to be happy in their second life. Filipinos look beyond the termination of biological existence. Death is the transition from life in the present to eternal life in the spiritual world. Filipinos believe that the personality of the dead person has not ceased to exist and that spiritual life has no end. The spirit of the dead will always be around—never forgotten, always remembered.

Death is also seen as the last cure for those who are incurably ill. More prayers are offered to the Lord to end their long sufferings and take them to heaven to attain pure spirit. Death is preferred over painful sufferings.

Coping

Filipinos are known culturally as shy people. Being frank, assertive, and talkative are not seen as positive contributors to smooth inter-personal relations with others. However, Filipinos are overwhelmingly open to discussing death. Open discussion has always been helpful in the initial coping with the situation. Even the community takes part in carrying out the discussion about the death of a particular person. The more the situation is shared and discussed, the more sympathy and help are provided to the bereaved family. Anger, shame, guilt, help-lessness, and inadequacy are shared among the family and the community.

Filipinos believe that the more you share of the situation, the easier the grieving will be. It is almost expected of every family to share the burden of death with the community. Some families prefer to main-tain silence and privacy about the dead. However, some people in the community would become suspicious and negatively interpret the deci-sion as refusing community sympathy and help. Or they might believe that something is bad about the dead person that should be kept hid-den. In this situation, it is useful to have bilingual medical and social workers. Even when clients are proficient in English, they may prefer to speak in their native language when communicating with their doc-tor, social worker, or clergy (Cook and Jenkins, 1982).

In addition, one's economic background dictates how open one wants to be with regard to discussing the situation. Rich families will usually keep the event rather private and family oriented. Families with less financial resources will depend more on the community for support and assistance.

Every family has their very own way of coping and dealing with a dying family member. The degree of acceptance, of course, varies from situation to situation. Factors such as family closeness, how much financial resources are available, timeliness of death, and age of the dying person all serve to measure how well a family copes with a dying person. Having financial resources at hand offers more opportunity to access needed medical treatment. Having limited financial resources, on the other hand, creates a greater need to depend on relatives and community for support.

Funeral Practices

Transition from life to death is achieved by means of funeral rites. The funeral reassures the living that immortality is a fact. Funeral practices decrease the intensity of the loss. These services actually serve the living more than the dead.

Preparing the dead for burial is an important matter. Again, the family's financial resources determine how the body will be prepared and how it will look for viewing. Those who have the money would have the dead embalmed, provide a decent casket, or maybe rent a vehicle to take the dead to the church for blessing.

The poor family, on the other hand, will be happy and content to have the dead person in a simple casket (usually made by the community people) and enough relatives and friends available to carry it on their shoulders to the church for blessing.

The dead person is viewed openly—a few days for those not embalmed or several days or sometimes weeks for those embalmed— until the last relative arrives to view the dead family member. When an older person dies, the children are encouraged to kiss the hand of the dead person as their last act of respect.

Taking pictures of the dead person with relatives and friends after the body is prepared for burial is something that has to be done. Photographs are kept for remembrance and become part of the family photo album.

The wake (*lamay*) is the most celebrated part of the funeral practice. It offers the family and friends the opportunity to be together, supporting and comforting each other in this time of loss—eating, dancing, playing table games, singing, reminiscing about good times and bad. Family members, friends, and community all participate as part of the wake. Food and refreshments are all donated by relatives and friends. Funeral expenses are usually covered by the money donated to the family.

The church offers mass and blessings for the dead. It is offered free for those who are poor, while a church fee is charged to those who can afford to pay it.

Families and friends accompany the dead from home, to church, and to the grave. The cemetery becomes the dead's fixed social place. Signs of upward and downward economic mobility are indicated by the size of the tomb. The manner of one's burial is as much a symbol of status as one's style of life.

An after-burial gathering is provided as a gesture of thanking everyone for their generosity, sympathy, support, and assistance.

The next nine days after burial are spent praying (*novena*). These rituals help decrease the guilt feelings of the living. The bereaved family is expected to dress in a certain way—all black for women and a white shirt and black pants for men. These garments are worn for a year to show their loss and grief.

After a year, it is expected that it is time to shed the grief and the sense of loss. It is after the fortieth day following the burial that Filipinos believe the spirit goes beyond earth. For the living, it is the time to let completely go, free of guilt, and rejoice for the dead. Also at this time, the dead are believed to be in a better world, and the living should be happy.

The dead are remembered as long as family and friends exist. An annual religious reminder is on the calendar. "All Souls Day" is celebrated every first of November and is a time to thank the Lord for taking care of the dead. Relatives and friends get together and visit the cemetery; they bring food and refreshments and celebrate the occasion. Photographs are also a constant reminder of the dead people. It would appear that rituals are from Christian (Western) and Buddhist or Shinto (Eastern) religions. Thus, those who provide care for dying patients must respect the patients' spiritual beliefs and preferences and must develop the resources necessary to meet the spiritual needs of patients and their families (Doka and Morgan, 1993).

Death of Children

The death of a child is the most difficult situation a family can face. Severe guilt is experienced by the parents. Coping and grieving do not come easily for the family and friends. To decrease the pain of the parents, rituals for children are much simpler and shorter. Children are perceived as "angels." Filipinos believe that children are innocent and have not committed sins, so they go directly to heaven after they die. They are also expected to wait and meet their parents in heaven when their turn comes.

Acculturation

The degree of acculturation plays an important role in determining how in tune Filipinos are with mainstream America when it comes to death practices. The older generation of Filipinos is still tied to the traditional values and practices and would like the tradition preserved as long as possible. The difficulty they face is that the longer they stay in America, the more they have to fight to preserve their traditional values and practices. Acculturation weakens their hold on traditional beliefs. In order for them to carry out their traditions, older generations prefer to be buried in the Philippines. This gives them the security and certainty that they will be long remembered.

Younger generations of Filipinos who are already much acculturated and have never witnessed a traditional funeral practice have difficulty understanding the values and importance of such rituals.

CHAPTER SEVENTEEN

Summary and Conclusion

One group that does not appear in this text is the Native American, or American Indian, who has, in the history of the United States, been severely oppressed. Today, family structures are losing key members who were previously responsible for passing on traditional matters, including death practices (Red Horse, 1988, p. 88). Native American traditional death beliefs are closer to those of the many Asian death practices described here. As Native Americans have become more acculturated and have married non-Indians, their death practices have become closer to mainstream American practices and beliefs (Parry, 1990).

This brief focus on Native Americans may be considered as a bridge between Eastern and Western beliefs. The central Buddhist belief system, examined in depth by Yeung in chapter 6, approaches death in a completely different way from the belief system of the Judeo-Christian tradition in the United States. Judaism, like Christianity, considers death to be the final stage of life. Thus, the Judeo-Christian differs from the Hindu-Buddhist tradition, which views death as a single event in a continuous chain of reincarnations (Markidas and Mindel, 1987, p. 173).

It is important for those of us who are helpers to understand the differences for persons whose reality of death and dying is more closely allied to a belief system that varies from our own. When such information is available to us, it improves clinical skills and can lead to improved social policy and further research. "Death is an inescapable aspect of each person's reality. Across time and culture, men have devised a variety of ways of handling the psychological, social, economic, and political

221

consequences of death and the processes of dying and of grieving" (Kalish and Reynolds, 1976, p. 187).

We commented in the Introduction that no book on death, dying, and religion can ignore AIDS. This epidemic has hit certain minorities very heavily, and the stigma society puts on gays and intravenous (IV) drug users creates additional problems for these groups. Whitmore (1988) says there is a cruel dimension to AIDS which churns up terror, shame, and guilt, and "at its most rudimentary, AIDS denial reflects the tacit judgment of society that AIDS happens only to an outcast few people who somehow deserve the disease" (p. 70). These ideas are thoroughly documented by Gerty and by Housel in their chapters. Both chapters provide an in-depth perspective of the problems AIDS creates for gays and for the Roman Catholic church.

The Catholic, Protestant, Jewish, Islamic, Christian Fundamentalist, and other religions are all "minority" groups within the United States. The death, dying, and grief belief systems described within each of these religious groups are different from each other. It is important for clinicians to understand the guidelines of each religion. Muslim immigration to the North American continent is increasing, is relatively recent, and includes "new immigrants from diverse cultural and linguistic backgrounds who are coping with a strange language, strange customs, and separation from their ancestral lands and traditions" (Abu-Laban, 1991, p. 6).

Gender

We believe it is important to emphasize again the gender difference as it relates to death and dying practices. Women are the caretakers, women are the mourners/criers, and women are often those who dress the deceased. This gender difference is noted across cultures and groups. In the description of an African group, the women have a "house of tears," and the men have a "male house." When discussing what women do in this group, it is stated that "the closest kinswomen begin to cry and the others gradually join in, and as they wail, the women cover their heads and faces" (Platt and Persico, 1992, p. 181).

African-American women, Mexican-American women, Puerto Rican women, Anglo or white women, and Cambodian women are the major mourners in their cultures (Parry, 1990). While there are differences among groups in death, dying, and grief practices, there are also similarities among groups. Gender roles ascribed during the dying, at the point of death, during the funeral, and in bereavement are similar. Ritual is present for all of the groups. The elaborateness of the ritual is not necessarily related to whether a society is more or less accepting of death. As ethnic groups become more acculturated within the United States, their death practices begin to take on some of the mainstream practices. There is often a mixture of traditional and mainstream practices.

Children

One major difference between Eastern and Western approaches to death and dying is how the death of a child is treated. In many Eastern cultures, the death of a child is dealt with quickly and seemingly without great sadness, since the child is without sin and considered a little angel. Since Western thinking is more linear than Eastern, the families who experience the death of a child feel it is an "off-time" death, and more painful. In fact, Ponzetti (1992) says the impact of a child's death upon the family is powerful and pervasive: "It is particularly traumatic because the death of a child violates one's expectations of the natural order; that the young are not supposed to die before the old" (p. 63). In African-American families, the death of a child creates excessive anxiety (Meagher and Bell, 1993). Also, parents often believe they are responsible for the death of their child.

Ritual

The similarities can also be observed in religious practice and ritual, particularly when certain Western religions have migrated around the world. As people accepted these new religions, they continued to use traditional practices when people died. Death practices are the most pervasive in most cultures. Sometimes traditional rituals were mixed with the new rituals. As Silva points out in her chapter, the Indian culture mixed with the Spanish (Roman Catholic) culture to create a mix of death practices.

Funeral Practices

Funeral practices vary in many areas; the Jews bury their deceased as rapidly as possible, with some emphasis on the funeral and graveside prayers but more emphasis on the period after death (*Shiva*). The fundamentalist Christians do not have a formal wake; the funeral itself is the only ritual. A funeral for Muslims is a transition from life in this world to life in the grave. Complete silence is recommended for the funeral, and no music or singing is allowed. The Mexican funeral brings the "whole" family together from many places; the bigger the crowd, the better. A big crowd indicates reverence for the deceased but also serves as a protection against death for the survivors. A Chinese funeral service is not elaborate, and public display of grief is strongly discouraged. The Korean funeral in the United States is a combination of Korean traditions and contemporary Protestant Christian practices. The African-American funeral is always a communal affair but may vary in content in different areas. In the Filipino culture, the deceased may be viewed for as many days as it takes for people to arrive for the funeral.

These are some of the differences in funeral practices, and as clinicians/helpers, we need to be open to learning varying death practices as they are needed to help those with whom we work. There are differences to consider between persons of minority groups who have newly immigrated to the United States and those minority groups such as Blacks, Mexicans, Puerto Ricans, and Native Americans who have been here for many generations. Chau (1991) states that what practitioners are expected to do in cross-cultural helping encounters may be considered more demanding and complicated than what they are expected to do in a monocultural setting.

Conclusion

We have put this book together with the expectation that many professional helpers could make use of the information in these chapters to help with the demanding and complicated job of assisting cross-cultural/minority-group individuals and families/lovers/friends with the overwhelming business of dying and bereavement. There is a need for more research and examination into these thanatology areas as U.S. minority populations change and increase steadily.

A final comment is a caveat: There are differences among groups and differences within groups, and the uniqueness of each family and person with whom we work must always be considered paramount.

REFERENCES

Introduction

Bowker, J. (1970). *The Problems of Suffering in Religions of the World*. London: Cambridge University Press.

Bynner, W. (Trans.). (1944). *The Way of Life: According to Lao Tzu*. New York: Capricorn Books.

Capra, F. (1984). *The Tao of Physics*. New York: Bantam.

Chan, W. T. (1963). *Sourcebook of Chinese Philosophy*. Princeton, NJ: Princeton University Press.

Cooklin, A. (1989). Tenderness and toughness in the face of distress. *Palliative Medicine, 3*(2), 89–95.

Cullinan, A. (1993). Spiritual care of the traumatized: A necessary component. In K. J. Doka with J. D. Morgan (Eds.), *Death and Spirituality*. New York: Baywood.

De La Cancela, V., and McDowell, A. (1992). AIDS: Health care intervention models for communities of color. *Journal of Multicultural Social Work, 2*(3), 107–122.

Doka, K. J., and Jendreski, M. (1986–87). Spiritual support for the suffering: Clergy attitudes toward bereavement. *Loss, Grief and Care, 1*(1–2), 155–160.

Fox, R. C. (1981). The sting of death in American society. *Social Service Review, 55*(1), 42–59.

Grollman, E. A. (1993). Death in Jewish thought. In K. J. Doka, with J. D. Morgan (Eds.), *Death and Spirituality*. New York: Baywood.

Huber, J. T. (1993). Death and AIDS: A review of the medico-legal literature. *Death Studies, 17*(3), 225–232.

Humphreys, S. C., and King, H. (Eds.). (1981). *Mortality and Immortality: The Anthropology and Archeology of Death*. London: Academic Press.

Irish, D. P. (1993). Multiculturalism and the majority population. In D. P. Irish, K. F. Lundquist, and V. J. Nelsen (Eds.), *Ethnic Variations in Dying, Death and Grief*. Washington, DC: Taylor and Francis.

225

Irish, D. P., Lundquist, K. F., and Nelsen, J. V. (Eds.). (1993). *Ethnic Variations in Dying, Death and Grief.* Washington, DC: Taylor and Francis.

Kapleau, P. (1989). *The Wheel of Life and Death.* New York: Doubleday.

Kapp, M. B. (1993). Living and dying in the Jewish way. *Death Studies, 17*(3), 267–276.

Leary, W. E. (1990). Uneasy doctors add race-consciousness to diagnostic tools. *New York Times,* Sept. 25, p. 13.

Miller E. J. (1993). A Roman Catholic view of death. In K. J. Doka with J. D. Morgan (Eds.), *Death and Spirituality.* New York: Baywood.

New, P. K. (1965). Another approach to professionalism. *American Journal of Nursing, 65*(2), 124–126.

Parry, J. K. (1989). *Social Work Theory and Practice with the Terminally Ill.* New York: Haworth.

Parry, J. K. (1990). *Social Work with the Terminally Ill: A Transcultural Perspective.* Springfield, IL: Charles C. Thomas.

Peoples, E. H., and Francis, G. M. (1968). Some psychological obstacles to effective health care practice. *Nursing Forum, 7*(3), 28–37.

Platt, L. A., and Persico, V. R., Jr. (1992). *Grief in Cross-Cultural Perspective: A Casebook.* New York: Garland.

Richard E., and Shepard, A. C. (1981). Giving up smoking: A lesson in loss theory. *American Journal of Nursing, 81*(2), 755–757.

Rosenblatt, P. C. (1993). Cross-cultural variation in the experience, expression and understanding of grief. In D. P. Irish, K. F. Lundquist, and V. J. Nelsen (Eds.), *Ethnic Variations in Dying, Death and Grief.* Washington, DC: Taylor and Francis.

Ryan, D. (1993). Death: Eastern perspective. In K. J. Doka with J. D. Morgan (Eds.), *Death and Spirituality.* Baywood.

Schoeneck, T. K. (1991). *Hope for the Bereaved.* Syracuse, NY: Hope Press.

Stillion, J. (1985). *Death and the Sexes.* Washington, DC: Hemisphere.

Truitner, K., and Truitner, N. (1993). Death and dying in Buddhism. In D. P. Irish, K. F. Lundquist, and V. J. Nelsen (Eds.), *Ethnic Variations in Dying, Death, and Grief.* Washington, DC: Taylor and Francis.

Tseng, W. S., and Hsu, J. 1991. *Culture and Family.* New York: Haworth.

Vachon, M. L. S. (1987). *Occupational Stress in the Care of the Critically Ill, the Dying, and the Bereaved.* New York: Hemisphere.

Watson, B. (Trans.). (1968). *Chuang Tzu: The Complete Works.* New York: Columbia University Press.

Yang, C. K. (1973). The role of religion in Chinese society. In J. Meskill (Ed.), *An Introduction to Chinese Civilization.* Lexington, MA: D. C. Health.

Chapter 1: Women, Death, and Dying

Aiken, L. (1985). *Dying, Death and Bereavement.* Boston: Allyn and Bacon.

226

Belle, D. (1982). The stress of caring: Women as providers of social support. In L. Goldberger and A. Breznitz (Eds.), *Handbook of Stress* (pp. 496–505). New York: Free Press.

Broverman, I., Vogel, S., Broverman, D., Clarkson, F., and Rosencrantz, P. (1972). Sex-role stereotypes: A current appraisal. *Journal of Social Issues, 28,* 59–78.

Brown, J. (1990). Social work practice with the terminally ill in the Black community. In J. Parry (Ed.), *Social Work Practice with the Terminally Ill* (pp. 67–82). Springfield, IL: Charles C. Thomas.

Campos, A. (1990). Social work practice with Puerto Rican terminally ill clients and their families. In J. Parry (Ed.), *Social Work Practice with the Terminally Ill* (pp. 129–143). Springfield, IL: Charles C. Thomas.

Cartwright, A., Hockey, L., and Anderson, J. (1973). *Life before Death.* London: Routledge and Kegan Paul.

Devore, W. (1990). The experience of death: A Black perspective. In J. Parry (Ed.), *Social Work Practice with the Terminally Ill* (pp. 47–66). Springfield, IL: Charles C. Thomas.

Gottlieb, N. (1980). The older woman. In N. Gottlieb (Ed.), *Alternative Social Services for Women* (pp. 280–319). New York: Columbia University Press.

Hirayama, K. (1990). Death and dying in Japanese culture. In J. Parry (Ed.), *Social Work Practice with the Terminally Ill* (pp. 159–174). Springfield, IL: Charles C. Thomas.

Holden, K. (1989). Women's economic status in old age and widowhood. In M. Ozawa (Ed.), *Women's Life Cycle and Economic Insecurity* (pp. 143–169). New York: Praeger.

Hooyman, N., and Ryan N. (1987). Women as caretakers of the elderly: Catch-22 dilemmas. In J. Figueira-McDonough and R. Sarri (Eds.), *The Trapped Woman* (pp. 143–171). Newbury Park, CA: Sage.

Hoschild, A. (1989). *The Second Shift: Working Parents and the Revolution at Home.* New York: Viking.

Kalish, R. (1985). *Death, Grief and Caring Relationships* (2nd ed.). Monterey, CA: Brooks/Cole.

Kastenbaum, R., and Kastenbaum, B. (1989). *Encyclopedia of Death.* Phoenix, AZ: Oryx Press.

Kessler, R., and McLeod, J. (1984). Sex differences in vulnerability to undesired life events. *American Sociological Review, 49,* 620–631.

King, A. (1990). A Samoan perspective: Funeral practices, death and dying. In J. Parry (Ed.), *Social Work Practice with the Terminally Ill* (pp. 175–189). Springfield, IL: Charles C. Thomas.

Kübler-Ross, E. (1969). *On Death and Dying.* New York: Macmillan.

Lang, L. (1990). Aspects of the Cambodian death and dying process. In J. Parry (Ed.), *Social Work Practice with the Terminally Ill* (pp. 205–211). Springfield, IL: Charles C. Thomas.

Lopata, H. (1987). Women's family roles in life course perspective. In B. Hess and M. Ferree (Eds.), *Analyzing Gender* (pp. 381–407). Newbury Park, CA: Sage.

Miller, D. (1981). The "sandwich" generation: Adult children of the aging. *Social Work, 26,* 419–423.

Mor, V., Greer, D., and Kastenbaum, R. (1988). *The Hospice Experiment.* Baltimore, MD: Johns Hopkins University Press.

Parry, J. (Ed.). (1990). *Social Work Practice with the Terminally Ill: A Transcultural Perspective.* Springfield, IL: Charles C. Thomas.

Rando, T. (1984). *Grief, Dying and Death.* Champaign, IL: Research Press.

Rando, T. (1985). Bereaved parents: Particular difficulties, unique factors, and treatment issues. *Social Work, 30,* 19–23.

Salcido, R. (1990). Mexican-Americans: Illness, death and bereavement. In J. Parry (Ed.), *Social Work Practice with the Terminally Ill* (pp. 99–112). Springfield, IL: Charles C. Thomas.

Schor, J. (1991). *The Overworked American: The Unexpected Decline of Leisure.* New York: Basic Books.

Stillion, J. (1985). *Death and the Sexes.* Washington, DC: Hemisphere.

Stroebe, M., and Stroebe, W. (1983). Who suffers more? Sex differences in the health risks of the widowed. *Psychological Bulletin, 93,* 279–301.

Stroebe, W., and Stroebe, M. (1987). *Bereavement and Health.* Cambridge: Cambridge University Press.

Ta, M., and Chung, C. (1990). Death and dying: A Vietnamese cultural perspective. In J. Parry (Ed.), *Social Work Practice with the Terminally Ill* (pp. 191–204). Springfield, IL: Charles C. Thomas.

Teltsch, K. (1992). Men at care. *San Jose Mercury News,* July 17, pp. C1, 8.

Veroff, J., Douvan, E., and Kulka, R. (1981). *The Inner American: A Self-Portrait from 1957 to 1976.* New York: Basic Books.

Weisman, A. (1972). *On Dying and Denying: A Psychiatric Study of Terminality.* New York: Behavioral Publications.

Wethington, E., McLeod, J., and Kessler, R. (1987). The importance of live events for explaining sex differences in psychological distress. In R. Barnett, L. Biener, and G. Baruch (Eds.), *Gender and Stress* (pp. 144–156). New York: Free Press.

Wilson, B., and Ryan, A. (1990). Working with the terminally ill Chinese-American patient. In J. Parry (Ed.), *Social Work Practice with the Terminally Ill* (pp. 145–158). Springfield, IL: Charles C. Thomas.

Chapter 2: The Roman Catholic/Christian Church and AIDS

Called to compassion and responsibility, a response to the HIV/AIDS crisis. (1989). Washington, DC: National Conference of Catholic Bishops.

Church and Friary of Saint Francis of Assisi. (1993). *Bulletin,* Jan.-Feb. (135 West 31st Street, New York, NY 10001)

How Uganda battles AIDS. (1993). *Maryknoll Mission Journal,* April, p. 34.

New York Times. (1993). April 30.

Perelli, R. J. (1991). *Ministry to Persons with AIDS.* Minneapolis, MN: Augsburg Press.

The many faces of AIDS, a gospel response. (1987). Washington, DC: United States Catholic Conference.

Trinity Missions. (1993). Silver Spring, MD.

Chapter 3: Judaism and Death: Practice Implications

Abrahams, I. (1926). *Hebrew Ethical Wills.* Philadelphia, PA: Jewish Publication Society.

Baeck, L. (1948). *The Essence of Judaism.* New York: Schocken.

Bogot, H. (1987). *AIDS: A Glossary of Jewish Values.* New York: Union of American Hebrew Congregations.

Getzel, G. S. (1983). Older people: A functional view of their reminiscence. *Journal of Jewish Communal Service, 59,* 318–325.

Goodman, A. (1981). *A Plain Pine Box: A Return to Simple Funerals and Eternal Traditions.* New York: Ktav.

Herzberg, W. (1960). *Protestant, Catholic, Jew.* New York: Doubleday.

Heschel, A. J. (1954). *Man's Quest for God.* New York: Schocken.

Heschel, A. J. (1974). Death as homecoming. In J. Reimer (Ed.), *Jewish Reflections on Death* (pp. 58–73). New York: Schocken.

Kaplan, A. (1974). Life and death as partners. In J. Reimer (Ed.), *Jewish Reflections on Death* (pp. 126–133). New York: Schocken.

Lamm, M. (1969). *The Jewish Way of Death and Mourning.* Middle Village, NY: Jonathan David.

Liebman, J. L. (1946). *Peace of Mind.* New York: Simon and Schuster.

Malcolm, A. H. (1991). Spanning cultural canyons: Counseling interfaith couples. *New York Times,* Oct. 1, p. B2.

Meier, L. (1988). *Jewish Values in Psychotherapy: Essays on Vital Issues on the Search for Meaning.* Lanhan, MD: University Press of America.

Milligram, A. (1977). *Jewish Worship.* Philadelphia, PA: Jewish Publication Society of America.

Plaut, W. G. (1981). *Torah: A Modern Commentary.* New York: Union of American Hebrew Congregations.

Reimer, J. (1974). Introduction: Modernity and the Jewish way of death. In J. Reimer (Ed.), *Jewish Reflections on Death* (pp. 5–14). New York: Schocken.

Reimer, J., and Stampfer, N. (1983). *Ethical Wills: A Modern Anthology.* New York: Schocken.

Rosenbloom, M. (1988). Lesson of the Holocaust in mental health practice. In R. L. Brahm (Ed.), *The Psychological Perspectives on the Holocaust and Its Aftermath* (pp. 145–159). New York: Columbia University Press.

Rosner, F. (1991). *Modern Medicine and Jewish Ethics.* Hoboken, NJ: Ktav.

Schlindler, A. M. (1989). Jewish community service in support of people with AIDS. Sermon delivered at Leo Baeck Temple, March, Los Angeles.

Selzer, R. (1980). *Jewish People, Jewish Thought: The Jewish Experience in History.* New York: Macmillan.

Silver, D. J. (1974). The right to die. In J. Reimer (Ed.), *Jewish Reflections on Death* (pp. 117–125). New York: Schocken.

Solveitchik, J. B. (1974). The Halakah of the first day. In J. Reimer (Ed.), *Jewish Reflections of Death* (pp. 76–83). New York: Schocken.

Trepp, L. (1962). *Eternal Faith, Eternal People: A Journey into Judaism.* Englewood Cliffs, NJ: Prentice Hall.

Zborowski, M., and Herzog, E. (1952). *Life Is with People: The Culture of the Shetl.* New York: Schocken.

Chapter 4: Walking through the Valley of Death: Grief and Fundamentalism

Abbott, D., Berry, M., and Meredith, W. (1990). Religious belief and practice: A potential asset in helping families. *Family Relations, 39*(4), 443–448.

Adams, J. (1971). *Competent to Counsel.* Nutley, NJ: Presbyterian and Reformed Publishers.

AIDSline. (1982). In service, prayer, religious communities seek role. New Brunswick, NJ: Robert Wood Johnson Foundation.

Becker, E. (1975). *The Denial of Death.* New York: Free Press.

Bergin, A. (1991). Values and religious issues in psychotherapy and mental health. *American Psychologist, 46*(4): 394–403.

Birenbaum, L. (1990). Family coping with childhood cancer. *Hospice Journal, 6*(3), 17–33.

Coles, R. (1990). *The Spiritual Life of Children.* Boston, MA: Houghton Mifflin.

Denton, R. (1990). The religiously fundamentalist family: Training for assessment and treatment. *Journal of Social Work Education, 26*(1), 6–14.

Dobson, E. (1986). Learning from our weaknesses. *Fundamentalist Journal, 5*(4), 12.

Doka, K. (1989). *Disenfranchised Grief: Recognizing Hidden Sorrow.* Lexington, MA: Lexington.

Ellison, C. (1991). Religious involvement and subjective well-being. *Journal of Health and Social Behavior, 32*(3), 80–99.

Falwell, J. (1986). What is a good church? *Fundamentalist Journal, 5*(4), 10.

Family living: Explaining death to a child. (1986). *Fundamentalist Journal,* 5(4), 54.

Farrell, J. (1982). The dying of death: Historical perspectives. *Death Education,* 6(2), 105–123.

Galanter, M., Larson, D., and Rubenstone, E. (1991). Christian psychiatry: The impact of evangelical belief on clinical practice. *American Journal of Psychiatry,* 148(1), 91–93.

Griffith, J. (1986). Employing the God-family relationship in therapy with religious families. *Family Process,* 25(12), 609–618.

Hunsberger, B. (1991). Empirical work in the psychology of religion. *Canadian Psychology,* 32(3), 497–503.

Hyles, J. (1974). *How to Rear Children.* Hammond, IN: Hyles-Anderson.

Koenig, N. (1988). Religious behaviors and death anxiety in later life. *Hospice Journal,* 4(1), 3–24.

Leming, M. (1980). Religion and death: A test of Homan's thesis. *Omega,* 10(4), 347–363.

Lifton, R., and Stozier, C. (1990). Waiting for Armageddon. *New York Times Book Review,* Aug. 12, p. 1.

Lightner, R. (1986). A plea to fellow Fundamentalists. *Fundamentalist Journal,* 5(6), 14–15.

Lowenberg, F. (1988). *Religion and Social Work Practice in Contemporary American Society.* New York: Columbia University Press.

Marty, M. (1981). Morality, ethics, and the new Christian Right. *Hastings Center Report,* 8, 14–17.

Millison, M., and Dudley, J. (1990). The importance of spirituality in hospice work. *Hospice Journal,* 6(3), 63–78.

Mollica, R., Streets, F., Boscarino, J., and Redlich, F. (1986). A community study of formal pastoral counseling activities of the clergy. *American Journal of Psychiatry,* 143(3), 323–328.

Ness, R. and Wintrob, R. (1980). The emotional impact of fundamentalist religious practice: An empirical study of intergroup variation. *American Journal of Orthopsychiatry,* 50, 302–315.

Rando, T. (1984). *Grief, Dying, and Death.* Champaign, IL: Research Press.

Rando, T. (1988). *Grieving: How to Go On Living When Someone You Love Dies.* Lexington, MA: Lexington.

Rice, J. (1971). *God in Your Family.* Murfreesboro, TN: Sword of the Lord Press.

Thiessen, H. (1969). *Introductory Lectures in Systematic Theology.* Grand Rapids, MI: Eerdmans.

Wiersbe, W., and Wiersbe, D. (1986). *Comforting the Bereaved.* Chicago: Moody Press. Adapted in *Fundamentalist Journal,* 5(4), 42.

Wilson-Ford, V. (1992). Health protective behaviors of rural black elderly women. *Health and Social Work,* 17(1), 28–36.

Young, M., and Daniels, S. (1980). Born-again status as a factor in death anxiety. *Psychological Reports,* 47, 347–370.

Chapter 6: Buddhism, Death, and Dying

Conze, E. (1975). *Buddhism: Its Essence and Development.* New York: Harper & Row.

Dhammananda, K. S. (1968). *Day to Day Buddhist Practices.* Kuala Lumpur: Buddhist Missionary Society.

Dhammananda, K. S. (1982). *What the Buddhists Believe.* Kuala Lumpur: Buddhist Missionary Society.

Fisher, J. (1985). *The Case for Reincarnation.* New York: Bantam Books.

Karma-glin-pa (1987). *The Tibetan Book of the Dead.* Trans. by F. Fremantle and C. Trungpa. Boston, MA: Shambhala.

KlinKenborg, V. (1992). At the age of eternity. *Life,* March, pp. 64–73.

Narada, M. T. (1972). *Facts of Life.* Kuala Lumpur: Buddhist Missionary Society.

Narada, M. T. (1973). *The Buddha and His Teachings.* Singapore: Buddhist Meditation Center.

Nyima, C. (1991). *The Bardo Guide Book.* Hong Kong: Rangjung Yeshe Publications.

Rahula, W. (1962). *What the Buddha Taught.* New York: Grove Press.

sGam-po-pa. (1986). *The Jewel Ornament of Liberation,* trans. by H. V. Guenther. Boston, MA: Shambhala.

Sheng, Y. (1991). *Questions on Buddhism* (Chinese). Taipei: Tung Chu Publications.

Smith, H. (1986). *The Religions of Man.* New York: Harper & Row.

Stevenson, I. (1977). The explanatory value of the idea of reincarnation. *Journal of Nervous and Mental Disease, 5,* 305–326.

Story, F. (1975). *Rebirth as Doctrine and Experience.* Sri Lanka: Buddhist Publication Society.

Suzuki, B. L. (1990). *Mahayana Buddhism.* Boston, MA: Unwin Paperbacks.

Wambach, H. (1979). *Life before Life.* New York: Bantam Books.

Weiss, B. (1988). *Many Lives, Many Masters.* New York: Simon & Schuster.

Willson, M. (1987). *Rebirth and the Western Buddhist.* London: Wisdom Publications.

Chapter 7: Death, Dying, and Religion among Dominican Immigrants

Acosta, F. X. (1980). Self-described reasons for premature termination of psychotherapy by Mexican Americans, Black Americans, and Anglo Americans. *Psychological Reports, 47,* 345–443.

Aguilar, I., and Wood, V. N. (1976). Therapy through a death ritual. *Social Work, 21*(1).

Anthony, S. (1972). *The Discovery of Death in Childhood and After.* New York: Basic Books.

Baekeland, F., and Lundwall, L. (1975). Dropping out of treatment: A critical review. *Psychological Bulletin, 82*(5), 738–783.

Bowen, M. (1978). Family reaction to death. *Therapy in Clinical Practice.* New York: Jason Aronson.

Bowlby, J. (1960). Grief and mourning in infancy and early childhood. *The Psychoanalytic Study of the Child.* New York: International Universities Press.

Bowman, L. (1959). *The American Funeral.* Westport, CT: Greenwood Press.

Boyd-Franklin, N. (1982). Family therapy with black families. In S. J. Korchin (Ed.), *Minority Mental Health.* New York: Praeger.

Brandon, E. (1976). Folk medicine in Louisiana. In W. D. Hand (Ed.), *American Folk Medicine: A Symposium.* Berkeley: University of California Press.

Burnell, G. M., and Burnell, A. L. (1989). *Clinical Management of Bereavement: A Handbook for Health-Care Professionals.* New York: Human Science Press.

Canda, E. R., and Phaobtong, T. (1992). Buddhism as a support system for Southeast Asian refugees. *Social Work, 37*(1), 61–67.

Canino, I., and Canino, G. (1982). Culturally syntonic family therapy for migrant Puerto Ricans. *Hospital and Community Psychiatry, 33.*

Comas-Diaz, L. (1981). Ethnicity and treatment: Puerto Rican espiritismo and psychotherapy. *American Journal of Orthopsychiatry, 51*(94).

Cornett, C. (1992). Toward a more comprehensive personology: Integrating a spiritual perspective into social work practice. *Social Work, 37*(2), 101–102.

Delgado, M. (1988). Groups in Puerto Rican spiritism: Implications for clinicians. In C. Jacobs and D. Bowles (Eds.), *Ethnicity and Race: Critical Concepts in Social Work.* Washington, DC: NASW.

Deutsch, H. (1937). Absence of grief. *Psychoanalytic Quarterly, 6,* 12–23.

Frank, J. D. (1961). *Persuasion and Healing: A Comparative Study of Psychotherapy.* Baltimore, MD: Johns Hopkins University Press.

Fulmer, R. H. (1983). A structural approach to unresolved mourning in single parent family systems. *Journal of Marital and Family Therapy, 9*(3).

Garcia-Preto, N. (1980). Puerto Rican families. In M. McGoldrick, J. K. Pearce, and J. Giordano (Eds.), *Ethnicity and Family Therapy.* New York: Guilford Press.

Garcia-Preto, N. (1989). Puerto Rican families. In M. McGoldrick, J. Pearce, and J. Giordano (Eds.), *Ethnicity and Family Therapy.* New York: Guilford Press.

Garrison, V. (1977a). Doctor, espiritista, or psychiatrist? Health seeking behavior in a Puerto Rican neighborhood of New York City. *Medical Anthropology, 1*(2), 69–191.

233

References

Garrison, V. (1977b). Puerto Rican syndrome in psychiatry and espiritismo. In V. Crapanzano and V. Garrison (Eds.), *Case Studies in Spirit Possession* (pp. 383–449). New York: Wiley.

Ghalis, S. (1977). Cultural sensitivity and the Puerto Rican client. *Social Casework, 58*(8), 459–468.

Harwood, A. (1977). Spiritist beliefs and practices in the home and family: The wife and mother as caretaker of the family's spiritual protection. *Rx Spiritist as Needed* (pp. 144–149). Ithaca, NY: Cornell University Press.

Hessler, R. M., Nolan, B., and Ogbru, P. N. (1975). Intraethnic diversity: Health care of the Chinese Americans. *Human Organization, 34,* 253–262.

Joseph, M. V. (1988). Religion and social work practice. *Social Casework, 69*(7).

Kiev, A. (1968). *Curanderismo: Mexican American Folk Psychiatry.* New York: Free Press.

Kübler-Ross, E. (1969). *On Death and Dying.* New York: Collier.

Lacourciere, L. (1976). A survey of folk medicine in French Canada from early times to the present. In W. D. Hand (Ed.), *American Folk Medicine: A Symposium.* Berkeley: University of California Press.

Lazarus, R. S., and Folkman, S. (1984). *Stress, Appraisal, and Coping.* New York: Springer.

Lefley, H. P. (1984). Cross-cultural training for mental health practitioners: Effects on the delivery of services. *Hospital and Community Psychiatry, 35*(12), 1227–1229.

Levy, C. (1993). Survivors are some of neediest. *New York Times,* Jan. 7, B2.

Minuchin, S., and Fishman, C. (1981). *Family Therapy Techniques.* Cambridge, MA: Harvard University Press.

Monat, A., and Lazarus, R. (1991). *Stress and Coping* (3rd ed.). New York: Columbia University Press.

Nelson, J. (1975). Dealing with resistance in social work practice. *Social Casework, 56*(10), 587–592.

Patton, K. (1966). Science, religion, and death. *Zygon: Journal of Religion and Science, 14,* 332–341.

Rogler, L. N., and Hollingshead, A. (1961). The Puerto Rican spiritualists as a psychiatrist. *American Journal of Sociology, 67,* 17–21.

Rosen, H. (1991). Child and adolescent bereavement. *Child and Adolescent Social Work, 8*(1).

Sandoval, M. C. (1977). Santeria: Afrocuban concepts of disease and its treatment in Miami. *Journal of Operational Psychiatry, 8,* 52–63.

Snow, L. (1974). Popular medicine in a black neighborhood. In Spiecer, E. H. (Ed.), *Ethnic Medicine in the Southwest.* Tucson, AZ: University Press.

Sue, S. (1977). Community mental health services to minority groups: Some optimism, some pessimism. *American Psychologist, 32*(8), 616–624.

U.S. Bureau of the Census. (1991). *The Hispanic Population in the United States: March 1990.* Washington, DC: U.S. Government Printing Office.

Vastola, J., Nierenberg, A., and Graham, E. H. (1986). The lost and found group: Group work with bereaved children. In A. Gitterman and L. Shulman (Eds.), *Mutual Aid Groups and the Life Cycle*. Itasca, IL: Peacock.

Chapter 8: Mexican-American Women: Death and Dying

Alegria, D., Guerra, E., Martinez, C., and Meyer, G. G. (1977). El hospital invisible: A study of Curanderismo. *Archives of General Psychiatry, 34,* 1345–1357.

Asuncion-Lande, N. (1979). Problems and strategies for sexual identity and cultural integration: Mexican-American women on the move. *International Journal of Intercultural Relations, 3*(4), 497–505.

Becker, E. (1973). *The Denial of Death.* New York: Macmillan.

Blea, I. I. (1992). *La Chicana and the Intersection of Race, Class, and Gender.* New York: Praeger.

Clark, M. (1959). *Health in the Mexican-American Culture.* Berkeley: University of California Press.

Cuellar, J. (1990). *Aging and Health: Hispanic-American Elders.* Stanford, CA: Stanford Geriatric Center.

Del Castillo, A. R. (1977). Malintzin Tenepal: A preliminary look into new perspective. In R. Sanchez and R. M. Cruz (Eds.), *Essays on La Mujer* (pp. 124–149). Los Angeles, CA: Chicano Studies Center Publications, UCLA.

Edgerton, R. B., Karno, M., and Fernandez, I. (1970). Curanderismo in the metropolis. *American Journal of Psychotherapy, 24,* 133–134.

Elsasser, N., MacKenzie, K., Tixier, Y., and Vigil, Y. (1980). *Las Mujeres: Conversations from a Hispanic Community.* New York: Feminist Press.

Franz, C. (1979). *The People's Guide to Mexico.* Santa Fe, NM: John Muir Publications.

Gonzales, S. (1977). The white feminist movement: The Chicana perspective. *Social Science Journal, 14*(2), 68–76.

Kalish, R. A., and Reynolds, D. K. (1976). *Death and Ethnicity: A Psychocultural Study.* Los Angeles: University of Southern California Press.

Kaplan, B. H., Cassell, J. C., and Gorse, S. (1977). Social support and health. *Medical Care, 15,* 47–57.

Madsen, W. (1964). *Society and Health in the Lower Rio Grande Valley.* Austin, TX: Hogg Foundation.

Manzanedo, H. G., Walters, E. G., and Lorig, K. R. (1980). Health and illness perceptions of the Chicana. In M. B. Melville (Ed.), *Twice a Minority: Mexican-American Women* (pp. 1991–2007). St. Louis, MO: Mosby.

Paz, O. (1951). *The Labyrinth of Solitude.* New York: Grove.

Saunders, L. (1954). *Cultural Differences and Medical Care: The Case of the Spanish-Speaking People of the Southwest.* New York: Russell Sage Foundation.

Stein, H. D., and Cloward, R. A. (1958). *Social Perspectives on Behavior.* New York: Collier-Macmillan.

Chapter 9: Spirituality and Death and Dying from a Gay Perspective

Andersen, H., and MacElveen-Hoehn, P. (1988). Gay clients with AIDS: New challenges for hospice programs. *Hospice Journal, 4*(2), 37–54.

Becker, E. (1973). *The Denial of Death.* New York: Free Press.

Biller, R., and Rice, S. (1990). Experiencing multiple loss of persons with AIDS: Grief and bereavement issues. *Health and Social Work, 15*(4), 283–290.

Boykin, F. (1991). The AIDS crisis and gay male survivor guilt. *Smith College Studies in Social Work, 61*(3), 247–259.

Bullough, V. (1975). Sex and the medical model. *Journal of Sex Research, 11*(4), 291–303.

Clark, J. M., Brown, J. C., and Hochstein, L. M. (1989). Institutional religion and gay/lesbian oppression. *Marriage and Family Review, 14*(3–4), 265–284.

Fortunato, J. E. (1987). *AIDS: The Spiritual Dilemma.* New York: Harper & Row.

Lovejoy, N. (1989). AIDS: Impact on the gay man's homosexual and heterosexual families. *Marriage and Family Review, 14*(3–4), 285–316.

Nelson, J. B. (1981–82). Religious and moral issues in working with homosexual clients. *Journal of Homosexuality, 7*(2–3), 163–175.

Roscoe, W. (Ed.). (1988). *Living the Spirit: A Gay American Indian Anthology.* New York: St. Martin's.

Tibier, K. B., Walker, G., and Rolland, J. (1989). Therapeutic issues when working with families of persons with AIDS. *Marriage and Family Review, 13*(1–2), 81–128.

Weitz, R. (1989). Uncertainty and the lives of persons with AIDS. *Journal of Health and Social Behavior, 30*(3), 270–281.

Williams, W. L. (1986). *The Spirit and the Flesh: Sexual Diversity in American Indian Culture.* Boston, MA: Beacon Press.

Chapter 10: The Lesbian Perspective on Death and Dying

Berube, A. (1989). *Coming Out Under Fire: The History of Gay Men and Women in World War II.* New York: Free Press.

Coleman, E. (1982). Developmental steps of the coming-out process. *Journal of Homosexuality, 7,* 31–43.

Cornell, G. (1992). Reconstructionist Jews condone same-sex unions. *Santa Cruz Sentinel,* March 7.

Cruikshank, M. (Ed.). (1982). *Lesbian Studies, Present and Future.* New York: Feminist Press.

Grahn, J. (1984). *Another Mother Tongue: Gay Words, Gay Worlds.* Boston, MA: Beacon Press.

Hite, S. (1976). *The Hite Report.* New York: Macmillan.

Horn, S. (1991). *Gaia's Guide.* New York: Inland Book Co.

Kinsey, A. C., Pomeroy, W. B., Martin, C. E., and Gebbard, P. H. (1953). *Sexual Behavior in the Human Female.* Philadelphia, PA: Saunders.

Martin, D., and Lyon, P. (1991). *Lesbian Woman.* Volcano, CA: Volcano Press.

Ollenburger, J. C., and Moore, H. A. (1992). *A Sociology of Women.* Englewood Cliffs, NJ: Prentice Hall.

Potter, S. J. (1985). Social work, traditional health care systems and lesbian invisibility. In M. Valentich and J. Gripton (Eds.), *Feminist Perspectives on Social Work and Human Sexuality.* Binghampton, NY: Haworth.

Potter, S. J., and Darty, T. E. (1981). Social work and the invisible minority. An exploration of lesbianism. *Social Work, 26,* 187–192.

Slater, S., and Mencher, J. (1991). The lesbian family life cycle: A contextual approach. *American Journal of Orthopsychiatry, 61*(3).

Chapter 12: May the Circle Be Unbroken: The African-American Experience of Death, Dying, and Spirituality

Boyd-Franklin, N. (1989). *Black Families in Therapy: A Multisystems Approach.* New York: Guilford.

Kamalu, C. (1990). *Foundations of African Thought.* London: Karnak House.

Lattanzi, M. E. (1984). Professional stress: Adaptation, coping, and meaning. In J. C. Hanson and T. T. Frantz (Eds.), *Death and Grief in the Family* (pp. 95–106). Rockville, MD: Aspen Systems.

Martin, J., and Martin, E. (1985). *The Helping Tradition in the Black Family and Community.* Silver Spring, MD: NASW.

Pennington, D. L. (1985). Time in African culture. In M. K. Asante and K. W. Asante (Eds.), *African Culture: The Rhythms of Unity* (pp. 123–140). Westport, CT: Greenwood Press.

Richards, D. (1985). The implications of African-American spirituality. In M. K. Asante and K. W. Asante (Eds.), *African Culture: The Rhythms of Unity* (pp. 207–231). Westport, CT: Greenwood Press.

Chapter 13: Understanding Death, Dying, and Religion: A Chinese Perspective

Asamoah, Y., Garcia, A., Hendricks, C., and Walker, J. (1991). What we call ourselves: Implications for resources, policy, and practice. *Journal of Multicultural Social Work, 1*(1), 7–22.

Bloom, M. (Ed.). (1992). *Changing Lives: Studies in Human Development and Professional Helping.* Columbia: University of South Carolina Press.

Blunden, C., and Elvin, M. (1983). *Cultural Atlas of China.* Oxford: Phaidon Press.

Discourses and Sayings of Confucius, The. (1982). Taipei: Overseas Chinese Affairs Commission.

Fairbank, J. K. (1992). *China: A New History.* Cambridge, MA: Harvard University Press.

Four Books, The. (1977). Taipei: Culture Book Company.

Glaser, B., and Strauss, A. L. (1984). The ritual drama of mutual pretense. In E. S. Schneidman (Ed.), *Death: Current Perspectives* (pp. 161–171). Palo Alto, CA: Mayfield.

Hinton, J. (1984). Speaking of death with the dying. In E. S. Schneidman (Ed.), *Death: Current Perspectives* (pp. 152–161). Palo Alto, CA: Mayfield.

Hsu, F. L. K. (1981). *Americans and Chinese: Passage to Differences.* Honolulu: University Press of Hawaii.

Kaleidoscope: Current World Data. (1990). Santa Barbara, CA: ABC-CLIO.

Keys, P. R. (1991). Ethnic and multicultural concerns in social work. *Journal of Multicultural Social Work, 1*(1), 1–6.

Kotre, J., and Hall, E. (1990). *Seasons of Life: Our Dramatic Journey from Birth to Death.* Boston MA: Little, Brown.

Kung, H., and Ching, J. (1989). *Christianity and Chinese Religions.* New York: Doubleday/Collins.

Lee, P. (1992). Social work in Hong Kong, Singapore, South Korea, and Taiwan: Asia's four little dragons. In M. C. Hokenstad, S. K. Khinduka, and J. Midgley (Eds.), *Profiles in International Social Work* (pp. 99–114). Washington, DC: NASW.

Lin, D. (1992). Hospice helps make death a time of dignity. *Free China Journal, 5.*

Lum, D. (1992). *Social Work Practice and People of Color: A Process-Stage Approach.* Pacific Grove, CA: Brooks/Cole.

Reischauer, E. O., and Fairbank, J. K. (1960). *East Asia: The Great Tradition.* Boston, MA: Houghton Mifflin.

Stephenson, J. S. (1985). *Death, Grief, and Mourning: Individual and Social Realities.* New York: Free Press.

Tai, H. (Ed.). (1989). *Confucianism and Economic Development: An Oriental Alternative.* Washington, DC: Washington Institute Press.

Wolf, A. (Ed.). (1974). *Religion and Ritual in Chinese Society.* Stanford, CA: Stanford University Press.

Yang, C. K. (1961). *Religion in Chinese Society.* Berkeley: University of California Press.

Chapter 14: Death, Dying, and Grief in the Chinese-American Culture

Cassidy, H. (1977). Helping the social work student deal with death and dying. In E. Prichard, J. Collard, B. Orcutt, and A. Kutscher (Eds.), *Social Work with the Dying Patient and the Family* (pp. 313–321). New York: Columbia University Press.

Foster, G. M. (1978). *Medical Anthropology.* New York: Wiley.

Fried, M. N., and Fried, M. H. (1980). *Transitions: Four Rituals in Eight Cultures.* New York: Norton.

Fujii, S. M. (1976). Elderly Asian Americans and use of public services. *Social Casework, 57*(3), 202–208.

Hessler, R. M., Nolan, M. F., Ogbru, B., and Kong-Ming-New, P. (1975). Intraethnic diversity: Health care of the Chinese-Americans. *Human Organization, 34*(3), 253–262.

Hom, G. S. (1971). *Chinese Argonauts.* San Jose, CA: Foothill Community College District.

Kleinman, A. (1980). *Patients and Healers in the Context of Culture.* Berkeley: University of California Press.

Lefley, H. P., and Pedersen, P. B. (1986). *Cross-Cultural Training for Mental Health Professionals.* Springfield, IL: Charles C. Thomas.

McGoldrick, M., and Carter, B. (1989). *The Changing Family Life Cycle.* Needham Heights, MA: Allyn and Bacon.

Parry, J. K. (1990). *Social Work Practice with the Terminally Ill: A Transcultural Perspective.* Springfield, IL: Charles C. Thomas.

Rando, T. A. (1984). *Grief, Dying, and Death.* Champaign, IL: Research Press.

Tsai, M., Teng, L. N., and Sue, S. (1981). Mental health status of Chinese in the United States. In A. Kleinman and T. Lin (Eds.), *Normal and Abnormal Behavior in Chinese Culture.* Boston, MA: Reidel.

Watson, J. L., and Rawski, E. S. (1988). *Death Ritual in Late Imperial and Modern China.* Berkeley: University of California Press.

Chapter 15: The Korean Perspective on Death and Dying

Choi, J. S. (1982). Family system. In S. Y. Shin (Ed.), *Korean Society* (pp. 15–33). Seoul: Si-sa-yong-o-sa Publishers.

Chung, D. (1990). *Three Day Promise.* Seoul: Chung Ahm Printing.

Han, S. B. (1982). Village conventions in Korea. In S. Y. Shin (Ed.), *Korean Society* (pp. 103–126). Seoul: Si-sa-yong-o-sa Publishers.

Lee, D. B. (1992). Divided Korean families: Why does it take so long to remedy the unhealed wounds? *Korea Journal of Population and Development, 21*(3).

Levy-Warren, M. H. (1987). Mourning to a new culture: Cultural identity, loss, and mourning. In J. Bloom-Feschbach et al. (Eds.), *The Psychology of Separation and Loss* (pp. 300–315). San Francisco, CA: Jossey-Bass.

Roh, C. S. (1987). The traditional funeral ritual in Korea. Paper presented at the Annual Meeting of the Pennsylvania Sociological Society, Oct. 23–25.

Sands, R., and Lee, D. B. (1985). Teaching death and dying in the early part of the life cycle. *Areta, 10*(2), 50–56.

Yoon, Y. S. (1987). *Korea the Beautiful: Treasures of the Hermit Kingdom.* Carson, CA: Golden Pond Press.

Chapter 16: The Filipino Perspective on Death and Dying

Cook, A. S., and Jenkins, L. E. (1982). Implications of ethnicity in the care of the terminally ill. *Social Case Work, 63*(4), 215–219.

Doka, K., and Morgan, J. B. (Eds.). (1993). *Death and Spirituality.* New York: Baywood.

Wagner, N. (1973). Filipinos: A minority within a minority. In S. Sue and N. Wagner (Eds.), *Asian-Americans: Psychological Perspectives.* Ben Lomend, CA: Science and Behavior Books.

Chapter 17: Summary and Conclusion

Abu-Laban, S. M. (1991). Family and religion among Muslim immigrants and their descendants. In E. H. Waugh, S. M. Abu-Laban, and R. B. Qureshi (Eds.), *Muslim Families in North America* (pp. 6–31). Edmonton: University of Alberta Press.

Chau, K. L. (1991). Social work with ethnic minorities: Practice issues and potentials. *Journal of Multicultural Social Work, 1*(1), 23–39.

Doka, K. J., and Morgan, J. D. (1993). *Death and Spirituality.* New York: Baywood.

Kalish, R. A., and Reynolds, D. K. (1976). *Death and Ethnicity: A Psycho-cultural Study.* Los Angeles: University of Southern California Press.

Markidas, K. S., and Mindel, C. H. (1987). *Aging and Ethnicity.* Newbury Park, CA: Sage.

Meagher, D. K., and Bell, C. P. (1993). Perspectives on death in the African-American community. In K. J. Doka and J. D. Morgan (Eds.), *Death and Spirituality*. New York: Baywood.

Parry, J. K. (1990). *Social Work Practice with the Terminally Ill: A Transcultural Perspective*. Springfield, IL: Charles C. Thomas.

Platt, L. A., and Persico, V. R., Jr. (1992). *Grief in Cross-Cultural Perspective: A Casebook*. New York: Garland.

Ponzetti, J. J. (1992). Bereaved families: A comparison of parents' and grandparents' reactions to the death of a child. *Omega, 25*(1), 63–71.

Red Horse, J. (1988). Cultural evolution of American-Indian families. In C. Jacobs and D. D. Bowles (Eds.), *Ethnicity and Race* (pp. 86–102). Silver Spring, MD: NASW.

Whitmore, G. (1988). Accepting AIDS as fatal helps victims. In B. Leone, M. T. O'Neil, C. Debner, and B. Szumski (Eds.), *Death and Dying* (pp. 67–73). St. Paul, MN: Greenhaven Press.

EDITORS

Joan K. Parry, D.S.W., retired in 1992 as professor in the School of Social Work, San Jose State University, California. She has also taught at Hunter College School of Social Work and Fordham University, and was director of social work at Community Hospital at Glen Cove, New York. Her major interests are work with the terminally ill, group work, and multicultural counseling.

Angela Shen Ryan, D.S.W., is professor of social work at Hunter College, City University of New York. She has taught social work practice with substance abusers, research, and cross-cultural counseling. She has received several training grants from federal, state, and city governments for programs focusing on cultural competence and has also written in the areas of immigration and refugees.

CONTRIBUTORS

Gary R. Anderson, M.S.W., Ph.D., is a professor at Hunter College School of Social Work. He has extensive experience in child welfare and family services, and has written articles and books on child welfare issues, children with AIDS, and ethical issues in social work practice.

John L. Bolling, M.D., is a child psychiatrist and a psychiatrist consultant for the Interfaith Counseling Center and Graham Windham Children's Services. He is also the founding director of the Mandela Center, which provides spiritual and religious counseling to members of the African-American community.

Julia A. Carter, M.S.W., is a mental health client specialist at Santa Cruz Community Health Services. She has had fourteen years experience working with the terminally ill in hospitals and nursing homes.

Idella M. Evans, Ph.D., is a clinical psychologist recently retired from private practice in Santa Cruz, California. She has also taught psychology in the Oregon System of Higher Education, at San Jose State University, and in the extension at the University of California in Santa Cruz.

Ursula M. Gerty, D.S.W., is professor emeritus, Fordham University School of Social Service. She taught at Fordham for over twenty-five years, and currently serves on dissertation committees for the Graduate School of Social Service. She also is engaged in private practice in social work counseling and serves on the boards of several voluntary social service agencies, the American Red Cross, and UNICEF.

George S. Getzel, D.S.W., is professor of social work at Hunter College, where he has taught social work practice with groups and social policy for twenty-five years. He has written extensively on social work practice with the aging, people with AIDS, victims of violence, and issues in health care. He has served as consultant to the U.S. Public Health Service, the Canadian Centre on AIDS, McGill University, the University of Maryland, the Veterans Administration, and other health and social agencies.

David A. Housel, M.S.W., is a social worker in the AIDS Center Program at St. Luke's/Roosevelt Hospital Center, New York City. He conducts educational forums on a variety of subjects, including HIV/AIDS and safer sex, to diverse audiences in the United States and abroad, and has been a consultant to several AIDS organizations.

Daniel B. Lee, Ph.D., is a professor in the School of Social Work, Loyola University of Chicago. He has also taught in the College of Social Work, The Ohio State University. He is particularly interested in the fields of marriage, family, mental health, and cross cultural issues. He is in private clinical practice and consults in these areas.

Peter Ching-Yung Lee, Ph.D., is a professor of social work and director of the Center for Human Services Research and Development at San Jose State University. He is also secretary-general for the Inter-University Consortium for International Social Development, an organization of educators and practitioners from over sixty-five countries.

Joan M. Merdinger, D.S.W., is professor and director of Field Education in the College of Social Work, San Jose State University. She has also taught at the University of Pennsylvania and Rhode Island College. Her research interests include women's issues, transcultural practice, and field education and instruction.

Ana Paulino, M.S.W., Ed.D., is associate professor at Hunter College School of Social Work and director of Puerto Rican Family and Children Services. She has also taught at Columbia University School of Social Work. She has extensive clinical experience with Hispanic clients and their families. Her primary interests are cross cultural counseling and culture-sensitivity training for social work students and human service workers.

Ahmed H. Sakr, Ph.D., an educator and Muslim scholar, has taught in Lebanon and the United States. He was a founding member of the Islamic Society of North America and of the World Council of Mosques. He was the first director and representative of the Muslim World League to the United Nations and is currently president of the Foundation for Islamic Knowledge and director of the Islamic Education Center in California, among other interests.

Juliette S. Silva, Ph.D., is professor and associate dean of the College of Social Work, San Jose State University. She teaches transcultural social work, human

244

behavior, and women's issues. She is also a core faculty member of the Stanford University Gerontological Education Center.

Martha Adams Sullivan, D.S.W., is director of geriatric services, Department of Psychiatry, Gouverneur Hospital, in New York City. She is also on the faculty of Hunter College School of Social Work, where she teaches social work practice. She is also chairperson of the Citywide Geriatrics Committee. Her areas of interest are mental health management and program development, minority mental health, family treatment, homelessness, the treatment of women, and the aged, especially the family in later life.

Jane G. Tanner, M.S.W., is faculty field instructor for San Jose State College of Social Work. She has also worked as a medical social worker at the San Jose Medical Center.

Ihande Weber, M.S.W., is a psychiatric social worker at Agnew's Developmental Center, San Jose, California. She has also worked for a homeless project in San Jose.

Wing Yeung, M.D., is the medical director of Richmond Area Multi-Services, Inc., in San Francisco. He has also served as a psychiatrist in New York City at St. Vincent's Hospital and at mental health agencies in the Asian community. In 1990, he entered a Buddhist monastery to become a monk.

INDEX

247